AMERICAN CIVILIZATION SINCE 1900

About the Author

Arnold S. Rice received his B.A. from the State University of New York at Albany, his M.A. from Columbia University, and his Ph.D. from Indiana University. He is Professor of History and a former Chairperson of the Department of History at Kean College of New Jersey. During the 1964–1965 academic year he was a Fulbright Exchange Professor in the Netherlands. In 1980 he received the Distinguished Alumnus Award from his undergraduate school. He belongs to the American Historical Association and the Organization of American Historians. In addition to having made many contributions to a variety of journals and reference works, he is the author of four other books: *The Ku Klux Klan in American Politics; Herbert Hoover; Newark, 1666–1970;* and *United States Since 1865* (with John A. Krout).

AMERICAN CIVILIZATION SINCE 1900

ARNOLD S. RICE

BARNES & NOBLE BOOKS
A DIVISION OF HARPER & ROW, PUBLISHERS
New York, Cambridge, Philadelphia,
San Francisco, London, Mexico City, São Paulo, Sydney

Portions of this book are drawn from *United States Since 1865* by John A. Krout and Arnold S. Rice (Barnes & Noble Books/A Division of Harper & Row, Publishers, New York, 1977).

FIRST EDITION

Designer: C. Linda Dingler

Library of Congress Cataloging in Publication Data

Rice, Arnold S.
    American civilization since 1900.
    Includes index.
    1. United States—Civilization—20th century.
I. Title.
E169.1.R55   1983   973.9   82-48255
ISBN 0-06-460145-5 (pbk.)

83 84 85 86 87 10 9 8 7 6 5 4 3 2 1

*For
my wife, Marcia,
and
my son, Noah,
with love*

CONTENTS

PREFACE

American Civilization Since 1900 focuses on social and cultural developments.

Although such an undertaking must be to some extent arbitrary, it is instructive to divide the decades of the twentieth century into a series of compact social-cultural eras, each with its own social ambience and its own cultural aura.

In preparing this book I have attempted to give appropriate emphasis to the social and cultural developments of the past quarter of a century, many of which could well serve as guides to the future of the nation. Thus the chapter on the period 1960–1980 treats comprehensively such topics as the new sexual morality, the struggle by blacks and other minority groups for equal treatment, the women's liberation movement, the exploration of space, and the entertainment and informational revolution wrought by television.

Since chronology is the basic structure of the treatment of civilization, a chronological arrangement determines the pattern of this book. In addition, a topical sequence for all important subjects can be easily traced through use of the index.

The bibliography lists special works with which every attentive observer of American society and culture should become acquainted.

I hope that students will find that *American Civilization Since 1900* will not only provide a social-cultural framework for courses in American history but also serve as a digest of social and cultural material for courses in American government; American society; and American art, literature, or music.

ARNOLD S. RICE

Chapter 1

THE CONFIDENT YEARS: 1900–1920

The period 1900–1920 is a social-cultural era that has a flavor all its own—an all-pervading confidence in the future of the nation with the coming of the new century. The era's social and cultural conditions grew out of two sets of historical circumstances. First, the tremendous industrial expansion in the three decades after the Civil War produced a mass society with new needs and values. Second, a late-nineteenth-century direction in foreign policy resulted in the emergence of the United States as an empire-rich global power. This imperialism added to the characteristics of mass society and mass culture a chauvinistic awareness of the nation's power and potential.

HISTORICAL BACKGROUND

For some time after the Civil War the United States attempted to pursue its past intention—professed, at least—of isolationism. But gradually Americans turned their attention to active participation in international affairs and overseas expansion until the United States became a world power. On the domestic scene, from about the time Theodore Roosevelt assumed the presidency in 1901 until Woodrow Wilson started his second term in 1917, a widely accepted reform movement called "progressivism" held sway. During World War I Wilson tried to maintain American neutrality, but after holding fast to this position for almost three years the United States entered the war.

The United States as a Global Power. Toward the end of the nineteenth century desire mounted in the United States for overseas expansion. The Spanish-American War of 1898 was the way to satisfaction. This war, won by the United States with few casualties and little cost in money and time, brought about a revision in American foreign policy. The acquisition, as a result of the war, of island territories in the Caribbean Sea and the Pacific Ocean presented a new challenge: to establish principles and procedures for governing overseas possessions. The United States was forced to deal extensively not only with nations in Latin America and the Far East but also with the European powers that had established their imperial presences in the regions. This territorial acquisition was quickly followed by military intervention and commercial penetration, something deeper than the considerable trade activity that had previously taken place. In the first fifteen years of the twentieth century the United States thus emerged from semi-isolation to become a world power—with all the benefits and hazards accruing to that status.

Theodore Roosevelt personally handled the nation's foreign affairs to a degree that none of his predecessors had even approached. His always dynamic and sometimes flagrantly aggressive manner of doing this ensured that other nations would regard with care the role of the United States in world affairs. Roosevelt's style came to be known as "big-stick diplomacy" (from a favorite West African maxim of his: "Speak softly and carry a big stick"). William H. Taft, succeeding Roosevelt, fully embraced the goal of directing a foreign policy that would increase American participation and influence abroad. To attain that goal he relied on business and financial pursuits, a method called "dollar diplomacy." Wilson, of the Democratic party, determined that the expansionist objectives and techniques pursued by his two Republican predecessors be promptly discarded. He began his administration resolved that its diplomatic basis would be anti-imperialism. He rejected both military intervention in the affairs of weak countries and the use of diplomatic relations to foster American economic enterprise overseas. The new conduct of dealing with the nations of the world would rest on morality. However, despite his declared idealistic approach to diplomacy, realities both at home and abroad were such that Wilson eventually found himself directing a foreign policy that was virtually indistinguishable from that of Roosevelt and Taft.

The Progressive Movement. Progressivism developed as a doctrine for dealing with the far-reaching impact of the enormous industrialization after the Civil War. The United States had to contend with, among other things, the monopolistic practices of the large manufacturing firms; the abuses of the rapidly extending railroad systems; the changing status of the labor force that was being transformed from skilled craftsmen into factory workers; the plight of farmers as they cultivated more efficiently with better machines and thus increased production with consequent declining prices for their crops; and the demanding problems brought about by the vast growth of cities. The adherents of the progressive movement (called progressives whether their party affiliation was Democratic or Republican) endeavored to make government organization and processes on the federal, state, and local levels more democratic and to foster social legislation that would directly benefit the people.

In the White House for almost eight years, Theodore Roosevelt gave a new meaning to the presidency with his exuberant style. He manifested a lively concern that his administration should afford what he referred to as a "square deal" for all Americans—businessmen, laborers, farmers, and consumers. The reason for Roosevelt's impact lay in his unusual ability to arouse the people to an awareness of their civic duties, rather than in any notable progress toward social justice under his leadership. His handpicked successor, Taft, although much more conservative in temperament than Roosevelt, nevertheless sympathized with the political reformers of his time and approved of many of their objectives. In listing the achievements of his term, his admirers included the vigorous prosecution of combinations in restraint of trade, the extension of the merit system in the civil service, the adoption of the eight-hour workday for employees on government contracts, and the passage of legislation reserving additional public lands from private enterprise. But Taft frequently took issue with the reformers' methods and criticized the haste with which they attempted to implement their progressive ideas.

In his campaign for the presidency in 1912 the Democratic candidate Woodrow Wilson expressed a body of ideas for a program he called the New Freedom. In essence, it sought to curb any business that enjoyed a monopoly and to restore an earlier condition of competition. Wilson was victorious at the polls and entered the White House as the first Democrat after sixteen years of Republican rule. More significant than a switch of party control, however, is the fact that in his first term he brought the progressive movement to its zenith. In pursuing his domestic policy, Wilson totally rejected the concept that the American system should be scrapped. He desired to preserve that system, but also to strengthen it through reform. He had a strong sense of right and wrong, which he applied to the handling of domestic matters, supporting a number of reforms relating to the tariff, banking and currency, trusts, labor, and agriculture. When the United States entered World War I the attention and efforts of those imbued with progressive zeal switched from domestic reform to worldwide hostilities and their concomitant miseries. Progressive activity virtually ceased.

World War I. In 1914 World War I broke out in Europe between the Allies, headed by Great Britain, France, and Russia, and the Central Powers, led by Germany and Austria-Hungary. Wilson issued a neutrality proclamation, warning Americans not to be thrown off-balance by a "war with which we have nothing to do." However, public sympathy with the Allies and opposition to acts of the Central Powers eventually brought the United States into the war on the side of the Allies. American military and economic powers were swiftly mobilized and contributed greatly to the defeat of the Central Powers. Subsequently, the United States Senate refused to ratify the settlement reached at the peace negotiations— the punitive Treaty of Versailles—and in so doing failed to adopt the document's idealistic section containing the Covenant of the League of Nations. Thus the United States withheld its support from the world organization that had been conceived as the means of ensuring permanent security.

SOCIETY

A result of late-nineteenth-century industrialization and imperialism was the death of the old American society—insulated, detached, restrictive, prim—and the birth of a new. The period 1900–1920 meant to Americans that they were part of a "modern" mass society, to which each individual had a charge to adapt. (Of course there were some who, unwilling or unable to come to terms with this society, tried to salvage the customs and traditions of the old order.) A "modern" America meant, among other things, the following: a more humane approach in treating the Indians; the struggle of blacks for equality; the arrival and assimilation of large numbers of immigrants from eastern and southern Europe; the increased employment of women; the efforts of workers to develop effective unions to meet their needs; the tremendous growth of the cities; a new philosophy of and methodology for education; a testing of the old religious beliefs; and the extraordinary influence of new advances in science, technology, and medicine.

The Population. Between 1900 and 1920 the population of the United States rose from about 76 million to about 105 million—an increase of approximately 40 percent.

RACIAL AND ETHNIC BACKGROUND. Of the total population in 1900, 66.1 million (87 percent) were whites; 8.8 million (11.4 percent) were blacks; 250,000 were American Indians; 120,000 were Asians, mostly Chinese and Japanese. By 1920 whites numbered 93.3 million; blacks, 10.5 million; American Indians, 400,000; and Asians, 140,000. Of the white population in 1900, approximately 10.2 million (13.4 percent) had been born abroad, while another 15.6 million (20.5 percent) had at least one foreign-born parent. As a result of the large immigration (mainly from eastern and southern Europe) during the next two decades, the number of foreign-born increased to 14 million. Of the total black population in 1920, about 85 percent lived in the South. Of the total foreign-born population, more than 80 percent lived in the North.

EMPLOYMENT. The tremendous extent of American economic growth early in the twentieth century is reflected in the statistics of national income. In 1900 the total was $36.5 billion; by 1920 it had soared to $60.4 billion. During this period virtually everyone who sought work was able to find it. In 1920 close to 42.5 million persons (including approximately 8.5 million women) were employed. One of the most significant developments was the steady percentage decline of those who worked on farms, a trend begun in the last quarter of the nineteenth century. In 1900 fewer than 40 percent of those employed engaged in farm work; twenty years later fewer than 25 percent did so.

Indians. The settling of large numbers of white people in the West during the late nineteenth century quickly changed Indian life. War, introduction of diseases such as measles and tuberculosis, killing of the bison (commonly called buffalo), forced resettlement on reservations—by 1900 all these had created near-unendurable hardships for the Indians of the western plains.

After the Civil War hundreds of skirmishes took place between the Indian tribes and United States military forces. But the Indians' courageous campaign was eventually contained, and the frontier became relatively quiet. An important factor in the decline of militant resistance was the slaughter of buffalo by both professional hunters and sportsmen. By the beginning of the twentieth century only a few straggling herds remained of the millions of animals that had roamed the plains. Although the species survived under government protection, the main economic support of the Plains Indians was gone, for they had depended upon the flesh of buffalo for food, upon their hides for clothing, and upon other parts for additional articles of daily use.

THE RESERVATION SYSTEM. As actual warfare between Indian warriors and United States troops diminished, the government forced tribes onto reservations where they were almost completely dependent on the taxpayers' bounty, never adequate for their needs. The aim of the reservation policy was to assimilate the Indians into an agricultural economy. By 1900 there were reservations in more than twenty states and territories. But the administration of the reservation system was notoriously corrupt. Government agents made fortunes by supplying Indians under their jurisdiction with shoddy goods, selling them prohibited liquor, and cheating them out of their rightful lands through fraudulent real-estate deals. In the meantime, traders, miners, cattlemen, and railroad builders prodded the government into unwarranted encroachments on Indian reservations.

THE REFORM MOVEMENT. Humanitarians tried to modify or supplant the reservation system. However, among the reformers there was a sharp division between those who wanted to preserve old tribal customs and others who desired to hasten the Indians' assimilation.

In 1887 Congress passed the Dawes Act. This measure modified the reservation system by granting 160 acres of land and United States citizenship to the heads of Indian families who would agree to abandon their tribal allegiance. The right of disposal of land was withheld for twenty-five years. But land on the Indian reservation that was not allotted to former tribal members was opened to white settlers. Thus, cattlemen and farmers who sought new territory in the trans-Mississippi West profited more from the Dawes Act than did the Indians.

After some twenty years even the reformers admitted that title to private property and the rights of citizenship had not improved the status of many Indians. The Burke Act, designed to correct the defects of the Dawes Act, was passed in 1906. It provided new incentives for those making the transition from tribal membership to individual citizenship. Indians who proved competent in managing the land could become citizens in a shorter time than the twenty-five–year probationary period specified in the Dawes Act. In 1924 legislation was passed conferring citizenship on all Indians.

Blacks. In 1900, thirty-five years after emancipation, the vast majority of blacks still lived in the South, where all aspects of life— political, economic, and social—were hard. Blacks began to leave the South for northern cities in large numbers during World War I.

CONDITIONS IN THE SOUTH. By the turn of the century southern whites had undone virtually all black advancement of the Reconstruction period (1865–1877) and had restored "white supremacy." The number of blacks who could meet suffrage qualifications was steadily reduced, so that by 1900 hardly any blacks voted. Several devices were used: (1) the literacy test, so constructed that most blacks could not pass; (2) the poll tax, required for voting; (3) property requirements; (4) the "grandfather clause" of revised state constitutions, granting the suffrage only to those whose fathers or grandfathers had voted before 1867. (The last device, of course, barred blacks but made it possible for uneducated whites to vote.)

After the Civil War southern plantation owners lost their slaves and had insufficient money to hire laborers. Most tried a system of cultivation with tenants, who could not afford to pay a cash rental. Under this sharecropping plan which continued well into the twentieth century, the tenant agreed to give the landowner as rent a percentage (usually half) of his crop. If the landowner did not supply tools, seed, and draft animals, the sharecropper was often forced to pledge another share of his crop to the local merchant in order to secure credit. This was called the "crop-lien system." The majority of black farmers in the South were sharecroppers, who were virtually bound to the soil by heavy debts and lived in extreme poverty. The breakup of the large plantations into small farms often meant the loss of work for blacks, since many poor whites were given preference over blacks as sharecroppers. Those blacks who drifted into mill towns or got employment in mines and factories found their labor exploited almost as vigorously as it had been during slavery years.

Socially, blacks were kept separated from whites by so-called Jim Crow laws. (The name is believed to be derived from a character in a popular minstrel song.) Beginning in the 1880s statutes that legalized racial segregation were enacted by southern states and municipalities. Most public schools as well as stores, restaurants, hotels, and theaters were segregated by such laws. The Supreme Court in the *Plessy* v. *Ferguson* case of 1896 decided that a Louisiana law requiring "separate but equal" facilities for whites and blacks on railroad cars was constitutional. This doctrine was soon extended in the South to other public facilities, including educational institutions. The schools for whites were almost without exception superior to those for blacks.

LEADERS AND ORGANIZATIONS. There was disagreement among black leaders and black organizations on strategy to employ in the battle for equal treatment in a predominantly white society. The most prominent black leader was Booker T. Washington, who founded Tuskegee Institute in Alabama as a technical school for blacks, and was its president for almost thirty-five years. Washington advocated that blacks refrain from agitating for political rights and social advancement but instead strive for economic equality with whites through vocational training. Once blacks demonstrated diligence and competence in the nation's work force and played a positive role in the nation's economy, substantial gains along political and social lines would surely follow. Many black leaders bitterly opposed Washington's position. Among these was the militant and highly intellectual W. E. B. Du Bois, a professor at Atlanta University. Du Bois asserted that while vocational education was good for the majority of blacks, the "talented tenth" should study academic subjects in order to prepare for professional careers that would both satisfy them and enable them to guide their race. Meanwhile, blacks should agitate unflaggingly for complete equality—political, economic, and social.

In 1909 a group of whites and blacks, including Du Bois, founded the National Association for the Advancement of Colored People (NAACP) to combat racial discrimination. The NAACP employed a variety of methods, including lobbying and educational programs, but concentrated on legal action. Much of the organization's efforts was devoted to combatting lynching, an instrument of ugly terrorism used by some southern whites to keep blacks passive. There were more than 1300 lynchings between 1900 and 1920. In 1910 the National Urban League was organized by a biracial group to help blacks who migrated from the rural South adjust to city life.

MIGRATION TO THE NORTH. During World War I approximately 350,000 blacks moved from the South to the North to work in war plants. After the war blacks continued to come north. During the 1920s burgeoning business enterprises hired black workers as the white labor supply was curtailed by federal restriction of immigration.

Although blacks in the North enjoyed political rights, such as voting and running for office, they did encounter economic and social discrimination. They were the last employed in good times and the first dismissed in bad times. And when they worked, their pay was generally lower than that of whites who performed the same jobs. Opportunities for blacks to advance in a profession or industry were limited. Labor unions were on the whole disinclined to accept blacks, whether skilled or unskilled. The blacks who moved to the North crowded into cities. Soon ghettos were formed. Black sections containing large numbers of dwellers and limited housing quickly deteriorated physically. Because of their separation from whites through neighborhood housing patterns, black children attended schools that were segregated, not by law but in reality. And the schools for blacks were often inferior to those for whites.

"New Immigrants." Before the 1880s most immigrants to the United States came from northern and western Europe. They were "old immigrants." Attracted to the West by cheap land, thousands of the old immigrants, principally Germans and Scandinavians, swelled the population of the "prairie states" of the Mississippi Valley and the Great Plains. Since the old immigrants were like native-born white Americans in social practices, they adapted well to American society.

In the late nineteenth century industrial development with increasing opportunities for workers drew even larger numbers of immigrants from Europe. Beginning in the 1880s the "new immigrants," from eastern and southern Europe, predominated. From 1880 to 1920 close to 24 million persons entered the United States. Practically all had fled from poverty in the Old World, but many, notably Jews from Russia and Russian-controlled Poland, had fled also from political and religious persecution. The new immigrants, because of language barriers, their relatively poor education, and their tendency to cluster in cities, were considered more difficult than the old immigrants to assimilate into the dominant American culture. But the new immigrants filled the factories and the shops. Several national groups soon led in particular economic enterprises. Italians built bridges, laid railroad tracks, and dug sewers; eastern European Jews manufactured clothing; Poles, Czechs, and Hungarians mined coal and worked in the steel plants; Greeks operated restaurants. The new immigrants also gave to the older American culture an awareness of Europe's treasures in art, literature, and music. In addition, they enriched the language with expressive words and phrases and embellished the diet with ethnic foods that soon became staples of American cuisine.

Asians. During the late nineteenth century the American government began a long-continued policy of suspending immigration from China, and early in the twentieth century it effected a virtual prohibition of immigration from Japan.

CHINESE. Immigration from China increased rapidly after the mid-nineteenth century. Chinese laborers were welcomed on the West Coast so long as they were needed for such work as railroad construction. The Burlingame Treaty of 1868 between the United States and China granted Chinese subjects the right of unlimited immigration to the United States. In the 1870s, as it became apparent that, especially in California, the Chinese were competing for jobs with native-born Americans, a movement developed for a restriction of their immigration. It was maintained that the Chinese were socially unassimilable and that their low economic life-style endangered the American standard of living.

In 1879 Congress passed a bill restricting Chinese immigration, but President Rutherford B. Hayes vetoed it. Hayes then sent a commission to China to secure modification of the Burlingame Treaty. As a result of the negotiations, in 1880 the immigration of Chinese laborers was regulated but not prohibited. In 1882 President Chester A. Arthur signed the Chinese Exclusion Act, which suspended immigration from China for ten years. The exclusion principle was renewed periodically thereafter until 1965.

JAPANESE. Early in the twentieth century California discriminated against the large number of Japanese laborers who had come to the state seeking better job opportunities. Resentment flared in Japan over this situation. What rankled in particular was the action of the San Francisco School Board in ordering all Asian students to attend a separate school. Anticipating a rupture in American-Japanese relations, President Theodore Roosevelt decided to intervene. He invited the entire school board of San Francisco to a conference in the White House and a formula was found. The school board agreed to rescind the segregation order, and Roosevelt pledged that Japanese immigration would, in some way, be limited. What followed was a series of diplomatic notes during 1907–1908 between the United States and Japan, embodying the "Gentlemen's Agreement." Japan promised to deny passports to Japanese laborers seeking to emigrate to the United States, while the United States agreed not to prohibit Japanese immigration completely. Although Japan scrupulously observed the agreement, in 1924 the United States unilaterally ended it by a congressional act that totally prohibited Japanese immigration to the United States.

The Employment of Women. During the first two decades of the twentieth century the most notable change in the status of American women was their increased participation in the job market. In 1900 the vast majority of men opposed the employment of women, who, they asserted, were both mentally and physically unequal to most jobs. They believed that for married women to neglect home responsibilities for outside work was deplorable. Nevertheless, the number of employed women soared with the rapidly increasing demand for labor caused by tremendous industrial expansion. In 1900 approximately 1.3 million women worked; by 1920 about 8.5 million did so. Virtually all continued to attend to the housekeeping chores after work. Almost 40 percent of the women who went to work had as their primary goal adding to their husbands' income to meet family expenses.

Ordinarily, when a woman performed the same job that a man did, she would receive wages about half of his. For women factory workers in 1900, weekly wages of ten dollars or less and a workday of ten hours or more (six days a week) were common. Most men in labor unions vigorously opposed the unionization of women because they feared competition for jobs.

There were other job opportunities for women who had the required education. Women (in most places only if they remained unmarried) could pursue careers in teaching, nursing, or secretarial service. Women teachers not only usually received about half of what their male colleagues got for the same duties but also were closely restricted in their social conduct, being expected to maintain a decorous image. Women could become shop clerks, but they had little chance of rising to supervisory positions. Black women, discriminated against for most types of jobs usually became domestics, earning less than half the pay of white women factory workers and toiling almost twice the number of hours.

During World War I, for the first time in the nation's history, women were permitted to become members of the armed forces in fields other than nursing. The Army employed several thousand women in civilian capacities only, but the Navy officially recruited more than 10,000 women as "yeomanettes" and the Marine Corps some 300 as "marinettes."

The Labor Movement. By 1900 American workingmen had learned well that so far as they were concerned the most important effect of industrialization was the transformation of skilled craftsmen into factory workers. The consequences of this change for workers included the loss of the bargaining power that their skills and tools had given them; the impersonality of employer-employee relations in the new corporations; and increased competition for jobs resulting from the entry into the labor force of blacks, women, and the new immigrants. As industrialists formed ever-larger business units, workers tried to create organizations large and strong enough to bargain on equal terms with employers.

AIMS. Early in the twentieth century the labor movement had three principal aims that had been developed in response to the new industrial order: higher wages, shorter hours (the common demand was for an eight-hour workday), and safe and sanitary working conditions. But the labor movement was concerned with more than these goals. Among its secondary aims were the abolition of child labor; the recognition of the principle of collective bargaining (negotiation for employment terms between an employer or group of employers on one side and a union or unions on the other); the institution of compulsory arbitration of management-labor disputes; and the enactment of workmen's compensation laws (insurance for pay in case of an accident or illness arising out of work duties).

TACTICS. Among the tactics of organized labor were the strike; picketing; the boycott (a concerted refusal to deal with the products or services of an offending employer); and the closed shop (an establishment in which the employer hires and retains in employment only union members in good standing).

DIFFICULTIES. Facing numerous difficulties, the leaders of labor were less successful than the leaders of industry in mobilizing their forces. In their attempts to weld the nation's workers into a united and class-conscious group, the labor leaders had to cope with the entrance of blacks, both skilled and unskilled, into the ranks of paid labor; the presence of many poorly paid women in certain crafts; the increase in numbers of foreign-born workers, divided by language, religion, and national tradition; and the activities of radicals holding to abstract and frequently impractical theories for the reorganization of the social order.

THE AMERICAN FEDERATION OF LABOR. Skilled craftsmen were increasingly dissatisfied with the large post-Civil War union, the Noble Order of the Knights of Labor, primarily because it advocated industrial unions (membership in which was open to all workmen in any given industry) and focused on social-reform measures. This division resulted in the formation in 1881 of the Federation of Organized Trades and Labor Unions of America and Canada, reorganized in 1886 as the American Federation of Labor (AFL). The AFL became the most significant labor union of the early twentieth century. Samuel Gompers and Adolph Strasser, leaders of the Cigarmakers' Union, were influential in founding the AFL and formulating its philosophy. Elected the first president of the organization, Gompers held that position except for one term until his death almost forty years later.

The AFL was a league of separate and quite autonomous craft unions (membership in which was limited to workmen following the same craft), each of which retained strong local powers, with the authority of the central body strictly limited. The AFL concentrated its efforts upon the "bread-and-butter" issues: higher wages, shorter hours, and safer and more sanitary conditions of employment within the various crafts. The organization also vigorously advocated the restriction of immigrants, who competed for jobs with native-born Americans. The weapons of the AFL came to be the strike, the boycott, and collective bargaining. Refusing to sponsor an American labor party or to ally with any party, the organization used its political power to secure immediate objectives. Despite the pressure of a small Socialist minority among its members, the AFL remained conservative, defending the capitalist system while criticizing its imperfections.

Membership increased from about 100,000 in 1890 to about 550,000 in 1900 to more than 2 million in 1915. However, since the vast majority of the nation's industrial workers did not belong to the AFL, its victories had little direct effect on American labor in general. AFL achievements included the development within the national organization of strong craft unions with effective programs, aided by large funds, for sickness and unemployment benefits; the establishment of the eight-hour workday in several trades; the recognition by an increasing number of employers of labor's right to bargain collectively; and the slow but steady growth of labor's influence with the federal and state legislatures.

THE INDUSTRIAL WORKERS OF THE WORLD. In 1905 leaders of the radical wing of unionism together with militant Socialists founded the Industrial Workers of the World (IWW) to oppose conservative policies in the labor movement. William D. ("Big Bill") Haywood, who had been an officer in the Western Federation of Miners, was the organization's most prominent head. The IWW sought to bring all the nation's workers into a single industrial-type union. It strove to overthrow the capitalist system and establish socialism. Spurning the middle-class reformers and moderate Socialists alike, the IWW championed direct action—the mass strike and sabotage. The IWW appealed chiefly to migratory laborers in the lumber camps, mines, and the harvest fields of the Far West. Various states took legal proceedings against the organization because of its radical views and actions, and in 1918 the federal government sentenced to prison its most influential leaders for opposition to American entry into World War I. By the mid-1920s the membership, which at its height numbered approximately 60,000, had disintegrated.

The Growth of Cities. One of the most significant social changes resulting from American industrial expansion was urban growth. As the cities began to offer more and better opportunities for employment, people left the rural areas for urban centers. The growth of cities had a tremendous influence on national thought and action.

At the turn of the century the United States was still predominantly rural. But over the next two decades urban growth was 650 percent greater than rural growth. In 1900 approximately 33 percent of the population lived in places with more than 8000 inhabitants; by 1920 the percentage had increased to 44. As for cities, in 1900 only thirty-seven had more than 100,000 residents; twenty years later the number of such cities was sixty-seven.

THE URBAN MIDDLE CLASS. Opportunities in the United States

drew from eastern and southern Europe millions of immigrants, most of whom settled in the cities. Some joined the native-born to swell the ranks of the middle class, composed principally of business and professional people, bureaucrats, and some skilled craftsmen. A segment of this class acquired wealth through "sharp" business methods.

REFORMERS. While most business leaders were involved in adding to their fortunes, acquiring town houses and country estates, and winning social recognition and prestige, a small group of other Americans in a variety of professions grappled with the difficult problems presented by the disorderly growth of the cities. They strove mightily, if not always effectively, to provide satisfactory housing, transportation, fire protection, and police service. A few individuals persisted in attacking the poverty, disease, alcoholism, and crime that thrived in the congested byways of the cities. Among the reformers in politics were Tom L. Johnson, Democratic mayor of Cleveland, and Samuel M. ("Golden Rule") Jones, Republican mayor of Toledo. In journalism were Joseph Pulitzer, publisher of the *New York World;* Jacob Riis, reporter for the *New York Evening Sun;* and Lincoln Steffens, writer for *McClure's Magazine.* Other reformers included in social work, Jane Addams, founder in Chicago of Hull House neighborhood center for the poor; in public health, Lillian D. Wald, organizer in New York City of a visiting nurse program; in the temperance crusade, Carry Nation, a hatchet-wielding smasher of saloon property first in Kansas and subsequently in several other states; and in architecture, Louis H. Sullivan, a Chicago-based practitioner of a modern architectural style.

THE URBAN INFLUENCE. If much of the city's population was drawn from the rural districts, conversely the farms and villages fell more and more under the influence of urban manners and standards. Despite the antagonism toward the cities often manifested by rural people, they succumbed gradually to urban standardization in habits and thought as well as to uniform factory-made goods.

Education. Americans were beginning to realize that the home and the church were becoming less influential in educating the young. They thus made an ever-increasing commitment to public education to prepare their children for the challenges of a vibrant society.

ELEMENTARY EDUCATION. In the first two decades of the twentieth century elementary education underwent an extraordinary change both in curriculum and in teaching methods. Administrators and teachers began to doubt the traditional belief that the value of education lies in developing mental discipline through arduous abstract learning. By far the most influential individual in establishing a new direction for elementary schools was John Dewey, a professor at Columbia University. Dewey maintained that rather than preparing a child for life, a classroom should be life itself. A child will best develop mentally if he participates in activities that are purposeful and meaningful to him within this microcosmic society. The teacher should be a knowledgeable and sympathetic guide of the classroom activities. At teachers colleges across the nation hundreds of professors who had become dedicated followers of Dewey's philosophy prepared elementary schoolteachers to implement that philosophy in the classroom.

SECONDARY EDUCATION. Between 1900 and 1920 the enrollment in the nation's secondary schools increased remarkably, from approximately 500,000 to about 2 million. The only goal of secondary education before the turn of the twentieth century was to prepare students for study at a college or university. After 1900 secondary schools assumed other purposes. First, they attempted to develop in every adolescent both intellectual and social skills to meet the challenges of a complex and rapidly changing nation. Second, they catered to students' occupational aims by adding to the college preparatory course other programs, such as commercial, industrial technology, and home economics.

Further significant developments were extension of the high school downward through the establishment of the junior high school and upward through the creation of the junior college. The development of the two- or three-year junior-high-school program was intended to ease the transition of youngsters from the (former eight-year) elementary-school program to the (former four-year) high-school program, each of which was correspondingly shortened. Junior colleges had a twofold purpose: first, to extend general education for those who were not bound for a four-year college and to give those who desired it training in nonprofessional occupations; second, to offer a course of study that would prepare, in more refined fashion than high school was equipped to do, those headed for higher learning at a college or university. The first public junior college opened in 1902 in Joliet, Illinois. By 1920 there were a few hundred of them in the nation.

HIGHER EDUCATION. In 1900 there were approximately 240,000 students in American colleges and universities; by 1920 the number had increased to more than 530,000. The major trend in higher education was the replacement of a fixed curriculum by elective study programs that eventually included elective courses. This idea had received some attention during the late nineteenth century, but after 1900 it gained acceptance at an ever-accelerating pace. The reasons for the trend to let college and university students decide what they would study were, first, a belated acceptance of the idea that individuals at that educational level ought to know what their own needs and interests are and, second, a recognition that certain traditional subjects were not in keeping with modern social and scientific developments.

With the growing awareness of the value of deep and specialized study at the graduate level, enrollment in graduate schools increased from approximately 500 in 1900 to more than 2500 by 1920. It was not until the turn of the century that European academicians in significant numbers began to affiliate with institutions of higher education in the United States; they had previously considered American contributions to scholarship much less sophisticated than the European.

Religion. At the beginning of the twentieth century, within the two wings of Christianity—Protestantism and Roman Catholicism—and also within Judaism, there was a split between the conservatives, or traditionalists, who clung to the old doctrines and rituals of their faith, and the liberals, or modernists, who were inclined to test old religious beliefs by the standards of recent social and scientific advances.

PROTESTANTISM. The modernists within Protestantism were drawn to a recent movement called the "social gospel." Its most influential leaders were two ministers, Congregationalist George Washington Gladden and Baptist Walter Rauschenbusch. The social gospel meant the application of biblical teachings to the social problems resulting from industrialization. Affirming that preaching individual salvation and engaging in charitable works were proper but limited church enterprises, the social-gospel movement attempted to heal economic and social ills, indeed ultimately to reform industrial society itself. In 1908 the Federal Council of the Churches of Christ in America was organized by more than thirty Protestant denominations and adopted the "social creed." Among other things, this creed espoused the abolition of child labor, the implementation of safer and more sanitary working conditions for women, the institution of a shorter workday, and the establishment of pensions for the retired.

The conservatives among Protestant clergy and laymen were apprehensive about this liberal trend. They held tenaciously to a fundamentalist (literal) acceptance of every biblical idea and a denial of scientific discoveries that seemed contrary to traditional religious beliefs. Conservative Protestants, whose numerical strength lay in the rural areas, eagerly welcomed traveling evangelist preachers who, in highly charged revival meetings, summoned sinners to repent. Among revivalists who proclaimed "old-time" religion, none had more drawing power than the energetic and colorful Reverend William A. ("Billy") Sunday.

ROMAN CATHOLICISM. In striking contrast to the segmentation within Protestantism, containing as it did a deep conservative-liberal division and a number of sects, Roman Catholicism had a notable unity brought about by the church's highly refined structure and close control of its affairs. In a 1907 papal encyclical the Roman Catholic church expressly and vigorously repudiated "modernism" in so far as it would weaken traditional religious beliefs; however, the church did accept the role of trying to ameliorate harsh economic and social conditions resulting from industrialization. The most striking development within Catholicism in the United States was the increase in the number of its adherents, from approximately 9 million in 1890 to approximately 12 million in 1900 to more than 18 million in 1920. Much of this increase was due to the "new immigration" wave from the largely Catholic regions of eastern and southern Europe. Some of the more impassioned members of the conservative wing of Protestantism participated in anti-Catholic organizations, such as the American Protective Association, founded in the Midwest in the late 1880s. But such outbursts never approached the extent of nativism that existed in the decades before the Civil War.

JUDAISM. From 1900 to 1920 far-reaching developments took place within American Judaism. During the first three-quarters of the nineteenth century most Jewish immigrants came from Germany. As a group they quickly became Americanized and soon achieved a good measure of economic and social status. In keeping with their reputation for liberalism, they developed by 1900 under the leadership of Rabbi Isaac Mayer Wise of Cincinnati a branch within their faith called Reform Judaism. Although the moral principles of the religion were retained, many rituals and traditions were abandoned, such as the strict prohibition of all nonreligious activities on the Sabbath, the observance of dietary rules, the separation of men and women in the synagogue, and the wearing of the yarmulke (skullcap) and prayer shawl during services. In the "new immigration" wave of 1880 to 1920 approximately 2 million Jews entered the United States, the majority from Russia and Russian-controlled Poland. Fleeing from persecution in the Old World, they tended to cling to Orthodox Judaism with its emphasis on strict observance of ancient religious laws, rituals, and traditions. During the early twentieth century an ever-larger group of American Jews, believing that Reform Judaism had gone to extremes and that Orthodox Judaism was not adjusting to the realities of twentieth-century culture, brought forth a program of Conservative Judaism—a position between the other two branches. The Jews, as a minority group (numbering in 1920 some 3.5 million in a population of about 105 million), found themselves rapidly supplanting Roman Catholics as the main object of whatever religious discrimination there was in the nation.

Science. From the late nineteenth century on, most of the great achievements in pure science emanated from Europe. In 1895 the German Wilhelm Konrad Roentgen discovered X-rays; three years later the Frenchman Pierre Curie and his Polish-born wife Marie discovered radium; in 1900 the German Max Planck introduced the quantum theory, which revolutionized physics; in 1905 the German Albert Einstein presented his Special Theory of Relativity; six years later the Englishman Ernest Rutherford developed the nuclear theory of the atom. American scientific contributions were mainly in the applied areas, such as engineering, and, to a notable but lesser extent, medicine.

Technology. As the twentieth century began, Americans were confident, even exhilarated, that technology would soon solve all problems, bringing about "the good life"—comfortable and pleasant. By 1900 the American people were quite used to marvelous everyday objects that had been invented during the previous quarter of a century, such as electric lighting, the telephone, and the phonograph. The railroad system, developed during the latter half of the nineteenth century, continued to be instrumental in maintaining a thriving economy. Other inventions—the automobile, the airplane, and the radio—appeared whose influence upon the nation not many envisaged.

THE RAILROADS. In the eastern United States railroad construction proceeded rapidly in the 1850s. It was checked by the Civil War, but even before hostilities ceased construction was resumed and it continued at a rapid rate over the next few decades. The trend toward consolidation of the shorter rail lines established many of the nation's great rail systems, such as the New York Central, which was organized by Cornelius Vanderbilt and which ran from New York City to Chicago; the Pennsylvania, which reached Cleveland, Chicago, and St. Louis; and the Illinois Central, which was managed by Edward H. Harriman and which traversed the Mississippi Valley from Chicago to New Orleans. By 1890 a dozen important rail systems had pushed into the region between the Mississippi River and the Pacific Coast; they included the Union Pacific, which ran from Omaha, Nebraska, to near Ogden, Utah; the Central Pacific, which was controlled by Collis P. Huntington and Leland Stanford and which pushed from Sacramento, California, eastward to meet the Union Pacific near Ogden; and the Great Northern, which was under James J. Hill and which traversed the Northwest from St. Paul, Minnesota, to Seattle, Washington. The railroads were of paramount importance in the development of a modern industrial and commercial America with an ever-growing population. They united all sections of the nation, bringing raw materials and foodstuffs to the industrial centers and carrying finished products to the domestic markets and to ports for shipment in foreign trade.

The shrewd and powerful entrepreneurs who organized and managed the great rail systems frequently used unscrupulous methods to secure domination. Despite the obvious benefits from the rapid extension of the railroad lines, criticism increased against those responsible for the management of the great rail systems. The owners were charged with a number of abuses in promotion, construction, and operation. These protests led to the passage of a number of stringent federal regulatory measures: the Interstate Commerce Act of 1887, which created the Interstate Commerce Commission

(ICC) to implement the provisions of the law and was the first attempt by the federal government to control private business enterprise in the public interest; the Elkins Act of 1903, which struck closely at the railroad practice of rebates that had been declared illegal by the Interstate Commerce Act; the Hepburn Act of 1906, which by increasing the power of the ICC made a great advance toward government regulation of the railroads; and the Mann-Elkins Act of 1910, which corrected certain defects in the Hepburn Act. During World War I the railroads were placed under government control by presidential proclamation. The Railroad Administration, with the secretary of the treasury as director general, operated the lines as a unified system. Coordination of rail transportation during this period resulted in marked savings of time and energy.

THE AUTOMOBILE. The first practical automobiles were built in the 1890s in both the United States and Europe. A number of American inventors produced steam-driven vehicles. By 1900 over a hundred different makes of this type were being manufactured; the best-known was the Stanley Steamer. Soon the electric car overtook the steam car in popularity. Throughout the period, meanwhile, American automakers experimented with vehicles containing an internal combustion engine that used gasoline. The first operable American gasoline-powered car was built in 1893 by the brothers Charles E. and J. Frank Duryea. But American car manufacturers lagged behind their European counterparts, continuing to produce mostly steam and electric automobiles after Europeans had developed the gasoline-powered car to the point of demonstrating its advantages over the other types of vehicles. In 1901 Ransom Olds, who made the Oldsmobile, established the assembly-line system of manufacturing cars. A few years later Henry M. Leland, who produced the Cadillac, began to use interchangeable parts. Both these techniques were fully exploited by automaker Henry Ford.

In 1908, in a chassis he called the Model T, Ford installed a simple gasoline engine he had invented. Within five years he was producing over five hundred a day of these small, inexpensive cars, popularly referred to as "flivvers" and "tin lizzies." Production mounted rapidly to keep up with the demand. In 1914 Ford introduced a moving assembly line, in which the car's frame moved on a main conveyor belt while other belts brought parts to be used by workmen in assembling the vehicle. By such amazingly efficient production methods, Ford managed to decrease the price of his cars almost every year. By 1916 they were selling for less than $400. The Ford Motor Company would soon be able to boast that the Model T could be found on the roads of every continent. The American people enjoyed a mobility that they had never before experienced. Young as it was, the automobile industry by 1920 was already the third largest in the nation. In that year close to 2 million automobiles were sold in the United States.

THE AIRPLANE. From the middle of the nineteenth century on, inventors in the United States and Europe attempted in earnest to build a machine that would carry human beings into the air. The American Samuel P. Langley made some notable progress in experiments with flight. Wilbur and Orville Wright, while operating a bicycle-repair shop in Dayton, Ohio, immersed themselves in the study of and experimentation with flying. On December 17, 1903, at Kitty Hawk, North Carolina, the Wright brothers made the first human flight in a power-driven, heavier-than-air machine. Orville piloted the gasoline-powered airplane, staying in the air for twelve seconds and traveling 120 feet. This achievement was an impetus to other inventors to construct and fly airplanes. But the development of aviation was slow until its military possibilities were perceived. During World War I the infant United States airplane industry produced about 1,000 military craft. In the war, airplanes—canvas-covered, relatively slow-moving, and capable of holding one or two fliers—were used mostly for observation of enemy movements and for light bombing raids. Squadrons of fighter pilots from the leading belligerents contended for air supremacy. The cancellation of government contracts for military aircraft at the end of World War I was a severe setback to the aviation industry. The Post Office Department helped a bit by opening in 1918 an airmail route between New York City and Washington, D. C., but it was eight years before Congress granted subsidies to commercial airlines for carrying the mails.

THE RADIO. As was the case with the automobile and the airplane, inventors in several nations took part in developing the radio. Among them was the Italian Guglielmo Marconi, who in 1901 built a sending station in England and a receiving station in Newfoundland and then picked up the first overseas wireless signals. In 1906 the American Lee De Forest broadcast the human voice for the first time. The following year De Forest patented a three-element vacuum tube, called a "triode," which amplified the signals emitted by radio stations, making possible long-distance radio communication. (Some decades later the triode served the same purpose in television communication.) In 1910 the first musical broadcast took place in New York City from the Metropolitan Opera House. Woodrow Wilson became the first president to speak over the radio when from a ship he addressed American troops aboard other vessels returning from Europe after World War I. But the radio did not realize its full potential until the 1920s, when commercial broadcasting began.

Medicine. Early in the twentieth century medicine in the United States was making such progress that the people were becoming unquestionably healthier. Americans were convinced that medicine would eventually cure all ills of the body. A major indication of progress was the reform of medical schools. In 1910 Abraham Flexner conducted a comprehensive survey of medical education for the Carnegie Foundation for the Advancement of Teaching. As a result of the report's revelations of inferior practices and its recommendations, approximately half the nation's medical schools were forced to close, while those remaining greatly improved their courses of study and methods of instruction.

Between 1900 and 1920 American medicine made tremendous progress. The national death rate declined from 17.7 per 1000 to 13.1 per 1000. These striking statistics reflect the near-eradication by medical science of malaria, diphtheria, and smallpox. Based on the research on malaria-bearing mosquitoes during the construction of the Panama Canal, effective action was taken within the United States to wipe out the breeding places of mosquitoes and to quarantine people infected with the disease. In 1913 the Hungarian-born Béla Schick introduced a skin test that played a significant role in eliminating diphtheria. The nation conducted an intensive campaign to give children the century-old smallpox vaccination. There was much more effective control (assisted by state and municipal boards of health through improved sanitation programs) of typhoid fever and typhus. Physicians achieved success against syphilis with a European-developed chemical preparation and against tuberculosis with an ever-refined sanatorium treatment. In 1909 the industrialist John D. Rockefeller donated $1 million for the elimination of hookworm disease, from which more than half the children of the South suffered. In 1912 two biochemists, the Englishman Frederick

G. Hopkins and the Polish-American Casimir Funk presented the theory that a lack of specific vitamins in the diet causes certain diseases. Three years later Joseph Goldberger of the United States Public Health Service proved that lack of vitamin B-complex causes pellagra, a debilitating disease then prevalent in the South.

CULTURE

Early in the twentieth century many of the nation's leaders in art, literature, and music made a determined effort to produce works that would appeal to the masses of Americans, not, as heretofore, merely to the elite. At the same time they strove to retain the quality of their output. There were two significant movements in art and literature: realism and naturalism. As for orchestral and operatic music, the nation had not yet come into its own in terms of native-born composers and performers. The musical theater, well loved by so many, was still greatly influenced not only by American vaudeville but also by European operetta. By 1920 motion pictures were well on their way to becoming the most influential art form— the true art of a mass culture. As art, literature, music, and motion pictures reflected the values of mass culture, so too did the developing popular team sports.

Art. At the turn of the century painting and sculpture in the United States seemed to give little evidence of a new direction. Patrons of art demanded the works of the "masters." Yet in painting itself there were important stirrings of a movement called "realism," whose roots lay in nineteenth-century European art. American painters in this genre, who portrayed, without romanticizing, scenes of ordinary life, were quickly followed by the naturalists, who delineated on their canvases what could be called the ugliness of life. And American architecture struck out in excitingly significant changes.

PAINTING. In 1900 the most influential painters of the late nineteenth century were still at work. These artists subscribed to the doctrine of art for art's sake. Central to this idea was that *what* the artist painted did not matter; what mattered was *how* it was painted. This doctrine was popularized by the writings and lectures of James A. McNeill Whistler, who is regarded by many as the most original American painter of the period. Although Whistler subscribed to realism in painting, he asserted that it was the privilege of any artist to turn an actual scene of misery into a scene of beauty. He maintained that the proper arrangement of form and color was the most significant aspect of his work; he was admired as a superb colorist. His most famous painting is a portrait entitled *Arrangement in Gray and Black, No. 1* (1871) but popularly known as *Whistler's Mother*. John Singer Sargent, who lived in England during his most productive years, achieved a reputation as a brilliant portraitist. His renditions of members of American and English high society are radiantly flattering. Considered the founder of mural painting in the United States, John La Farge also committed himself to the design of brightly colored stained-glass windows. A man of deep religious conviction, George Inness, in his consistently romantic and spiritual paintings sought atmosphere rather than form.

Two of the greatest realists of the period were Thomas Eakins and Winslow Homer. In Eakins's work, much of it pertaining to outdoor activity such as hunting and swimming, an honesty of detail is achieved without sacrifice of depth of feeling. The emotional impact of his paintings, particularly those in which the human figure is rendered, is such as to place Eakins in the first rank of American artists. Winslow Homer became well known as a marine painter. He attempted to convey the sea objectively and directly in dramatic color.

Younger American painters extended the realism of Eakins and Homer to naturalism. A movement arose called The Eight or the Ashcan School. They painted naturalistic urban scenes with a notable absence of sentimentality, choosing as their subjects such aspects of seamy city life as saloons, poolrooms, and sweatshops. The Ashcan School included Robert Henri, art teacher as well as painter, and John Sloan. Sloan's portrayals of teeming New York City life, executed with broad, powerful brush strokes, are considered the finest expression of the Ashcan School. Greatly influenced by the Ashcan School was the young painter George Bellows, who left the Midwest to study with Henri. Bellows's work, much of it, such as *Dempsey and Firpo* (1924), dealing with boxing matches, exudes rough strength that fills the canvas with a unique excitement.

In 1913 a group of forward-looking American artists, including Henri and Bellows, organized the International Exhibition of Modern Art at the Sixty-ninth Regiment Armory in New York City.

Popularly called the Armory Show, the exhibition was a precipitate introduction of modern art to the American people. The works of American artists accounted for approximately two-thirds of the more than 1500 pieces shown, but what gained the greatest amount of attention was the collection of paintings and sculptures representing European avant-garde movements: fauvism (in which objects were presented in a flat distorted manner and in intense brilliant colors) and cubism (in which the traditional attempt to present an object three-dimensionally by use of perspective was abandoned in favor of presenting the object two-dimensionally, fragmenting it and redelineating it from a number of points of view simultaneously through use of many overlapping, interlocking often transparent geometric planes).

SCULPTURE. The last art in the United States to develop a contemporary mode was sculpture. Most American sculptors continued to imitate the style of nineteenth-century European sculptors well into the twentieth century. Although the works of Daniel Chester French varied greatly in both subject matter and style, French excelled in rendering the human figure along realistic lines. His most notable achievement is the stupendous figure of Abraham Lincoln (1922) in the Lincoln Memorial in Washington, D.C. The preeminent sculptor of the period was Augustus Saint-Gaudens, whose figures are distinguished by an energetic lifelike expression. Among the most characteristic examples of his style are the statues of naval officer David G. Farragut (1881) in New York City and President Lincoln (1887) in Chicago.

ARCHITECTURE. Dominating American architecture from the latter nineteenth century through the early twentieth century was the revival of the Renaissance style and, to a somewhat lesser degree, the classic Greek and Roman styles from which it was derived. These styles were popularized by McKim, Mead & White, an architectural firm that exercised tremendous influence upon American building for many decades. Headed by Charles Follen McKim, William Rutherford Mead, and Stanford White, the firm in its many structures turned the tide from the immoderate mid-nineteenth-century romanticism to a restrained classicism. Stanford White had a particular concern and became famous for rich and graceful interior ornamentation. Two of the greatest achievements of McKim, Mead & White were the Boston Public Library (1895) and the no longer existing Pennsylvania Railway Station (1910) in New York City.

There was a movement among some American architects to free themselves from imitation of traditional styles that dominated the architecture of the time. Louis H. Sullivan, the head of the movement, propounded the theory that "form follows function"; that is, a building's architecture should be organically related to its use. Although this theory was rejected by most architects during Sullivan's career, it eventually became *the* spirit of architecture not only in the United States but also throughout the world.

Sullivan created a style that was both functional and distinctly American. This was readily observable in the early skyscrapers that he designed. The American architectural concern in the latter nineteenth century was to construct large office buildings for the nation's burgeoning cities. The solution was found in the skyscraper, which could hold many stories in a steel framework. The first skyscraper was built in 1884 in Chicago. The design of the sixty-story Woolworth Building (1913) in New York City, produced by architect Cass Gilbert, greatly influenced the construction of skyscrapers for a number of years.

Literature. The major development in literature during the early twentieth century was the firm rooting of realism and naturalism, which, originating in mid-nineteenth-century Europe, were introduced to the United States in the latter part of the century. Realism in literature is the attempt to portray life objectively. The writer makes every effort to describe his observations of society without subjectivity, every effort to refrain from idealizing or romanticizing his material. Although realism was definitely established in the United States during the early 1900s, the writing style retained much of the gentility that had been a trait of American literature for decades. Following close on realism was naturalism. The naturalistic writers in a sense extended realism as far as possible, portraying life in all its harshness, indeed sordidness.

THE NOVEL. During the late nineteenth century William Dean Howells was a pioneer of realism. Through his articles, reviews, and his own novels, he enormously influenced younger writers and introduced new trends to the American public. His best-known work is *The Rise of Silas Lapham* (1885). Professionally influenced by Howells and a close friend of his was Henry James, who was to become the most skilled writer of realism, achieving a solid reputation for his novels and short stories. In 1876 the thirty-three-year-old James decided to make his permanent home in England, and ultimately he became a British subject. His treatment of the subtle-

ties of character and his highly complex style that conveyed intricate shades of thought had a great impact on contemporary authors
both in the United States and Great Britain. Two of his most
praised works are *The Ambassadors* (1903) and *The Golden Bowl*
(1904). A friend of James's was Edith Wharton, whose own writing
was influenced by his. In such novels as *The House of Mirth*
(1905) and *The Age of Innocence* (1920) Wharton deals with the
emptiness of rigid social convention among wealthy New Yorkers in
the early twentieth century.

A notable regionalist author was Willa Cather. Her novels *O
Pioneers* (1913) and *My Antonia* (1918), both stylistically lovely,
exalt the strength of spirit of immigrant families on the Great
Plains. Booth Tarkington established himself as an amiable delinea-
tor of the genteel life in the small towns of the Midwest.

Credited with introducing naturalism into American literature is
Stephen Crane, who died in 1900 at the age of twenty-nine. Crane
was exceedingly adept at imagery. His novel *Maggie: A Girl of the
Streets* (1893) deals with a young woman who ultimately commits
suicide in the hopelessness of life in a slum; his novel *The Red
Badge of Courage* (1895) portrays a young Civil War soldier who
gradually rises above cowardice as he sheds his illusions about war
and encounters its realities. An influential practitioner of naturalistic writing was Frank Norris. His *McTeague* (1899) is a grim study
of San Francisco slum life. *The Octopus* (1901), which treats the
struggle between wheat growers and railroad owners, and *The Pit*
(1903), which deals with speculation on the Chicago grain market,
are significant contributions to the early-twentieth-century "muckraking" movement, which searched out misconduct in the fields of
business and politics. Another muckraker was Upton Sinclair,
whose novel *The Jungle* (1906) graphically exposes unsanitary conditions in the Chicago meat-packing plants. Jack London also contributed to the development of the naturalistic tradition. London
subscribed to the philosophy of the "survival of the fittest," and his
works celebrate ruthless individualism and brutal power. His most
famous novel, *The Call of the Wild* (1903), relates how a tame dog
is forced to revert to the ways of his savage forebears.

POETRY. The best-known poets of the early twentieth century
were William Vaughn Moody, Edwin Markham, Vachel Lindsay,
and Joyce Kilmer. Moody, a college English instructor, wrote verse
distinguished for its soaring idealism and its lyrical beauty. Mark-

ham won praise for his poem "The Man With the Hoe" (1899),
which condemns the exploitation of labor. Lindsay's poetry is characterized by brilliant onomatopoeic effects and intense rhythms.
Kilmer, who was killed in World War I, achieved fame for "Trees"
(1914), containing the well-known lines "Poems are made by fools
like me,/But only God can make a tree."

DRAMA. During the early twentieth century the plays produced in
the United States were overwhelmingly those by Europeans. The
works of the realists, the Norwegian Henrik Ibsen and the Swede
August Strindberg, and the naturalist German Gerhart Hauptmann
were exceedingly popular with sophisticated American playgoers.
Meanwhile, American dramatists were attempting to establish a
distinctly native drama. Clyde Fitch was the period's most successful playwright. His work was mainly of the melodramatic sort reminiscent of the latter nineteenth century. However, in plays such as
The Girl with the Green Eyes (1902) he dipped into realism, fore-
shadowing the realistic and naturalistic playwrighting that was
soon to come. But playgoers would have to wait until the 1920s for
the advent of a new and vibrant, unmistakably American drama.

Of course, a play, fully to realize its potential, requires the com-
municative skill of actors. Some of the most competent and appreciated actors of the period were John Drew, who in 1887 starred in
Shakespeare's *The Taming of the Shrew;* Ethel Barrymore, who in
1901 appeared in Clyde Fitch's *Captain Jinks of the Horse Ma-
rines;* and Maude Adams, who in 1905 played for the first of many
times the title role in James M. Barrie's *Peter Pan.*

NEWSPAPERS AND MAGAZINES. A new trend in American journalism began in 1895 when William Randolph Hearst purchased
the *New York Journal* and sought to surpass the circulation of Joseph Pulitzer's *New York World,* a well-written newspaper of high
standards. Hearst introduced a style of reportage that held reader
interest by dealing with sensational items or ordinary news sensa-
tionally distorted.To retain its own readers and capture others, the
New York World felt compelled to do the same. This newspaper
style of coverage came to be called "yellow journalism," after the
"Yellow Kid," the first comic strip printed in color. The "yellow
press" was characterized by such techniques as large blatant headlines and an abundance of pictures. After 1898 Pulitzer withdrew
from the race with Hearst and returned the *New York World* to its
more responsible traditions.

During the heyday of the sensationalist press a half-a-century-old newspaper with a lagging circulation was purchased and developed into one of the world's most distinguished newspapers. This was the *New York Times* under the ownership of Adolph S. Ochs, who introduced the slogan "All the News That's Fit to Print." Ochs saw to it that his newspaper became a model of dignity, objectivity, accuracy, and thorough coverage. The *New York Times* was to become the nation's newspaper of historical record.

A development in American journalism that had widespread effects was the emergence of newspaper chains. Edward Scripps started the first chain, which eventually included more than thirty newspapers in fifteen states of the Middle and Far West. However, the most prominent newspaper chain was Hearst's. With an empire that eventually included forty large-circulation newspapers, Hearst exercised a tremendous influence on American society and culture.

A highly important aspect of early-twentieth-century periodical publishing was the appearance of the "muckraking" magazines. The term "muckrakers" was applied to a group of writers who stirred public opinion to the point of action by exposing abuses in business and corruption in politics. The word originated with President Theodore Roosevelt, who, while concurring with the basic accusations of the crusading writers, criticized them for their focus on sensationalism. He compared them with a character in John Bunyan's seventeenth-century allegory *Pilgrim's Progress* who was so intent on piling up the filth with his muckrake that the only way he looked was downward. Several popular magazines of the period, including *Collier's, The Cosmopolitan, Everybody's Magazine,* and most prominently *McClure's Magazine,* provided the muckrakers with a forum for some of their most startling disclosures. Two major series of articles carried by *McClure's Magazine* were Ida M. Tarbell's "History of the Standard Oil Company," which condemned the monopolistic practices of that corporation, and Lincoln Steffens's "Shame of the Cities," which exposed corruption in various municipal governments across the nation.

Although President Roosevelt was unwilling to recognize his indebtedness to the muckrakers, his own crusade for social justice was significantly aided by their work. One can trace to the muckrakers such results as legislation for the protection of consumers and suits by the federal government against various large business consolidations.

Music. During the early twentieth century a number of American symphony orchestras and the Metropolitan Opera House ranked with the world's best musical organizations. But few of the musicians, singers, and conductors and even fewer of the composers were Americans. The musical theater in the United States was greatly influenced by a European source, the operetta, but also by American vaudeville, which had a particular impact on the shows of George M. Cohan and Florenz Ziegfeld.

ORCHESTRAL COMPOSERS AND COMPANIES. At the turn of the century most of the great orchestral music was still being produced by European composers. The most important American composers were the romanticist Edward MacDowell and the avant-gardist Charles Ives. MacDowell is best known for his piano pieces, the most popular of which is *Woodland Sketches* (1896). However, he wrote numerous orchestral works, including the esteemed *Indian Suite* (1892), which uses American Indian melodies. Ives was a daring innovator in twentieth-century music, employing dissonance and unusual rhythms. Although all of these stylistically advanced pieces were written before 1920, they had no influence on musical composition of the time, since the vast majority of his works lay unpublished and unperformed until the 1940s. His works frequently embody American folk music. Included in his output were symphonies, among them the acclaimed *Third Symphony* (1904); orchestral suites; chamber music; and choral works.

The New York Philharmonic Symphony Orchestra, which began in 1842 and is the oldest symphony orchestra in the world, attracted two outstanding conductors: the German-born Walter Damrosch and the Austrian Gustav Mahler, who was not only one of the greatest conductors of the period but also a world-renowned composer. In 1900 the Boston Symphony Orchestra (founded in 1881) occupied its new headquarters, Symphony Hall, whose brilliant acoustics immediately placed it in the ranks of the world's greatest concert halls. That same year the Philadelphia Orchestra was founded. Under the dynamic and flamboyant leadership of the London-born Leopold Stokowski, beginning in 1912, the orchestra quickly assumed a place as one of the world's finest orchestras.

OPERA. The Metropolitan Opera House in New York City, which was established in 1883, quickly became the foremost operatic company in the United States. It was in a class with the leading opera houses of the world. In 1908 Giulio Gatti-Casazza came from

Italy to become its general manager. He served forcefully in that capacity for twenty-seven years, attracting great singers to the company. The Italian tenor Enrico Caruso made his debut at the Metropolitan in 1903. Possessor of one of the most brilliant voices in opera history, Caruso was the preeminent star of the house until shortly before his death in 1921. His repertory included more than fifty roles in Italian and French operas; his interpretation of Canio in Leoncavallo's *I Pagliacci* is widely considered unequaled. Other outstanding singers of the Metropolitan Opera Company were soprano Geraldine Farrar, acclaimed for her singing of the title role in Puccini's *Madama Butterfly*; soprano Emma Eames, who triumphed in the title role of Puccini's *Tosca*; and the Italian baritone Giuseppe de Luca, who mastered about one hundred roles from the Italian and French operas.

MUSICAL THEATER. Performances of orchestral music and opera were attended by a small segment of the population, but millions of Americans took delight in the lighter tunes of musical theater.

American operettas, like those of Europe (where they originated), had by and large a frankly sentimental plot and contained many highly pleasant, sweeping melodies. The most successful composer of operettas during the early twentieth century was the Irish-born Victor Herbert. Some of his most popular works were *Babes in Toyland* (1903), *The Red Mill* (1906), and *Naughty Marietta* (1910). "Ah! Sweet Mystery of Life" and "I'm Falling in Love with Someone" are two songs from *Naughty Marietta* that have remained constant favorites.

Former vaudevillian George M. Cohan became the jack-of-all-trades in the early-twentieth-century American musical theater— he frequently produced; directed; wrote the book, music, and lyrics for; and starred in the same show. Among the most successful of his typically exuberant shows were *Little Johnny Jones* (1904) and *Forty-five Minutes from Broadway* (1906). He composed a host of highly esteemed songs, including "The Yankee Doodle Boy" (1904), "Give My Regards to Broadway" (1904), "You're a Grand Old Flag" (1906), and the most popular American song of World War I, "Over There" (1917).

As a theatrical producer Florenz Ziegfeld brilliantly fathomed what an audience wanted and gave it to them. He was noted for productions that featured elaborate sets, beautiful women in lavish costumes, and topflight comedians. In 1907 he introduced the first of his annual Ziegfeld Follies, revues that remained popular for almost twenty-five years. Among his stars were Fannie Brice, who went through her comedy routines with involved face-mugging; Eddie Cantor, whose singing was accompanied by an inimitable rolling of eyes, clapping of hands, and skipping of feet; Al Jolson, who in blackface introduced many popular songs, among them "Mammy" and "Swanee"; Will Rogers, who while dressed as a cowboy and performing rope tricks made homely but shrewd comments on current political and social topics; W. C. Fields, who, with bulbous nose, while speaking from the side of his mouth performed intricate feats of juggling; and the black Bert Williams, who with his light-skinned face covered with burnt cork and in a shabby dress suit portrayed a sad victim of hard luck, telling stories and singing songs of his woe in an exaggerated black dialect.

MODERN DANCE. Starting early in the twentieth century, and emanating in large part from the creative ideas of American performers, modern dance was in its ascendancy during the late 1930s. The new form's exponents (there were not many in the beginning) rejected completely the artificial formality with which dance, particularly ballet, had become encumbered. The first and the most influential leader of the movement to free dance from its long-standing restrictions was Isadora Duncan, who early in the twentieth century won recognition touring throughout first Europe and then her native United States. Clad in a tunic patterned after that worn in ancient Greece, with scarves enveloping her neck and shoulders, and with feet bare, she gave performances conveying the ultimate in flowing simplicity and naturalness and seeking to express the innermost feelings of the human mind and body. Ruth St. Denis, a contemporary of Duncan's, choreographed dances based mainly upon Asian and American Indian themes, which she and the performers associated with her, stunningly costumed, executed in a most "free" manner, attempting to convey to the audience a feeling that it had been witness to, and indeed part of, a religious experience.

In 1915 St. Denis and her husband, the innovative and stylistically virile dancer Ted Shawn, founded the Denishawn dance company, which was until its closing in the early 1930s both a performing troupe and a school. The former made many successful tours throughout the United States and abroad and helped to gain public acceptance for modern dance; the latter trained performers, choreographers, and teachers not only to serve in the troupe but also to carry on the cause of modern dance.

BANDS. An important facet of American musical activity consisted of band concerts. Many communities organized their own bands, made up of unpaid local citizens, which gave open-air performances weekly throughout the summer season. But paramount in this genre were the professional bands that during national tours and resort engagements provided the American people with their best opportunity to listen to a large ensemble of highly skilled instrumentalists led by able directors. The repertory of these bands consisted mostly of marches (attesting to the band's military origins), but they also performed selections from orchestral music, opera, and the musical theater.

By far the most famous bandmaster was John Philip Sousa. After leading the United States Marine Corps Band for twelve years, Sousa formed his own concert band in 1892. In addition to frequent tours of the United States, the Sousa band made four European tours and a world tour, all of which were widely acclaimed. Sousa also became the nation's best-known composer of band music. His approximately a hundred vigorous and melodic marches, which earned him the title the "March King," include such exceedingly popular compositions as "Semper Fidelis" (1888), "The Washington Post March" (1889), and what is almost the official American patriotic march "The Stars and Stripes Forever" (1897).

After World War I the popularity of concert bands diminished rapidly as the American people's taste in lighter music shifted from the simple sounds of these bands to the sophisticated rhythms of dance bands.

Motion Pictures. In 1900 few imagined that the embryonic motion pictures would become the most influential art form (as well as a far-reaching method of communication) of the first half of the twentieth century.

BEGINNINGS. Toward the end of the nineteenth century attempts to first produce and then project motion pictures were made by numerous inventors, including Thomas A. Edison of the United States, William Friese-Greene of Great Britain, and the brothers Louis and Auguste Lumière of France. Who was the first to succeed is uncertain, since several experimenters achieved this goal during the same period. In the United States motion pictures were first projected on a screen in a New York City theater by Edison in

1896. Included in the short program were a dance sequence and part of a boxing match. The first film to relate a sustained story was *The Great Train Robbery* (1903), directed by Edwin S. Porter. In 1905 there opened in McKeesport, Pennsylvania, the first nickelodeon, a name given to a theater (often a converted storeroom) that showed a motion-picture program, usually with piano accompaniment, for five cents. Within two years approximately 5000 nickelodeons had begun operation. Soon companies were formed to meet the increasing desire for motion-picture entertainment. Company heads, such as Louis B. Mayer, Jesse Lasky, and Samuel Goldwyn, earned reputations as pioneers in American film production. Hollywood quickly became the nation's movie center as early film directors went to California because of its good weather, necessary since filming had to be done outdoors.

DIRECTORS. Two famous film directors were D. W. (David Wark) Griffith and Mack Sennett. Griffith was one of the most creative directors in motion-picture history; he introduced such techniques as the flashback, the fade-out, the close-up, panning, and montage. Griffith's masterpiece is *The Birth of a Nation* (1915), a work on the Civil War and Reconstruction whose high technical and artistic merit is unfortunately marred by antiblack bias. Sennett specialized in slapstick comedies. Hallmarks of his films are the wild chasing after wrongdoers by the Keystone Kops and the prancing about of bathing beauties at the seaside.

STARS. By 1920 a number of motion-picture actors and actresses had become "stars"; their faces and names were known by virtually everyone in the nation. One of the very biggest stars was the incomparable comedian Charlie Chaplin. He created the character of a gentle little tramp with a funny mustache, wearing a derby, a skimpy jacket, baggy pants, oversize shoes, and carrying a bamboo cane. Mary Pickford ("America's Sweetheart") invariably portrayed endearing innocent girls. Theda Bara was the "Vamp" (a slang term for a sultry woman who uses her wiles on men). The handsome and muscular Francis X. Bushman was the first "lover" to adorn the screen. Pearl White earned a wide popular following as the heroine in breathtaking serials, such as *The Perils of Pauline* (1914). William S. Hart played the grim-faced, strong-willed cowboy in more than twenty-five westerns.

Sports. From the beginning of the twentieth century the developing popular team sports, exhibiting as they did the worth of group cooperation on the one hand and group competition on the other, both reflected and influenced mass culture, affecting participants and spectators.

BASEBALL If any sport can be said to be the national game of the United States it is baseball, an outgrowth of the English game of cricket. Abner Doubleday, a career Army officer, is credited by some with originating baseball in 1839 at Cooperstown, New York (a claim that is open to dispute). The first professional baseball team, organized in 1869 in Cincinnati, Ohio, was soon joined by a host of teams in other cities. In 1876 the National League was established; in 1900 the American League was organized. The major leagues began to achieve much success as a number of first-rate players drew fans to baseball parks. Among these were Honus Wagner, Christopher ("Christy") Mathewson, and Tyrus ("Ty") Cobb. Wagner, who played for the Pittsburgh Pirates, is widely considered the greatest shortstop in baseball history. Mathewson, perhaps the best pitcher of his period, won close to four hundred games for the New York Giants. Cobb, a superb outfielder for the Detroit Tigers, was noted for his batting prowess and base running.

BOXING During the post–Civil War period boxing was a less than popular American sport; indeed, it was illegal in most states. In the 1880s it came into its own, largely through the efforts of John L. Sullivan. The world heavyweight boxing champions during the 1890s were Sullivan, who in 1889 had defended his title in the last bare-knuckle championship fight; the technically skilled James J. Corbett; and Robert P. ("Bob") Fitzsimmons, who originated the solar-plexus punch. The first heavyweight champion of the new century was James J. Jeffries, who retired undefeated after six years. John Arthur ("Jack") Johnson won the heavyweight championship in 1908, becoming the first black to hold the title. In 1915 he lost the crown to Jess Willard. Boxing gained wide acceptance during World War I as an integral part of the physical-training program for servicemen.

FOOTBALL American football developed from the English game of rugby. In 1869 Princeton and Rutgers played the first intercollegiate game. In 1869 the recently organized American Intercollegiate Football Association established a body of rules for the game. Walter C. Camp, football coach and later athletic director at Yale University, is often called the father of American football. In 1889 he originated the practice of selecting an annual All-American col-

lege football team. More significantly, he devised many of the rules
and patterns of play associated with the modern game.

BASKETBALL. In 1891 James A. Naismith, a Young Men's Christian Association physical-education instructor, invented basketball.
Seeking a game that could be played indoors in cold weather, he
gave his students, divided into two teams, a soccer ball to play with,
and hung a peach basket at each end of the gymnasium. Most of
the rules he devised have remained unchanged. In 1896 the first
intercollegiate game was played between Yale and Wesleyan. At
the beginning of the twentieth century the game rapidly became
popular in high schools and colleges throughout the nation among
both young men and young women.

Chapter 2

THE ROARING TWENTIES: 1920–1930

The decade after World War I—"the Roaring Twenties"—was marked by an almost frenzied acceleration in the tempo of American life. The people tended to discharge their energies not by attempting to deal with serious issues but by gratifying a desire for personal pleasure. The prosperity that characterized the Roaring Twenties proved insecurely founded. And the decade ended with the stock-market crash—prelude to the worst depression in the nation's history.

HISTORICAL BACKGROUND

In the postwar decade the Republican party and its newfound conservatism held the loyalty of most Americans. During this period of unprecedented prosperity the people turned away from the liberal philosophy that characterized the progressive movement. In domestic matters the federal government embraced a philosophy of laissez-faire. But under three Republican presidents (Warren G. Harding, Calvin Coolidge, and Herbert C. Hoover) who believed that the government should actively promote prosperity, the avowed policy of "hands off" became in reality one of "hands out-stretched"—to business and at the expense of labor and agriculture. Tired of war and disillusioned by the treaty-making, the people attempted to withdraw from international commitments. Even so, the three Republican administrations did not allow the United States to retreat into full isolationism.

Politics saw the old issues go. Progressive reform, imperialism, war, treaty-making—all were forgotten. Yet the game of politics is never ended. The rules remain the same. The object is to win each round. A Republican party that was reunited after a deep split in the election of 1912 became once more the party of the majority of Americans. Most voters, desiring to escape from the challenge of Wilson's idealism and the responsibilities of world leadership, believed they were returning to "normalcy" (a campaign term used by Republican presidential candidate Harding in 1920) by restoring the Republican party to power.

SOCIETY

The social ambiance of the 1920s was largely determined by the effects of World War I. During the war there was a suspension of the old-fashioned absolute moral code, and then a disinclination to return to it, and subsequently the substitution for that code of a more free and individual morality. Another result of the war was the increased independence of women. They had engaged in many new types of jobs as part of the war effort and quickly began to demand greater freedom as their right. As a result of their wartime opportunities, blacks showed a newfound dignity. The strict conservation policies of the government during the war included confining the use of grains almost exclusively to food, thus greatly limiting their use for liquor production. This gave impetus to the ultimate success of the long drive for prohibition, which could not be effectively enforced and gave rise to a large-scale illicit liquor traffic. Also, during the war Americans allowed the government to suppress criticism, mobilize labor and other resources, and raise money through bond drives and increased taxation. After the war the nation permitted itself to deport aliens, to mistrust and mistreat political radicals, and to accept the idea of "one hundred percent Americanism."

A New Morality. The 1920s saw the sudden end of an old way of life and the beginning of a new. The decade meant a new morality. This meant, among other things, the weakening of religious influence and parental authority and the supplanting of the traditional absolute moral code by a more free and personal one, which permitted such activities as drinking illicit liquor, doing the Charleston and other extreme dances, engaging in uninhibited discussions of sexual matters, and petting in public. Those Americans who refused to adapt to this way of life tried to retain the old religious-moral standards—but in the face of overwhelming odds.

Fads. Every era has its fads, but in the 1920s they were conspicuously abundant. During these ballyhoo years people used their leisure time to experience new amusements, including the following: marathon dancing, in which couples agonizingly clung together for thousands of hours; flagpole sitting, with Alvin ("Shipwreck") Kelly setting a record of twenty-three days and seven hours; goldfish swallowing, indulged in particularly by college students; solving crossword puzzles, for which the "addicted" were required to know esoteric two-letter words; playing Mah-Jongg (an ancient Chinese game), in which devotees, overwhelmingly women, drew and discarded 144 ivory tiles in trying to secure a winning hand of four sets of three tiles and a pair.

As for attire, young men affected low-crowned, flat-topped, pork-pie hats with a turned-up brim, bell-bottomed trousers, and long raccoon coats; young women took to bobbed hair, plucked eyebrows, mascaraed eyelashes, rouged cheeks, and—the ultimate in cosmetic achievement—a mouth turned bow-shaped with bright red lipstick, as complements to straight, long-waisted dresses so short that they exposed the knees (sometimes rouged), below which were rolled-down stockings.

The period was notably prolific in the coining of imaginative words and phrases. Some popular expressions were "the bee's knees" and "the cat's meow" for a transcendentally impressive person or thing, "applesauce" and "banana oil" for anything nonsensical, "flapper" for a young woman who rejected constraint and convention in conduct and apparel, "neck" for caress intimately, and "speakeasy" for a place where illicit liquor was sold.

The Independence of Women. During the decade American women achieved an increased independence—political, economic, and social.

THE SUFFRAGE. The egalitarian philosophy of the far-western frontier, the entrance of women into certain trades and professions, the opening of institutions of higher education to women—all these gave impetus to the campaign for woman suffrage after the Civil War. Wyoming was the first state to grant the ballot to women, having been admitted to the Union in 1890 with the provision already established by law. The progressive era was marked by a notable extension of woman suffrage. By the end of the Taft administration in 1913 eight states (Kansas, Colorado, Idaho, Utah, Arizona, Washington, Oregon, and California) had given women the right to vote. Many advocates of women's rights believed that a constitutional amendment was the solution to the issue. Susan B. Anthony, a social reformer and leader in the woman suffrage movement, proposed such an amendment in 1869; nine years later it was introduced in Congress. There it languished for more than forty years. In 1919 Congress passed the Nineteenth Amendment to the Constitution, granting nationwide woman suffrage. Ratification in August 1920 permitted women to vote in the presidential election that year. This result was testimony to the effective work of such feminists as Anthony, Elizabeth Cady Stanton, and Carrie Chapman Catt. But in general women did not soon "take" to politics. They did fulfill their newly acquired civic responsibility by voting in large numbers, but very few became candidates for public office. Even so, the granting of the ballot to women was a tremendously important psychological advance in the movement to attain full equality between the sexes.

NEW OPPORTUNITIES IN EMPLOYMENT. There were opportunities for women previously denied them in the business sector. (Careers in teaching and nursing were still the most commonly pursued.) In years past women had been relegated to secretarial service, but they could now aspire to being, for example, writers for advertising concerns, editors for publishing houses, agents for realty firms, or buyers for department stores.

RELIEF IN HOUSEKEEPING. Perhaps the most significant independence that women achieved was that of being relieved of many tedious and time-consuming housekeeping chores. This permitted them to devote more energy to other activities, such as employment, community services, and leisure. Many married couples were deciding to have fewer children and thus bought smaller homes or rented apartments, which required less housework. Also, the coming into general use of housekeeping appliances had a revolutionary impact upon women's lives. Although the first electric irons and electric toasters had appeared in the late nineteenth century and the first refrigerators and washing machines early in the twentieth century, they were not widely manufactured and sold until the 1920s. In addition to those appliances, a few others, including the vacuum cleaner, were available. Within half a century more than seventy-five household appliances would be marketed. Further, new processing methods increased the amount and variety of foods in cans, jars, and boxes. The rapid increase in commercial bakeries eliminated the necessity for housewives to devote a day each week to making breads, cakes, and pies.

Blacks. The performing of military duty and the association with whites in France by black servicemen during World War I and the high wages earned by large numbers of blacks employed in war industries gave the nation's blacks a feeling of dignity that they had never before experienced. White racist organizations exploited the resulting feeling of those whites who resented the developing black pride.

The most significant movement among the black masses during the 1920s was racial nationalism. Its most ardent proponent—and the most influential black leader of the period—was Jamaican-born Marcus Garvey. In 1914 he founded the Universal Negro Improvement Association (UNIA), and two years later he set up the headquarters of the organization in New York City. The UNIA espoused worldwide black unity and emphasized the worth and glory of African civilization. Its appeal was directed to the lower classes of the black community. Firmly believing that blacks would never be able to attain equality with whites in nations where they were in the minority, the UNIA dismissed as futile any efforts to achieve integration. Garvey advocated a "back-to-Africa" program and established the Black Star Line comprising three ships to carry his followers to Africa. But he was convicted and then jailed in 1925 for mail fraud in his attempts to get investors for his steamship company. The UNIA quickly disintegrated and Garvey's influence declined. But his persuasive appeal to pride in race gave blacks an enhanced self-esteem that had a lasting effect.

Restriction of Immigration. Before 1914 the United States permitted virtually unrestricted immigration from Europe, barring only those aliens considered likely to affect adversely public health, safety, or morals. The United States was proud to be an asylum for the oppressed of the Old World. Also, the nation needed cheap labor to exploit its abundant mineral wealth, to build railroads, and to operate the machinery in its factories. Yet there was a growing demand for a selective immigration policy.

THE LITERACY TEST ACT Bills providing for a literacy test for immigrants had been vetoed by Grover Cleveland in 1896, William H. Taft in 1913, and Woodrow Wilson in 1915. Finally, in 1917 Congress succeeded in passing over Wilson's veto an act requiring immigrants to be able to read and write a language, whether English or another.

QUOTA ACTS. When it appeared at the close of World War I that "the world was preparing to move to the United States," Congress rather hastily adopted a policy of restriction. The Emergency Quota Act of 1921 limited immigration from Europe in any one year to 3 percent of the number of each nationality resident in the United States according to the census of 1910. The total number of immigrants permitted to enter the United States was set at approximately 357,000 annually.

The Quota Act of 1924 limited immigration from Europe in any one year to 2 percent of the number of each nationality resident in the United States according to the census of 1890, with the total number of immigrants set at approximately 164,000 annually. The changing of the census base from 1910 in the act of 1921 to 1890 in the act of 1924 drastically reduced the quotas of the "new immigrants" (those coming from eastern and southern Europe beginning in the 1880s) and automatically increased the proportion of the "old immigrants" (those arriving from northern and western Europe before the 1880s). As for the non-European nations, the act exempted the Western Hemisphere from its terms but totally prohibited immigration from Asia.

THE NATIONAL ORIGINS PLAN. The Quota Act of 1924 called for permanent regulations to take effect three years later, but the calculations for establishing new quotas proved so difficult that the regulations did not become operative until 1929. According to the National Origins Plan, the total number of immigrants from outside the Western Hemisphere was restricted to approximately 150,000 annually, with each country given a quota based on the proportion that the number of persons of that "national origin" residing in the United States bore to the total American population in 1920. But each European country was permitted to send at least a hundred people a year. All immigration from Asia was still prohibited. Although the quota system did not apply to Canada or the independent nations of Latin America, so wide was the latitude for administrative discretion that State Department and Labor Department officials were able to restrict selectively from even nonquota groups by requiring certain qualifications, such as the holding of property. (Mexican immigration, for example, was greatly reduced.) The National Origins Plan remained in effect until 1965, when the entire body of American immigration regulations was overhauled.

The Labor Movement. Quickly succumbing to the pleasant features of the higher standard of living that the prosperous 1920s made possible, the core of organized labor lost much of its militancy.

MODERATE UNIONISM. Before 1920 organized labor had grown steadily, but in the postwar decade it declined both in activity and prestige. The conservative American Federation of Labor reported more than 4 million members in 1920 and fewer than 3 million in 1930. Several circumstances explain the decline in moderate unionism: (1) it clung to its commitment to the craft-type labor organization in an evermore industrialized society; (2) it failed to come to grips with the problem of technological unemployment; (3) it was still disinclined to enroll blacks, who in larger numbers were entering into important trades; (4) it developed nothing to offer unskilled laborers; (5) it had difficulty making union benefits attractive in the face of increasing company programs of health protection, unemployment insurance, recreational facilities, and profit sharing.

RADICAL UNIONISM. The activities of labor's radical wing were curbed by the postwar anti-Communist campaign of the federal and various state governments. The leftist Industrial Workers of the World never recovered from this onslaught, and by 1925 had virtually disappeared. In labor circles, Communist workers at first strove to capture moderate unions by boring from within, but by the end of the decade they had begun a concentrated drive to form industrial unions committed to intensified class struggle. In 1928 radical workers were responsible for the establishment in the United States of the Communist party, which, however, was never able to pull more than 60,000 votes for its presidential candidate.

Prohibition. Probably no social issue was so widely discussed during the 1920s as the prohibition of the manufacture and sale of intoxicating beverages.

BACKGROUND. National prohibition was the culmination of a long campaign. From its inception early in the nineteenth century, the movement rested upon the conviction of an increasing number of Americans that intoxicants (1) had an injurious effect upon mind and body; (2) led users into vice and crime, thus constituting a menace to life and property; (3) sent many to asylums and prisons, the maintenance of which required heavy taxes; (4) reduced workers' efficiency, thus increasing management problems. The organizations particularly effective in the prohibition movement were (1) the Prohibition party, formed in 1869, whose platform placed destruction of the liquor traffic above every other issue; (2) the Woman's Christian Temperance Union, established in 1874, which undertook a spirited educational campaign; (3) the Anti-Saloon League, organized in 1893, which mobilized the sentiment of evangelical Protestantism so that it wielded great political influence.

THE EIGHTEENTH AMENDMENT. So successful were the tactics of the Anti-Saloon League that by the fall of 1917 the legislatures of more than half the states had banned the liquor traffic and fully two-thirds of Americans were living in areas that were "dry" by either state or local legislation. In December 1917 Congress passed the Eighteenth Amendment to the Constitution, prohibiting the manufacture, sale, or transportation of intoxicating liquors. Ratification by the required number of states was achieved with ease by January 1919.

THE VOLSTEAD ACT. This act, passed over President Wilson's veto in October 1919, provided the machinery for implementing the Eighteenth Amendment. It defined as intoxicating any beverage containing more than one-half of 1 percent alcohol. Administration of the act was assigned to the Bureau of Internal Revenue, a division of the Treasury Department.

There were major obstacles to enforcement of the Volstead Act, including (1) the opposition to national prohibition of some communities, especially large cities; (2) the lack of cooperation between federal and local authorities; (3) the corruption of some enforcement agents, who accepted bribes from illicit liquor traffickers; (4) the failure of the Treasury Department and the Justice Department to centralize control of enforcement services. Disrespect for law continually increased. The drinking of illicit liquor, much of it inferior and even harmful, became widespread, as did bootlegging (the illegal production or distribution of intoxicating beverages). There was extensive smuggling of liquor from other nations. Rival gangs involved in bootlegging, such as, in Chicago, those of Alphonse ("Al") Capone and Dion O'Banion, battled each other violently to retain or expand their areas of operation. The difficulties of implementing the Volstead Act caused many people to denounce the Eighteenth Amendment as a failure and to demand its repeal.

In 1929 President Hoover appointed the National Commission on Law Observance and Enforcement, with former attorney general George W. Wickersham as chairman, to conduct an investigation of prohibition and related problems of law enforcement. In 1931 this commission reported that prohibition was not being effectively enforced but recommended further trial of the Eighteenth Amendment and the Volstead Act.

THE TWENTY-FIRST AMENDMENT. In February 1933 Congress passed, and by December 1933 the required number of states had ratified, the Twenty-first Amendment, which repealed the Eighteenth Amendment. Thereupon, control of the liquor traffic reverted to the states. All but eight promptly permitted the manufacture and sale of intoxicating liquors under various types of regulation.

Antiradicalism. During the 1920s fear of radicalism pervaded the nation. Even the moderate reforms of the recent progressive era came under suspicion. As a result, some who had been reformers in their younger years now gained prominence as defenders of the social order.

THE "RED SCARE." The success of the 1917 Communist revolution in Russia convinced many Americans that the Communists ("Reds") and their sympathizers were using the postwar turmoil to secure political power elsewhere in the world, including the United States. Law enforcement agencies, both federal and state, were put on their guard against radical uprisings. In 1919 almost 250 aliens whose views were regarded as dangerously radical were deported. Early in 1920 Attorney General A. Mitchell Palmer authorized raids on both acknowledged and alleged Communists, resulting in the arrest of more than 4000 persons, many of whom were apprehended and held in violation of their constitutional rights. In the fall of 1920 a bomb exploded on Wall Street, killing thirty-eight people, sending a wave of fear across the nation, and contributing greatly to the antiradical fervor. Palmer asserted that the "Reds" were ready to "destroy the government at one fell swoop." By the beginning of 1921, however, the "Red Scare" had abated.

THE BOSTON POLICE STRIKE. In 1919 a dispute over the right of the Boston police force to affiliate with the American Federation of Labor led to a strike of about three-fourths of the force. To prevent the collapse of law enforcement, Calvin Coolidge, then governor of

Massachusetts, dispatched the state militia to the city. Although Coolidge had taken action after Boston was already under control, he won widespread approval for his statement "There is no right to strike against the public safety by anybody, anywhere, anytime."

THE SACCO-VANZETTI CASE. Fear of radicalism was evident in the handling of the case against two acknowledged anarchists, Nicola Sacco and Bartolomeo Vanzetti. In 1921, despite inconclusive evidence, the men were found guilty of murdering a paymaster and a guard in the course of a robbery at a shoe factory in South Braintree, Massachusetts. They received the death sentence, which was stayed by appeals from many people both in the United States and abroad who felt that the men had been convicted because of their anarchist beliefs rather than the evidence presented. They were finally executed in 1927. As a *cause célèbre,* the Sacco-Vanzetti case forced large numbers of Americans to reappraise their fears of radical views and those who held them.

The Ku Klux Klan. Fear created intolerance in the United States. The most notorious manifestation of organized hatred was the Ku Klux Klan. Founded in 1915 by a former itinerant preacher, William Joseph Simmons, in Atlanta, Georgia, the organization took firm root in the Deep South, then spread rapidly throughout the nation after 1920, achieving extraordinary success in the Midwest. The Klan drew its membership primarily from the villages and small towns that had been left rather undisturbed by the immigration, industrialization, and liberal thought of modern America. Although the secret order was to be a memorial to the Ku Klux Klan of the post-Civil War period, it had a wider program than the antiblack one of its precursor. To the original Klan's attacks on blacks, the Klan of the 1920s added anti-Catholicism, anti-Semitism, and antiforeign-bornism. Under a burning wooden cross and clad in white hoods and robes, Klansmen would listen to their officers (holding such titles as "Imperial Wizard," "Grand Dragon," and "Exalted Cyclops") preach an intolerance seldom matched in the nation's history. So many members, especially in the South, belonged to the evangelical sects that the public came to think that fundamentalism was a Klan article. The secret order was preoccupied with the question of morals. Some Klansmen (perhaps without approval of the local chapter) took vigilante action, including "night riding," that might culminate in tarring and feathering, whipping, branding, emasculation, hanging, or burning at the stake.

Although the Klan publicly denied playing a role in politics, it did control the political affairs of many local communities, did elect a number of state officials and some members of Congress, and was a force in the presidential races of 1924 and 1928. In the latter year, when the Democratic party's standard-bearer was the Catholic Alfred E. Smith, the spirit of the Klan was indeed a major factor in the desertion of almost half the states of the Solid South to the Republican candidate. At the height of its activity in the mid-1920s the Klan had an estimated 4 million members. But as a result of the nation's increasing wrath toward the organization, by the beginning of the 1930s the membership had withered away to scarcely 50,000. Since then the Ku Klux Klan, revived a number of times, has existed as a multiplication of splinter groups, as government on federal, state, and local levels has taken action against the order.

Religion. Conservative alarm over radicalism had a counterpart in the area of religion, as many were apprehensive that the changing mood of the nation would weaken traditional religious beliefs. The liberals among Protestant clergy and laypeople feared that a fundamentalist (literal) acceptance of every biblical idea and a denial of scientific discoveries would keep the Christian churches from interaction with modern culture. At times the liberals were inclined to test traditional religious beliefs by the standards of the twentieth century. The conservatives, or fundamentalists, feared that liberal interpretation of the scriptures would destroy the evangelical influence of Protestantism.

Among Protestant laypeople none defended the conservative position more forcefully than did the three-time Democratic presidential candidate William Jennings Bryan, who urged state legislatures to prohibit teaching the theory of evolution in the public schools. When John T. Scopes, a young teacher in Dayton, Tennessee, was indicted in a test case for presenting, contrary to state law, the evolutionary theory in his high-school biology class, Bryan himself served on the prosecution staff. Scopes's defense attorney was Clarence Darrow, the most famous trial lawyer of the period. The arguments of the two distinguished counselors focused the attention of the world on the trial in 1925. Scopes was found guilty of violating the state law and fined $100. Thereafter the fundamentalist cause steadily declined.

Technology. The railroads, facing new forms of competition, resorted to the consolidation of independent lines into large systems. The widespread use of automobiles brought about vast changes in the way Americans lived; and many people realized that before long airplane travel would have a similar effect.

THE RAILROADS. The placing of rail transportation under government control during World War I stimulated the demand in some quarters for government ownership and operation of the railroads. However, immediately after the war the executive branch recommended the return of the railroads to private control, while warning against the establishment of "the old conditions" without modifications.

During the 1920s the railroad operators, as hostile as ever to government regulation, nevertheless turned to the federal government for relief. After 1920 the railroads were alarmed over competition from improved internal waterways, trucking firms, expanding pipeline facilities, and airlines. The solution of the chronic railroad problem seemed to be the unification of independent lines into great systems based upon a careful analysis of the nation's needs. From railroad executives came insistent demands that Congress place their competitors under governmental regulation. The railroad operators explored the difficulties and possibilities of consolidation, but action was slow. Between 1920 and 1929 hundreds of short lines were acquired by the larger rail systems. Not until 1931 did the northeastern roads submit a plan for unification, which the Interstate Commerce Commission approved with certain changes in details. In the Northeast four great networks emerged: the New York Central, with almost 13,000 miles; the Pennsylvania, with more than 16,000 miles; the Baltimore and Ohio, with over 11,000 miles; and the unified Van Sweringen holdings, which included such subsidiary lines as the Erie and the Chesapeake and Ohio, with approximately 12,500 miles.

THE AUTOMOBILE. Car sales in the United States climbed from approximately 2 million in 1920 to about 4.5 million in 1929. Although automobile production greatly increased, the number of car manufacturers decreased, dropping from more than a hundred at the beginning of the 1920s to fewer than fifty at the end. Over half the cars purchased during the early 1920s were manufactured by the Ford Motor Company. In 1924 automaker Henry Ford, as a result of his efficient production methods, was selling the popular Model T for less than $300. Within a very few years, however, the

Chevrolet, manufactured by the General Motors Corporation, surpassed the Model T in sales. In 1929 three firms—General Motors, Ford, and the Chrysler Corporation—dominated American automobile manufacturing, producing approximately 80 percent of all vehicles. By the end of the decade over 21 million cars were on the roads. The coming of the automobile into general use in the 1920s revolutionized American society. It gave the people true mobility. It freed regions of the nation from isolation and thus standardized customs and manners. It brought rural and urban areas closer together. It created the new industry of tourism, in which millions of Americans on vacation participated. It stimulated the growth of the steel and rubber industries, both of which were important suppliers to car manufacturing. It promoted construction of paved roads.

THE AIRPLANE. In 1919 a New York hotel owner offered a $25,000 award to the aviator making the first nonstop flight from New York to Paris. For years the prize was without a recipient. Finally, airmail pilot Charles A. Lindbergh won the award. On May 20, 1927, he took off from Roosevelt Field, Garden City, Long Island, and made a 33½-hour solo flight across the Atlantic Ocean in his airplane *The Spirit of St. Louis;* he landed at Le Bourget Field near Paris amid pressing crowds. After being honored by many European nations, he returned to the United States to a wildly enthusiastic welcome. Nicknamed the "Lone Eagle," Lindbergh quickly became a symbol of what was the best in the 1920s. This thrilling flight impelled Americans to focus on the vast possibilities of aviation. Some months before Lindbergh executed his feat, the Department of Commerce, under the provisions of the Air Commerce Act of 1926, began to establish and regulate a nationwide system of airways (routes designated for regular travel by commercial aircraft carrying passengers, goods, and mail), to aid in the construction of municipal airports, and to set up intermediate landing fields. By 1929 there were forty-eight airways with a combined length of 20,000 miles, serving thirty-five cities that possessed airports. The United States was well on its way into the air age.

Medicine. One of the most significant developments in medicine during the 1920s was the use of insulin for the control of diabetes. In 1921 the Canadian Frederick G. Banting, assisted by three other researchers, isolated from the pancreas the hormone that was to be called insulin, which was immediately put to use by physicians in the United States. Another important medical development was the invention in 1928 of the iron lung by Philip Drinker and Louis A. Shaw at the Harvard University School of Public Health in Boston. Consisting of a metal drum in which the patient's entire body except for his head is enclosed, the device provides prolonged artificial respiration in diseases such as poliomyelitis. In surgery there were two notable advances: the extensive use of blood transfusions so that blood lost during an operation could be replaced, and improvements in anesthesia so that the chest cavity could be exposed for lung operations.

But perhaps the outstanding stride in American medicine during the 1920s had to do with the treatment not of physical but of mental dysfunction. Toward the end of the nineteenth century the Viennese physician Sigmund Freud developed psychoanalysis as a means for treating mental disorders and in 1909 he presented the tenets and methods of psychoanalysis in a series of lectures in the United States. But it was not until after World War I that the Freudian theories gained wide acceptance among American professionals. Freud maintained that mental illness originates in the repression of sexuality in the early stages of a person's physical and mental growth. He affirmed that in order to cure such illness, the subconscious memories of the sexual repression have to be drawn into consciousness. To accomplish this Freud evolved the two main techniques of psychoanalysis: the interpretation of the patient's dreams, which he believed are clues to the subconscious, and free association, in which the patient relates to the psychoanalyst his thoughts without any effort to control them.

The influence of Freudianism in the United States (as in the rest of the Western world) on the treatment of ills of the mind was, of course, enormous, but so too was its impact upon society and culture. Sex became a respectable topic for consideration in the fields of education and religion. Soon the popularizers seized upon psychoanalysis and in a myriad of books, magazines, and newspapers familiarized the people with the subject's essence (often less than precise) and terminology. The idea of investigating the unconscious mind was extensively employed in art, particularly painting, and in literature in the "stream-of-consciousness" device.

The Stock-Market Crash. From 1919 to 1929 the American people experienced a rise in their standard of living more remarkable than any change that had taken place in any previous decade.

The prosperity of the nation was marked by significant changes in the production, distribution, and sale of goods. Business statistics during the 1920s showed the following conditions: (1) a decline in manufacturing costs resulting from the use of standardized methods of operation and the making of uniform goods; (2) a greatly increased number of stockholders; (3) a proliferation of chain stores; (4) an extension of credit to customers through the use of the installment buying plan; (5) a significant increase of wages in most industries. The vast expansion of business enterprise concealed from many economists the highly speculative nature of this period of unprecedented prosperity.

Several features of those boom years were, however, becoming alarming at the beginning of the Hoover administration: (1) agricultural profits were lagging far behind industrial profits; (2) wages of factory workers were increasing, but not nearly so rapidly as the prices of manufactured goods; (3) the nation's factories and farms were producing more than American and foreign consumers were able to buy, while the recently passed high tariff was curtailing the overseas market; (4) consumers were buying an ever-increasing amount of goods on installment, thereby raising the total of outstanding private debts; (5) an extremely large proportion of the annual national income was being invested in highly speculative manufacturing, mining, and transportation enterprises.

Hundreds of thousands of Americans, for the first time, were buying securities (stocks and bonds) on the stock exchange, and many were acquiring their shares on credit. In late October 1929 panic developed in the New York stock market as securities prices dropped with startling rapidity. Over 13 million shares were traded on October 23 ("Black Thursday"). By November 14 approximately $30 billion in the market value of listed stocks had been wiped out. At no previous period had so many Americans been directly involved with corporate securities. The collapse of the New York Stock Exchange was thus the prelude to economic disaster.

CULTURE

Virtually all aspects of American art moved in courses that had been set during the period from the late nineteenth century to World War I. In literature, the novel was still bound by the realism and naturalism of the two preceding decades, but poetry and drama took new approaches both in subject matter and style. To the field of light music the United States made two important contributions: the musical comedy and jazz. A revolution occurred in the motion-picture industry with the invention of sound film. In sports, professional athletics became big business.

Art. Although painting, sculpture, and architecture continued in the same decades-old trends, there was one notable new development—the emergence of photography as an art form.

PAINTING. American painters were still influenced by the movements developed before World War I: the naturalism of the Ashcan School and the avant-garde thrust, particularly cubism, featured in the Armory Show of 1913. Edward Hopper carried on the tenets of the Ashcan School. He often painted run-down buildings on city streets, which if not deserted, have on them pitifully lonely figures. *Early Sunday Morning* (1930), evoking a feeling of stark emptiness, is a typical work. One of the many painters who held to the abstractionism or semiabstractionism presented in the Armory Show was John Marin. He worked in vivid watercolors, with scenes of New York City and the Maine seacoast, especially the latter, as his most frequent subjects. Each object, whether a skyscraper or a wave-dashed rock, is represented in semiabstract form by a few brush strokes.

SCULPTURE. Most American sculptors continued to copy the traditional nineteenth-century European style that had been so well executed by Daniel Chester French and Augustus Saint-Gaudens during the two preceding decades. Lorado Taft, who both worked in and taught sculpture in the Midwest, exerted great influence on that art. He was prolific, specializing in large-scale memorials and fountains, of which two notable examples are in Chicago. The best-known early sculptures of Gutzon Borglum include two studies of Abraham Lincoln: a head (1908) in marble in the rotunda of the Capitol in Washington, D.C., and the president (1911) in bronze, seated on a bench, in Newark, New Jersey. Borglum's masterpiece is the Mount Rushmore National Memorial in the Black Hills of South Dakota. Carved on the side of a mountain are the colossal busts of four presidents; Washington, Jefferson, Lincoln, and Theodore Roosevelt. He began the work in 1927 and had nearly completed it when he died fourteen years later. It was finished by his son Lincoln.

PHOTOGRAPHY. Perhaps the most significant development in

American art during the 1920s was the transition of photography, an approximately seventy-five-year-old science that produced a pictorial record, into an art form. The commanding figure in this movement was Alfred Stieglitz. Beginning in 1905 he operated in New York City galleries that for more than forty years were dedicated to the exhibition and promotion of photography as a creative art. His own photographs are considered masterpieces of artistic expression combined with technical proficiency. Immediately preceding and during the first half of the 1920s he produced his most critically acclaimed works, including portraits of his wife (the artist Georgia O'Keeffe), views of Manhattan, and studies of clouds.

ARCHITECTURE. The 1920s saw a continuation of architectural trends begun in the late nineteenth century. Virtually all public and commercial buildings, whether post offices and libraries or banks and railroad stations, were constructed in the late classic Greek and Roman and the Renaissance styles that had been popularized by the firm of McKim, Mead & White. More and more and higher and higher skyscrapers still based upon the functionalism of Louis H. Sullivan were erected. The American architects who were developing a distinctly contemporary style would have to wait for the following decade for their influence to be truly felt.

Literature. American novelists were still influenced by the realism and naturalism of the early 1900s, continually refining the techniques of these genres. The poets, however, rejected the older forms of their craft and sought innovative approaches. The playwrights produced truly American drama liberated from European influence.

THE NOVEL. With the works of novelists such as Sinclair Lewis, F. Scott Fitzgerald, and Ernest Hemingway, realism became so securely established that a return to idealizing or romanticizing material appeared almost impossible. Sinclair Lewis won fame for his works decrying the values and activities of middle-class life. In such novels as *Main Street* (1920) and *Babbit* (1922) he bitingly depicts the intellectual shallowness and cultural limitations of the hard-driving and assured business and professional people of the Midwest. Among his other major works are *Arrowsmith* (1925), which treats the frustration of a young physician's pursuit of his ideals, and *Dodsworth* (1929), which deals with the discord between an American businessman and his flighty wife on a tour of Europe. F. Scott Fitzgerald is regarded as the principal literary interpreter of the Roaring Twenties. His novels *This Side of Paradise* (1920) and *The Beautiful and the Damned* (1921) unerringly capture the wildness, recklessness, and overindulgence of a reveling post–World War I generation. *The Great Gatsby* (1925), in relating the story of a bootlegger, portrays the spiritual bankruptcy of the upper stratum of American society of the period. Ernest Hemingway established himself as one of the most highly praised writers of the 1920s with the publication of two novels, *The Sun Also Rises* (1926) and *A Farewell to Arms* (1929), both of which throw doubt upon the generally accepted values of American and European society. The former work describes a group of American expatriates in Paris, for whom their postwar life brings disillusionment and despair. The latter relates how an American ambulance driver in World War I is undone by a tragic love affair and by the war itself. Hemingway's well-known literary style, pointedly and elegantly concise, was greatly admired and much imitated by many contemporary writers.

Carrying on in the naturalistic tradition was Theodore Dreiser, who was to become the period's commanding novelist. His characters are the victims of their own actions, which are determined by two forces over which they have no control—their heredity and their environment. Rather than making decisions based on morality, his characters are impelled by their emotional and physical needs. Dreiser's most acclaimed novel, *An American Tragedy* (1925), is the story of a poor and weak-principled young man's quest for wealth and social position. Viewing his pregnant mistress, a lower-class girl, as an obstacle to attaining economic security and social status, he allows her to drown in a boating accident and is subsequently found guilty of and executed for murder.

Sherwood Anderson was a significant writer who rejected both realism and naturalism and focused on a psychological analysis of his characters. Throughout his work is the theme that the rigid rules of organized industrial society so inhibit the basic instincts of human beings that their emotions are warped. In his most impressive novel, *Winesburg, Ohio* (1919), he probes the loneliness and frustration of simple people in a small town.

Important for her influence on Fitzgerald, Hemingway, and Anderson is the American author Gertrude Stein, who had a salon in Paris that included these novelists among many European and American artistic and literary figures. Stein originated the phrase "lost generation" to characterize the disillusioned American intel-

lectual expatriates of the post–World War I period. Stein's own
writing is experimental; sound frequently takes precedence over
meaning, as in her most famous line, "Rose is a rose is a rose is a
rose."

POETRY. Most of the great poets of the 1920s produced works
that were so different in form from what had appeared before that
Americans of even the preceding generation would not have identified them as poetry. The new poets repudiated the traditional verse
form of systematized rhyme and measured rhythm in favor of what
came to be called "free verse," and they explored different approaches to accepted syntax and punctuation.

Still holding to the traditional verse form but employing a natural vernacular mode of expression rather than a formal literary one
were two New Englanders, Edwin Arlington Robinson and Robert
Frost. While Robinson's poems written before World War I are
mainly brief somber elegies on painful existence, his 1920s work
consists of long narrative poems that show a growing acceptance of
the human condition. Robert Frost, possibly the most widely read
twentieth-century American poet, wrote verse linked to the people
and land of New England. Although his poems are written in plain
language about simple people engaged in ordinary activities, his
themes are complex, noble, and symbolic. A common motif is that
since human beings can never conquer nature, or even comprehend
its design, the only course open to them is to carry on a productive
existence that accommodates itself to natural forces. Two of his
most famous poems are early works, "The Death of the Hired
Man" (1914) and "Mending Wall" (1914), the latter with the fa-
miliar opening line "Something there is that doesn't love a wall."

Expressing the ambiance of the Midwest were Carl Sandburg
and Edgar Lee Masters. Many of Sandburg's poems are about the
common people of farms and industrially developing cities; he
treats with a loving sensitivity their economic and social distress
and their yearning for a better future. His verse, which conveys a
sense of strength, makes no use of the conventional rhyme and
rhythm. The language employed is simple, yet at the same time
exalted. Among his collections of poems are *Smoke and Steel*
(1920) and *Good Morning, America* (1928). Edgar Lee Masters's
most important work is *Spoon River Anthology* (1915), a group of
epitaphs in free verse uttered by men and women buried in a ceme-
tery, and exposing—mostly in bitter tones—the deep recesses of

their lives and the closely guarded secrets of their midwestern village.

Singular in its pessimism is the poetry of Robinson Jeffers. To him the earth, full of natural beauty, is desecrated by the estrangement from it of human beings in anguished strivings to achieve their contorted goals. The inspiration for many of his works came from Greek tragedies.

Of the decade's great poets, Ezra Pound and T. S. (Thomas Stearns) Eliot were the most original and also the most influential. Their works marked a decisive break with the content and form of nineteenth-century poetry, and their styles became standards for other poets. The poems of both are characterized by profound scholarship. In 1907 the Idaho-born Pound traveled to Europe, soon settling in England, then in France, and finally in 1925 in Italy. His most significant work is a group of over a hundred poems called the *Cantos*, the first of which was published in 1925 and the last thirty-five years later. The work is an effort to reveal the long and varied story of all the divisions of humankind. The *Cantos* are extraordinarily difficult to comprehend, containing such diverse elements as myths, history, economic theory, medieval European songs, and Far Eastern verse.

Like Pound, the St. Louis–born T. S. Eliot spent most of his life in Europe. In 1927 he became a British subject. His poems are extremely complex, using language intricately and containing abstruse references to a diversity of literatures, myths, and religions. His early poetry reflects the belief that twentieth-century life is destitute of substance, that each human being, to some degree, is cut off from all others and suffers alone. These elements are found in his masterpiece "The Wasteland" (1922), which caused a stir in the literary world when it appeared.

DRAMA. The 1920s marked the "golden age" of American drama. In their successful attempt to free American theater from European influence and create a native drama, many playwrights, led by the towering Eugene O'Neill, engaged in bold experimentation.

O'Neill is considered the greatest playwright the United States has ever produced. He almost alone brought about a fundamental change in American drama. The realism and the naturalism in his plays gave their stamp to American drama from the early 1920s to the present. O'Neill discarded the well-known content and form of past drama and offered to American playgoers strikingly original works. His continued experimentation in subject matter and style encouraged other dramatists to follow suit. His more than a dozen plays of the 1920s exhibit, as do his later ones, an extraordinarily wide range of subject matter and form. *The Emperor Jones* (1920), a play containing exaggerated symbolism and suggesting subconscious elements, is about a black Pullman-car porter who becomes the power-mad dictator of a Caribbean island, then undergoes mental degeneration and is finally destroyed. *Anna Christie* (1921) deals with a prostitute's moral redemption in a fiercely realistic setting. *The Hairy Ape* (1922), a work filled with fantastic imagery, depicts society's destruction of a coarse and illiterate stoker on an ocean liner who has gloried in his physical energy. In the complexly constructed *The Great God Brown* (1926) the characters wear masks, which they change or sometimes remove, to convey the idea that human beings try to hide their true personalities. *Strange Interlude* (1928) is a detailed psychological study of a woman and her relationships with the three men in her life: her husband, her lover, and her longtime friend. In this play O'Neill uses the spoken "asides" of the Elizabethan drama to let the characters reveal their thoughts.

Two other major dramatists of the period, Sidney Howard and Elmer Rice, were also involved with experimentation. Howard is best known for *They Knew What They Wanted* (1924), a realistic play which deals tenderly with an aging immigrant Italian vineyard owner who courts a young waitress through the mails, brings her to California, and then accepts as his own a child she has with one of his hired men. Elmer Rice's most famous work, the naturalistic *Street Scene* (1929), graphically depicts tenement life in New York City.

Among the most celebrated dramatic performances of the decade were the playing of the title roles by John Barrymore in 1922 in Shakespeare's *Hamlet* and by Walter Hampden in 1923 in Edmond Rostand's *Cyrano de Bergerac*.

THE HARLEM RENAISSANCE. The 1920s saw a flourishing of culture, especially in literature, among black Americans. This surge of creativity is commonly referred to as the Harlem Renaissance, since it centered in the predominantly black section of New York City. Three outstanding writers of the Harlem Renaissance were James Weldon Johnson, Countee Cullen, and Langston Hughes. Although he was a well-respected novelist, James Weldon Johnson became best known as a poet. He won fame for *God's Trombones* (1927), a group of sermons in verse. Countee Cullen wrote lyric poetry that expresses pride in his race. Langston Hughes was a prolific author of poems, novels, plays, and short stories. He achieved prominence with the publication of *The Weary Blues* (1926), a collection of vividly descriptive poetry. His works focus on the economic and social plight of black Americans, especially in the cities.

NEWSPAPERS AND MAGAZINES. The most significant development in American journalism was the growing popularity of tabloids. The first one was the *New York Daily News*, founded by Joseph M. Patterson in 1919. Within half a dozen years it had the largest circulation of any of the nation's newspapers. In 1924 two more tabloids entered the field, William Randolph Hearst's *New York Daily Mirror* and Bernarr McFadden's *New York Daily Graphic*. The tabloids appealed to a mass audience by employing a short and narrow page with few columns, having a much compressed and simple style of writing, and using a surfeit of photographs and illustrations. Competing for reader interest, these tabloids gave extensive coverage to events dealing with crime, particularly murder, and sex. At the same time, newspapers with more responsible objectives, such as the *New York Times*, continued to report the news in dignified fashion.

In periodical publishing the most notable advance was the appearance of a large number of general-interest magazines in addition to the established ones that catered to a special-interest readership. Many of these new publications made a striking impact by using photographs and illustrations. Within a few years the general-interest magazines enjoyed large circulations. Among the most flourishing was the *Reader's Digest*, a pocket-size monthly, begun in 1922, that condensed articles from other periodicals. The *Reader's Digest* achieved enormous success. By 1935 the circulation was approximately 1 million; twenty years later it reached 17.5 million, of which 7.5 million copies were in eleven foreign-language editions. Another notable triumph in periodical publishing was *Time*, a weekly news magazine founded in 1923 by Henry R. Luce and Briton Hadden. *Time* became well known for a journalistic style that was breezy, rich with adjectives, and given to coining archly descriptive words. *Time*'s success motivated the founding of two other influential weekly news magazines, *Newsweek* and *U.S. News and World Report*, both of which began publication in 1933. Other magazines that, although remaining relatively small in circulation, were quite influential among sophisticated Americans were *The Saturday Review of Literature* and *The New Yorker*. The former appeared in 1924 as a weekly literary magazine. *The New Yorker*, which Harold Ross founded in 1925 and edited for more than twenty-five years, was launched as a weekly about New York City persons and events, but soon became national in scope. The magazine acquired renown for its discerning analytical essays, penetrating short stories, keen-witted cartoons, and eye-appealing advertisements.

Music. During the 1920s the nation's premier bodies engaged in the field of orchestral music and opera continued to perform at a high artistic level. The decade also saw the rapid shaping of the musical comedy.

ORCHESTRAL COMPANIES AND CONDUCTORS. During the 1920s three of the world's foremost conductors—Willem Mengelberg, Wilhelm Furtwängler, and Arturo Toscanini—held successive posts with the New York Philharmonic Symphony Orchestra. The Dutchman Mengelberg was well-known for his interpretations of the works of his contemporaries Gustav Mahler and Richard Strauss. A musician of deep knowledge and perception, the German Furtwängler won acclaim for his authoritative conducting of works of the nineteenth-century masters Beethoven, Wagner, and Brahms. Before his tenure as principal conductor of the New York Philharmonic Symphony Orchestra (which post, beginning in 1928, led to concentrating on orchestral music for the rest of his career), the Italian Toscanini distinguished himself as an operatic conductor, having been associated with La Scala in Milan, Italy, and the Metropolitan Opera House in New York City. Widely acknowledged as the greatest conductor of his time, Toscanini brilliantly interpreted the composers whose works he conducted and memorized the scores of virtually all the major compositions. He strove for perfection in the performance of the orchestras under his direction. Responding to the baton of their always exacting, often temperamental, and sometimes dictatorial maestro, the musicians would give a thrilling performance.

The Boston Symphony Orchestra appointed two distinguished conductors, Pierre Monteux and Serge Koussevitzky. The Frenchman Monteux was noted for his neatly disciplined renditions. The

Russian Koussevitzky was engaged as principal conductor of the orchestra in 1924. During the quarter of a century that he held that post he assiduously introduced the new works of contemporary composers, especially those of Americans. Whether or not the music was in the established repertory, Koussevitzky's rendition of it was strikingly energetic and forceful.

OPERA. Throughout the 1920s Giulio Gatti-Casazza, as general manager, maintained the high artistic standards of the Metropolitan Opera House. Among the company's celebrated singers were soprano Rosa Ponselle, who scored a notable success in Bellini's *Norma*; the Italian tenor Giovanni Martinelli (widely considered a worthy successor to the great Caruso), who sang approximately fifty roles from the Italian and French operas; and the Russian bass Feodor Chaliapin, whose incisive interpretation of the title role in Moussorgsky's *Boris Godunov* and of Mephistopheles in Gounod's *Faust* have remained unmatched.

MUSICAL THEATER. The traditional style of American operettas, as exemplified earlier in the works of Victor Herbert, was carried on by composers Rudolf Friml and Sigmund Romberg. Two of the Bohemian-born Friml's most successful operettas were *Rose Marie* (1924) and *The Vagabond King* (1925). The Hungarian-born Romberg composed more than seventy-five operettas, of which the best known were *Maytime* (1917); *Blossom Time* (1921), based on the life and music of Franz Schubert; *The Student Prince* (1924); *The Desert Song* (1926); and *The New Moon* (1928). Among the most popular of his hundreds of rapturous songs are "Sweetheart" from *Maytime;* "Deep in My Heart" from *The Student Prince;* and "Lover Come Back to Me" and "Stout-Hearted Men," both from *The New Moon.*

After World War I American operettas gradually yielded their hold on the public to musical comedies, in which dancing, both solo and chorus, assumed an importance equal to that of the singing. The musical-comedy form that quickly developed was to become one of the most important contributions to theater by the United States. Vincent Youmans wrote the scores for a number of successful musicals, among them *No, No, Nanette* (1925), which includes "Tea for Two" and "I Want to Be Happy," and *Hit the Deck* (1927).

Toward the end of the 1920s composers such as Jerome Kern and George Gershwin tended to select more realistic stories and to write more sophisticated songs, often with lyrics that conveyed a serious message. Kern was a master of melody. He wrote numerous successful musicals, including *Sally* (1920), for which he collaborated with Victor Herbert; *Show Boat* (1927); and *Roberta* (1933). His outstanding work was *Show Boat,* adapted from the novel of the same name by Edna Ferber. The musical featured the ever-favorite songs "Ol' Man River," "Only Make Believe," and "Why Do I Love You?" From *Roberta* comes one of the most popular songs of all times, "Smoke Gets in Your Eyes." The ingenious Gershwin composed several critically acclaimed exhilarating musicals, most of them in collaboration with his brother, lyricist Ira Gershwin. Among them were *Lady, Be Good!* (1924), which includes the song "Fascinating Rhythm"; *Oh, Kay!* (1926), with "Someone to Watch over Me"; *Funny Face* (1927), with "'S Wonderful"; and *Of Thee I Sing* (1931), with "Who Cares?" Gershwin's most ambitious and widely admired theater piece was *Porgy and Bess* (1935), a folk opera depicting southern black life and from which come the much-esteemed songs "Summertime," "I Got Plenty o' Nuttin'," and "It Ain't Necessarily So." Gershwin also turned his considerable talent to composing orchestral works, such as *Rhapsody in Blue* (1923) and *An American in Paris* (1928), both of which blend the elements of jazz with the classical musical forms.

JAZZ. Perhaps the only truly American art form in the history of world culture is jazz. This music is characterized by syncopated rhythm and contrapuntal ensemble playing, the interspersing of vocal renditions with instrumental performance, and most of all by improvisation of the players. Although the precise time and place of the beginning of jazz as it is now known is uncertain, it is a matter of record that toward the end of the nineteenth century it was being played in New Orleans by black brass bandsmen in parades and funeral processions. Throughout the 1920s black composers and performers dominated jazz. In the early years of its popularity, jazz was also called ragtime, although the latter term is more precisely applied to a style of piano music marked by similar spirited rhythmic structures. Among the best-known ragtime pianists was Scott Joplin, who composed about forty ragtime pieces for the piano, including "Maple Leaf Rag" (1899) and "The Entertainer" (1902). By 1910 another form of jazz, the slow melancholy blues, overtook ragtime in popularity. W. C. (William Christopher) Handy composed by far the most popular songs of this type, including "Memphis Blues" (1912) and "St. Louis Blues" (1914).

By the 1920s large numbers of southern black musicians had gone North, most to New York City and Chicago. Among them was Joseph ("King") Oliver, who played the cornet. In Chicago he led the much-acclaimed Creole Jazz Band, which included such brilliant musicians as trumpeter Louis ("Satchmo") Armstrong and cornetist Leon Bismarck ("Bix") Beiderbecke, one of the period's few white jazzmen. Armstrong became the preeminent figure in the history of jazz. In 1927 he formed his own band called the Hot Five, the first of several groups he organized over a more than fifty-year career. As a trumpeter with a bursting style (he was also an exuberant singer), the incomparable "Satchmo" achieved international renown and influenced virtually every jazz performer. Among the jazz vocalists, Bessie Smith is considered the greatest interpreter of the blues.

Motion Pictures. Early in the 1920s Hollywood developed from the movie center of the United States into the movie center of the world. Motion-picture stars came to be regarded as heroes and heroines. The introduction of "talkies" revolutionized the film industry.

DIRECTORS. Two great directors of the era were Cecil B. De Mille and Erich von Stroheim. De Mille specialized in the epic style. His films, often based on biblical themes, are noted for their lavish settings and crowd scenes. Of the more than seventy motion pictures that he produced and directed during a forty-year career, he achieved particular success with the biblical epics *The Ten Commandments* (1923) and *King of Kings* (1927). While De Mille's films are marked by their weighty mass, those of the Austrian-born von Stroheim are characterized by their imaginative subtlety. Von Stroheim was a perfectionist who concerned himself with meticulous detail in every scene he directed. He achieved wide fame with *Greed* (1923), a film, based on Frank Norris's naturalistic novel *McTeague*, that probed the deteriorating relationship between a boorish dentist and his avaricious wife.

STARS. Rudolph Valentino was the "Latin lover" of the silent motion pictures. Through such films as *The Sheik* (1921) and *Blood and Sand* (1922) this unabashedly romantic, sleekly handsome actor became the idol of millions of women. Douglas Fairbanks thrilled audiences as a swashbuckling hero in "costume" adventure films. Ever-smiling and breezy, with the agility of a skilled acrobat, he scaled walls, leaped over banisters, and jumped through windows in such popular movies as *The Mark of Zorro* (1921) and *The Thief of Bagdad* (1924).

As for female stars, "America's Sweetheart" Mary Pickford was joined by Clara Bow and Gloria Swanson. Clara Bow personified the Roaring Twenties. After the film *It* (1927), in which she danced the Charleston with more than the usual abandon, the boyish-bobbed saucy actress was called the "It" girl (a slang term suggesting sexual attractiveness). Gloria Swanson often portrayed the sophisticated, glamorous "woman of the world." Among her best roles was that in the early sound movie *Sadie Thompson* (1928), based on W. Somerset Maugham's short story about a prostitute and a missionary.

Lon Chaney was the "Man of a Thousand Faces." A master of makeup, he won acclaim for his horror films, in which he portrayed characters hideous of face and distorted of body. His best-known films are *The Hunchback of Notre Dame* (1923) and *The Phantom of the Opera* (1925). Charlie Chaplin's popularity as the nation's most beloved comedian still held. Joining him in the 1920s to form a triumvirate of superb funnymen of the silent moton pictures were Buster Keaton and Harold Lloyd. Deadpan, usually wearing a porkpie hat, surviving numerous pratfalls, Keaton persevered triumphantly in confrontations with human beings and inanimate objects, particularly machines. *The Navigator* (1924) and *The General* (1926) show him at his best. Harold Lloyd, in such movies as *Safety Last* (1923) and *The Freshman* (1925), played the shy, bumbling youth in horn-rimmed eyeglasses who continually got into frustrating or even perilous situations—but always extricated himself.

TALKIES. Soon after inventors had succeeded in projecting motion pictures they began to attempt to combine sound with films. But for more than two decades progress was slow and unsatisfactory. A notable development occurred in 1926 when the Warner Brothers motion picture company produced *Don Juan* starring John Barrymore; this was a silent film with a musical accompaniment on records. But the real breakthrough took place in 1927 when Warner Brothers presented *The Jazz Singer* with Al Jolson. Also through the use of records, Jolson sang three songs and engaged in a bit of conversation. By the following year the public would fill any theater presenting a sound motion picture—no matter how poor the quality—in preference to viewing a silent film—no matter how artistic the creation. Soon the use of records yielded to a method in which sound waves were transformed into electrical impulses that regulated the contact of light on the so-called sound strip to one side of the actual film itself. The revolution in the motion-picture industry had begun.

Radio. During the 1920s a combination of electronic skill and financial support from business firms advertising their products and services made possible the rapid development of radio for broadcasting news, public events, music, sports, drama, and comedy. The first American commercial station was KDKA in Pittsburgh, which began broadcasting in 1920, to be followed later that year by WWJ in Detroit. KDKA's coverage of the presidential election returns in 1920 was the first major public event to be broadcast. In 1926 the National Broadcasting Company, a coast-to-coast chain of radio stations, was established to increase the amount of programming and improve its quality; the following year a competing chain, the Columbia Broadcasting System, was inaugurated. In 1927 the government established the Federal Radio Commission to regulate the more than seven hundred stations then in operation. Seven years later this agency was replaced by the Federal Communications Commission, which was given authority to regulate all communication facilities: telegraph, telephone, cable, and radio. Although some influential leaders advocated the use of radio broadcasting as an instrument of mass education, most programs were designed to provide entertainment and to advertise products.

Achieving nationwide popularity were such radio personalities as a news and sports reporter, Graham McNamee; a comedy team, the Happiness Boys; and a dance band, the Clicquot Club Eskimos. The amount spent for radios increased from approximately $2 million in 1920 to about $600 million in 1930. With tens of millions of listeners tuned in to the same programs, the phenomenon of a nationwide appeal became a reality. More and more the American people listened to the same news reports, thrilled to the same dramatic sketches, laughed at the same comedy routines, and were persuaded through clever advertising to use the same brands of products. All this resulted in a greater uniformity in customs and manners than had ever before existed.

Sports. In the 1920s professional athletics became big business. Promoters found huge profits in baseball, boxing, football, tennis, and golf—all of which catered to the spectators' desire for excitement. Great crowds flocked to see professional athletes, who for the first time in the nation's history achieved the status of heroes.

BASEBALL. In 1920 the reputation of baseball was soiled by scandal. Eight members of the Chicago White Sox were accused of accepting money from gamblers to lose to the Cincinnati Reds in the 1919 World Series. Federal Judge Kenesaw M. Landis was then made commissioner of baseball by the club owners and was given wide authority to regulate the game. With the start of Landis's tenure, which was to last for almost a quarter of a century, baseball entered a "golden age."

Among the decade's most famous players were George Herman ("Babe") Ruth, Louis ("Lou") Gehrig, and Rogers Hornsby. Widely regarded as America's greatest baseball player, Ruth was an outfielder for the New York Yankees for fifteen years. (Yankee Stadium, which opened in 1923, came to be known as "The House That Ruth Built.") His personality and skill captured the imagination of millions of fans, who cheered on the incomparable slugger as he hit the ball out of the park, and then carried his powerful torso on spindly legs around the bases. He set two impressive major-league batting records: hitting a total of 714 home runs in regular-season play, a record that stood for close to forty years, and hitting sixty home runs during a single season (1927), a record that stood for thirty-four years. Lou Gehrig, who played first base for the Yankees for fourteen years, earned the nickname of the "Iron Horse." He appeared in 2130 consecutive major-league games, establishing an as yet unbroken record. Second-baseman Rogers Hornsby played for a number of teams, mostly for the St. Louis Cardinals. His 1924 batting average of .424 has remained the major-league record for a single season.

BOXING Like baseball, boxing enjoyed a "golden age" in the 1920s. Influential in popularizing the sport was promoter George L. ("Tex") Rickard, who in 1921 arranged the first championship fight to sell over $1 million in tickets. William Harrison ("Jack") Dempsey became one of the most celebrated heavyweight boxing champions. His announced appearance in the ring would always ensure capacity attendance. Dempsey won the title in 1919 from Jess Willard and lost it in 1926 to James J. ("Gene") Tunney. In a return match between Dempsey and Tunney the following year the famous "long count" occurred. Dempsey knocked Tunney down but did not go immediately to a neutral corner, causing the referee to delay starting the count over Tunney for approximately six seconds. Tunney rose just before the count of ten and continued to fight, finally winning the bout on a decision. He defended his crown once more and retired undefeated in 1928.

FOOTBALL In the decade after World War I college football achieved great popularity. The greatest coach of the period was Knute Rockne, head football coach at Notre Dame University from 1918 until his death in an airplane crash in 1931. Widely admired as a brilliant strategist, Rockne emphasized offensive play. During his career as coach, the Notre Dame football teams won 105 games, lost 12, and tied 5; he had five undefeated, untied seasons. Other famous coaches were Amos Alonzo Stagg and Glenn Scobey ("Pop") Warner. Stagg, the "Grand Old Man of Football," set a record by coaching for sixty seasons. After a forty-one-year tenure as athletic director and football coach at the University of Chicago, in 1933 he went on to coach other teams over the next nineteen years. The tackling dummy was his invention. Warner's career, which was pursued at several colleges and universities over a forty-seven-year span, included during the 1920s a position at Stanford University. where he shaped mighty teams.

Professional football also grew in importance. At the beginning of the 1920s the American Professional Football Association was established; its name was changed in 1922 to the National Football League. Large crowds started to attend games between professional teams once they had begun contracting for outstanding former college players. Turning to professional football and playing with the New York Yankees and the Chicago Bears was Harold ("Red") Grange, who had achieved wide fame for the number of touchdowns he scored and yards he gained as a halfback at the University of Illinois. By the time James Francis ("Jim") Thorpe started to play professional football in the 1920s, he had already achieved an international reputation. More than one of the greatest football players, he was perhaps the best all-around athlete in the history of American sports. A Sac Indian, he attended the Carlisle Indian School at Carlisle, Pennsylvania, performing spectacularly on its football team. In the 1912 Olympic games he became the first person ever to win both the pentathlon and decathlon. (The following year Thorpe was forced to surrender his medals when it was discovered that one summer he had played semiprofessional baseball; in

1982, however, the medals were restored posthumously.)

TENNIS. In 1873, in Great Britain, army officer Walter C. Winfield invented lawn tennis. The following year the game was introduced into the United States. In 1881 the United States National Lawn Tennis Association was founded, which soon changed its name to the United States Lawn Tennis Association, to regulate amateur playing. Perhaps the greatest player in the history of tennis was William Tatem ("Bill") Tilden, Jr. From 1920 to 1930 he won the United States men's singles championship seven times and the British three times. He turned professional in 1931 and played for ten years. Helen Wills is considered the best woman tennis player of her time. During the 1920s and 1930s she won seven United States and eight British women's singles championships.

GOLF. In 1887 what was probably the first permanent golf club in the United States, the Foxburg Country Club, in Foxburg, Pennsylvania, was established. In 1894 the United States Golf Association was organized to set up the rules for the game and to administer tournaments. The game grew rapidly and prospered strikingly in the decade after World War I. During that period Robert Tyre ("Bobby") Jones, Jr., dominated the sport. He was the only person ever to make the grand slam in golf, winning in 1930 the four major titles—the United States Open, the British Open, the United States Amateur, and the British Amateur. After accomplishing this feat he retired from tournament play.

The increasing popularity of golf transformed the once highly exclusive country club into a relatively common institution. In virtually every urban community the middle and upper classes strove to establish and maintain a private country club, and hundreds of thousands of business and professional men and women learned to play golf as an important part of the club's social programs. By 1929 there were more than 4000 private country-club golf courses in the United States, in addition to the hundreds of municipal public links.

Chapter 3

THE DEPRESSION DECADE: 1930–1940

During the 1930s the salient influence upon American society and culture was the Great Depression. Since the beginning of the twentieth century there had been three recessions, but each was relatively short and mild. However, the economic reversal that began in 1929 and continued for a decade was such that the American people came close to losing faith in their economic system.

HISTORICAL BACKGROUND

The economic expansion of the 1920s, with its increasing production of goods and high profits, culminated in an orgy of speculation that collapsed with disastrous results in 1929. President Hoover took the traditional American view that the surest and quickest way out of a depression is to rely mainly on individual initiative. He clung to the hope that self-help and private charity, with a minimum of governmental intervention, would restore prosperity. The federal government, however, was not entirely inactive. The Hoover administration tried several limited remedies which it believed would help businessmen, workers, and farmers. But it gradually became apparent that stronger measures would be necessary. In accepting the presidential nomination of the Democratic party in 1932, Franklin D. Roosevelt pledged that if elected he would give the nation what he called a New Deal. After he became president much of his approach to the difficult problems of the Depression was pure experimentation. But the experiments he tried convinced him that the best course for the nation was away from traditional principles of economic individualism toward a planned economy. The mission of the New Deal lay in, first, relief to persons in need by providing them with money, loans to make mortgage payments, or jobs; second, recovery for the nation as a whole by passing legislation to assist business, labor, and agriculture to reestablish themselves in strength; third, reform of institutions, such as banking, to provide greater economic and social stability. In many ways the New Deal represented a continuation of the reform movement begun toward the end of the nineteenth century. But in one sense it did constitute a new direction in government policy: during the 1930s the government turned from a primarily restrictive and coercive political philosophy to one of bold activism on behalf of the people.

SOCIETY

All Americans—rich and poor, rural inhabitants and urban dwellers, white and black, men and women—were subjected to the ravages of the Depression. Businesses failed. A great number of industrial plants stood idle. As factories locked their doors, millions of workers looked for jobs.

The Economic Effects of the Depression. The scope of America's suffering could be seen in the statistics of the gross national product*: in 1929 it was about $150 billion and in 1932 it was about $108 billion (a drop of almost 30 percent). Between 1929 and 1932 the total national income fell steadily from $81 billion to $41 billion. During that period savings in 9 million bank accounts were wiped out to meet current family expenses. From 1929 to 1932 approximately 85,000 businesses, with assets totaling about $4.5 billion, failed. During that period industrial production declined by almost 45 percent. Factories by the thousands stood idle, their doors locked and their machines rusting. By the end of 1930 over 5 million workers (almost 15 percent of the nonfarm labor force) were unemployed; by the end of 1931 close to 9 million (more than 25 percent of the force) were out of work; by the end of 1932 more

* The total value of the goods and services produced in a nation during a specific period plus the total of expenditures by both private and public sources and the total of investments by private sources.

than 12 million (almost 40 percent) were looking for jobs.

As might be expected, the group that was most severely affected by unemployment was that of nonunion unskilled laborers. Organized skilled workers, buttressed by the efforts of their craft unions, were usually able to survive better, often by agreeing to a reduction in the length of the workweek, with, of course, a consequent cutback in wages. White-collar employees, such as office workers and shop clerks, were laid off, and joined the ranks of those seeking jobs with a lesser social status. Persons employed by government enjoyed a measure of security, those on the federal level more so than those on the state or local. On the latter two levels dismissals as an economy measure were by no means rare. Salaries, such as for public-school teachers, were time and again reduced, and salary dispersal was frequently postponed until a defaulted payroll could be met through such devices as an advanced collection of taxes and a loan from a private business organization. The professional class, including physicians and lawyers, sustained a drastic reduction in income since its services were less frequently sought.

The circumstances of black workers and women workers were especially grim. By the end of 1932 more than half the nation's blacks were unemployed. Women—no matter how needy—who sought work had to contend with job discrimination, being reproached for taking employment away from men with families to support. Black women workers, whose plight had undoubtedly always been the worst of all working groups, found their position deteriorated even further with the onset of the Depression.

The "Bonus Army." In May 1932 approximately 1000 unemployed World War I veterans converged on Washington, D.C., declaring that they would remain there until Congress authorized the immediate cash payment of the twenty-year bonus voted them in 1924. Other veterans arrived in the city, bringing the total number to more than 15,000 by mid-June. By mid-July most of them had departed, but some 2000 refused to disband. Believing that the "Bonus Army" might eventually resort to some kind of violence, President Hoover ordered the use of infantry, cavalry, and tank corps to drive it from the capital.

The Nadir of National Morale. Perhaps the most serious injury sustained by the American people was spiritual rather than material. In the descent from "riches to rags" many of them lost self-confidence and felt that the old values had been destroyed.

Throughout the nation homeless men built shacks of flattened tin cans, cardboard, tar paper, and waste lumber, or they lived in abandoned industrial plants or idle freight cars. In New York City homeless men slept in subway stations. A few died from starvation, but in every community charitable agencies tried to care for the hungry by setting up soup kitchens and breadlines. Churches and synagogues, community centers, welfare societies, the Red Cross, and the Salvation Army all attempted to help people in need. An apple shippers' association devised a plan to market their surplus fruit and at the same time to help the jobless. Soon thousands of apple vendors took charge of the organization's stands on the sidewalks of large cities. The operation brought a pittance to a few, but it chiefly became a symbol of the people's will to survive on their own and of their reluctance to turn to the government for direct relief.

The First New Deal: Relief, Recovery, Reform. On March 9, 1933, Congress met in a special session called by President Roosevelt to deal with what seemed to be the impending collapse of the American banking system. After Congress passed an emergency act on banking it remained in special session, upon Roosevelt's request, to treat a variety of economic ills, including unemployment among laborers and falling prices for farmers. This session came to a close on June 16, 1933, after enacting a host of measures deemed essential by the Roosevelt administration. This special session of Congress, called the Hundred Days, was a remarkable period of cooperation between the executive and legislative branches of government. The Hundred Days launched the First New Deal, which had as its objectives the relief and recovery, and then the reform, of the various economic sectors of the nation.

The Second New Deal: Security for the Needy. Shortly after the Roosevelt administration received a tremendous vote of confidence from the American people in the congressional elections of 1934, it indicated that it was intent on sponsoring a group of new projects to help the needy throughout the nation. In his State of the Union Message to Congress in January 1935 President Roosevelt declared that his administration was ready to implement a comprehensive program of social reform, having as its basic objective to provide security against unemployment, illness, the cares of old age, and the uncertainty of dependency upon family or friends. This plan of action soon became known as the Second New Deal. Whereas the

First New Deal had instituted projects to help businessmen, laborers, and farmers, the Second New Deal gave assistance almost exclusively to laborers and farmers. In attempting to realize a fuller program of social action, the Second New Deal was decidedly more to the left in spirit than the First New Deal had been.

EXTREMIST PROPOSALS. One reason for Roosevelt's strong support of measures to give the people greater security was the appeal of several extremist proposals by groups that were hostile toward the Roosevelt administration. The Share-Our-Wealth movement, led by Democratic Senator Huey P. Long of Louisiana, advocated that the federal government guarantee every family a homestead worth $5000 and a minimum annual income of $2000. The Old-Age Revolving Pension plan, originated by Dr. Francis E. Townsend, a California physician, recommended that the federal government pay $200 a month to persons sixty years of age and over, who would be obligated to spend the entire sum within the month. The National Union for Social Justice, headed by the Reverend Charles E. Coughlin, a Roman Catholic priest in Michigan, who made effective use of the radio to spread his views, urged that the currency be extensively inflated through the use of silver.

THE SOCIAL SECURITY ACT. This act, passed by Congress in 1935, upon the recommendation of President Roosevelt, provided for (1) a federal program of benefits to retired workers beginning at the age of sixty-five and of benefits to the dependent survivors of deceased workers, based on the employees' earnings before the age of sixty-five, to be paid out of funds derived from a tax on employees and their employers; (2) a program of unemployment compensation administered by the state with grants from the federal government and financed by a similar payroll tax; (3) federal aid to the states for various projects, such as maternity and infant-care services and assistance to crippled children and the blind.

The Labor Movement. Quickly responding to the shattering effects of the Depression upon the working class, certain segments of organized labor assumed an activism like none before in order to achieve organized labor's aspirations for a higher status in American society. Great changes occurred within the labor movement.

THE NATIONAL LABOR RELATIONS ACT. The Roosevelt administration, extremely supportive of organized labor's goals, achieved some of its most substantial victories in the field of labor legislation. According to Section 7a of the National Industrial Recovery

Act (NIRA), passed by Congress in 1933, labor was guaranteed the right "to organize and bargain collectively through representatives of their own choosing." Section 7a stimulated the growth of unions, greatly increasing their membership. After the NIRA was declared unconstitutional by the Supreme Court in 1935, Democratic Senator Robert F. Wagner of New York initiated legislation to guarantee labor's right to bargain collectively. The result was the National Labor Relations Act (also called the Wagner-Connery Act), passed by Congress in 1935. The act created the National Labor Relations Board (NLRB), which was authorized to determine suitable units for collective bargaining, to conduct elections for labor's representatives, and to prevent interference with such elections. The NLRB was also empowered to investigate complaints of unfair labor practices, to issue orders that such practices be stopped, and to petition federal courts to enforce its restraining orders. The NLRB's work was made difficult by the hostility of employers, who felt that the National Labor Relations Act benefited the working class unfairly over the business class.

THE CONGRESS OF INDUSTRIAL ORGANIZATIONS. The activity of labor organizers in the early 1930s raised anew the issue of bringing into organized labor unskilled industrial workers. Within the American Federation of Labor (AFL) certain unions sponsored industrial unionism as opposed to craft unionism. The most notable of these unions were the United Mine Workers under John L. Lewis, the Amalgamated Clothing Workers of America under Sidney Hillman, the International Ladies' Garment Workers Union under David Dubinsky, and the International Typographical Union under Charles Howard. At the 1935 national convention of the AFL, the organization's president, William Green, and his associates blocked Lewis's attempt to commit the AFL to industrial unionism. A majority of the delegates favored the traditional structure based upon representation of the skilled crafts. However, eight unions affiliated with the AFL formed the Committee for Industrial Organization (CIO). Under the leadership of Lewis, the CIO defied the AFL executive committee and proceeded to organize along industrial union lines the automobile and steel industries. The CIO soon secured partial recognition from the General Motors Corporation and several subsidiaries of the United States Steel Corporation. In 1937 the AFL expelled the ten unions that were by then within the CIO, which was reorganized the following year as the Congress of Industrial Organizations.

Although most of the craft unions within the AFL continued their long-standing policy of excluding blacks from membership, the CIO from the outset endeavored to organize workers without regard to race. By 1939 approximately 200,000 black unskilled industrial workers had been enrolled in the CIO, where they experienced a new sense of kinship with white workers. Many women workers responded eagerly to the CIO's organizing drive, becoming union members for the first time in their lives. The International Ladies' Garment Workers Union, for example, in 1939 reported a membership of over 750,000, the vast majority of whom were women who had recently joined the organization and now made up approximately 75 percent of the rolls.

MANAGEMENT-LABOR STRIFE. The vigorous efforts of the CIO to organize workers in the automobile and steel industries brought strikes marked by violence. In the automobile industry dissatisfied workers used a new weapon—the sit-down strike. While ceasing work, they refused to leave plants against which their unions had called a work stoppage. This tactic spread rapidly to workers in many other industries. When employers began to use force to evict sit-down strikers, the labor organizers condoned meeting force with force. The firing by police upon union demonstrators in front of a steel plant in South Chicago in 1937 led to a pitched battled between the two groups in which ten men were killed. In 1939 the Supreme Court declared the sit-down strike illegal.

Education. During the 1930s the shortage of public funds and the high rate of unemployment had an impact upon education throughout the nation. Both elementary and secondary schools were seriously affected when boards of education felt the need to reduce their budgets to such an extent that in addition to removing the so-called frills from their programs they also eliminated essential services. With husbands out of work, married couples delayed having children, and elementary-school enrollment between 1930 and 1940 declined from about 23.6 million to about 21 million. High-school enrollment, on the other hand, rose from about 4.7 million to about 7 million, as many teen-agers, with little opportunity for employment, continued to attend school longer than they ordinarily would have. As for colleges and universities, their enrollment of approximately 1.1 million in 1930 began to dip for the first half of the decade, but then to grow to about 1.5 million by 1940.

To keep students in secondary schools and institutions of higher education the Roosevelt administration put a plan into operation. Established by executive order in 1935, under the provisions of the Emergency Relief Appropriation Act, the National Youth Administration (NYA) gave part-time employment to needy persons between the ages of sixteen and twenty-five in high schools, colleges, and universities so that they could continue their education. By the time the NYA was disbanded in 1943, it had helped more than 4 million young people.

Like elementary and secondary schools, institutions of higher education, as a result of severe budgetary cuts, experienced diminished effectiveness in fulfilling their obligations to students. With college and university graduates scrambling for the few jobs available in a depressed economy, career-preparation programs became increasingly popular, to the detriment of the traditional liberal-arts goal of producing "well-rounded" individuals.

Religion. During the 1930s the basic attitudes of Roman Catholicism and Judaism underwent no significant changes. However, the modernism that had been gathering momentum within Protestantism since the beginning of the twentieth century was challenged by neo-orthodoxy. This body of thought originated in Europe, where it was formulated primarily by the Swiss theologian Karl Barth. In the United States the leading figure of neo-orthodoxy was Reinhold Niebuhr, a professor at Union Theological Seminary in New York City, who through his many brilliant books, articles, and speeches was instrumental in gaining widespread acceptance for the new trend. While exhorting people to be involved in programs for social reform, neo-orthodox doctrine rejected the belief of the social gospel movement that the church itself should be a healer of social ills. Rather, the mission of the church should be to rescue a society fraught with immorality. Human beings, the neo-orthodox theologians argued, are sinners who can be saved only by the grace of God.

Technology. In 1939–1940 the New York World's Fair was held. Based on the theme "The World of Tomorrow" and symbolized by the dual structures of a trylon (a three-sided tapering pillar that rose to 700 feet) and perisphere (a globe 200 feet in diameter), the fair helped advance and popularize the technology of the period.

Although the first scientific air-conditioning system was designed by engineer Willis H. Carrier at the beginning of the twentieth century, the use of air conditioning did not become widespread until the 1930s when much-refined equipment began to be installed in motion-picture theaters throughout the nation. Soon many apartment dwellings and office buildings had central systems. Early in the 1930s room air conditioners were developed; these were a boon to healthy and comfortable living in private residences. Air-conditioning units in means of transportation were first used in trains in the 1930s.

In 1938 E. I. Du Pont de Nemours & Company introduced nylon, the product of a decade of research by a team of the firm's chemists, led by Wallace H. Carothers. Nylon, the first wholly synthetic fiber, is exceedingly versatile because each filament is strong, elastic, not affected by most chemicals, and absorbs little moisture.

Medicine. The inability during the Depression to buy sufficient and nourishing food and to pay for medical care resulted in a loss of health for millions of Americans. Nevertheless, the increase in life expectancy that had been the trend since the beginning of the twentieth century did continue, rising from 59.7 years in 1930 to 62.9 years in 1940. This fact attested to the high level of medicine and sanitation in the United States even when depression-ridden. Throughout the decade medical research suffered from a shortage of funds. However, the treatment of diseases was significantly advanced by the use of a group of chemicals developed in Europe early in the 1930s called "sulfa drugs," which function by curtailing the growth of bacteria in the body. The diseases against which the sulfa drugs are effective include pneumonia, meningitis, and dysentery. With the use of the sulfa drugs to prevent infection from bacteria introduced into the patient's body during the course of a surgical operation, physicians in the United States by the end of the 1930s had achieved a notable lowering of the heretofore high postoperative death rate.

CULTURE

The impact of the Depression on American culture was pervasive. Painters and writers in large numbers were propelled into dealing with social problems emerging from an economically distressed nation. The Works Progress Administration (WPA) was established by Congress primarily to give employment to manual laborers on construction projects. But the WPA also provided work for artists, writers, people of the theater, and musicians by creating the Federal Art Project, the Federal Writers' Project, and the Federal Theater Project. For example, under the auspices of the Federal Art Project murals were painted in public buildings, and under the auspices of the Federal Writers' Project state and local histories were written. In operatic music many native-born singers were engaged, in modern dance the height of public appreciation was reached, and in light music swing became the rage. Motion pictures continued to be the most influential art form. Radio reached its zenith, providing in the main a diversion from the Depression's ugly reality. With the alleviation during the second half of the 1930s of the economic impairment, professional sports regained the spectator attendance they had enjoyed in the prosperous 1920s.

Art. In painting, the nation's social ills as well as its regional variations were important themes; in sculpture, mere refinement of a long-standing style prevailed. It was in architecture that there occurred the most impressive development—a surge toward unabashed modernity.

PAINTING. Two movements—social criticism and regionalism—were paramount in American painting.

In response to the Depression many painters devoted themselves to themes of social significance. Influential in this group were Reginald Marsh, Ben Shahn, and Jack Levine. Marsh rendered candidly various aspects of New York City life, depicting such scenes as a knot of listless derelicts on the Bowery and a crowd of densely packed bathers on the beach at Coney Island. Shahn achieved recognition for intensely colorful works that convey his compassion for victims of social injustice. Levine was considerably more severe than Marsh or Shahn in his social protest. One of his best-known works, *The Feast of Pure Reason* (1937), shows three figures from the fields of government and law enforcement, each of whom through a studied distortion of face and body evokes a sense of corruption.

Among some American painters the desire to capture the nation's numerous regional distinctions was dominant. Regionalist Thomas Hart Benton was the decade's leading muralist, executing critically acclaimed works for numerous buildings of the federal and various state governments and of colleges and universities. Benton depicted rural life nostalgically on large expanses of wall, painting highly stylized figures engaged in their typical activities, such as midwestern farmers toiling in the fields or participating in an informal dancing party and a far-western sheepherder watching over his grazing animals. John Steuart Curry, with a dramatic ruggedness, painted views of simple agrarian life in his native Kansas. Grant Wood was a regionalist who filled his works with meticulously detailed renderings of rural midwestern landscapes peopled by prosaic men and women. His best-known painting, *American Gothic* (1930), satirically portrays a sober-visaged, overall-clad, pitchfork-wielding Iowa farmer and his equally sober-visaged, full-aproned daughter at his side.

Outside the movements of both social criticism and regionalism was Georgia O'Keeffe. She won distinction for representing her two most distinctive subjects, flowers that are executed in greatly enlarged fashion and bleached animal bones from the desert near her New Mexico home.

SCULPTURE. The prevailing influence upon American sculpture was still the commitment to realism. Jo Davidson created portrait busts that were incisively lifelike, and also seemed uncannily to reveal the individual psyche. Among the more than three hundred heads of prominent figures that established Davidson's reputation are those of Mohandas K. Gandhi (1931), Franklin D. Roosevelt (1933), and Albert Einstein (1934). The New York City–born Jacob Epstein became a British subject as a relatively young man and was knighted toward the end of a long, productive life. Both his large-scale monuments and his portrait busts, with their coarsely textured surfaces, exude a vigorously harsh, graceless reality.

ARCHITECTURE. By the end of the 1930s a few architects had developed an unequivocally contemporary style that for many years was to have a determinative influence upon American buildings. Leaders in the movement to modernity were Frank Lloyd Wright, Walter Gropius, and Ludwig Mies van der Rohe.

Frank Lloyd Wright is a titan among American architects. He strove against what was traditional and ordinary in architecture with an almost poetic inventiveness. During a career that began in the 1880s with an apprenticeship to Louis H. Sullivan (the proponent of functionalism) and lasted for almost seventy years, he created hundreds of buildings that were widely esteemed for the brilliant originality of their design. His guiding principle was that a building must be so compatible with its natural setting that it appears to stem from it. In the first decade of the twentieth century he designed a number of radically fashioned houses (some of the best known located in and near Chicago), with low horizontal lines that reflected the encompassing land. Among his many revolutionary techniques was the selective elimination of walls in order to attain both an aesthetic and a practical free-flowing interior space. Wright's "prairie style" had become the essence of residential design in the United States. Beginning in the 1930s an ever-growing respect for his conception of architectural aesthetics and practicality resulted in numerous commissions for nonresidential structures. For his office buildings he developed new techniques, such as using precast concrete blocks and glass walls. Wright's many notable nonresidential structures include the administration building (1939) and research tower (1950) of the S. C. Johnson & Son wax products company in Racine, Wisconsin, and the Solomon R. Guggenheim Museum (1959) in New York City. At his death he left designs for a number of imaginative structures, including a skyscraper for Chicago that would be a mile high—almost four times as tall as the highest existing building.

The 1930s might well have become notable for the design and construction of skyscrapers, but the Depression precluded that development. Nevertheless, the decade saw the creation of two splendors of skyscraper architecture in New York City. During 1930-1931 the Empire State Building was constructed; having 102 stories, it was for more than forty years the world's tallest building. Between 1931 and 1939 fourteen of the sixteen buildings that constitute the complex of skyscrapers known as Rockefeller Center were erected. The structures accommodated offices, stores, broadcasting facilities, and the world's largest motion-picture theater, the Radio City Music Hall. The furniture, paintings, sculptures, and ornamentation in the buildings of Rockefeller Center were magnificent examples of the period's popular style of design called "art deco" (from the title of the 1925 Paris exhibition that first promoted it). Art deco spurned both old-fashioned ornate decoration and current sparseness; it attempted to present sleekly streamlined forms of ornamentation as an expression of modern technology.

In 1932 the Museum of Modern Art in New York City held an exhibition of a new form of contemporary architecture. (The museum was founded in 1929 to collect and display, and to promote an appreciation for, visual arts of the late nineteenth and the twentieth centuries, including not only painting and sculpture, but also prints, photography, films, and architectural and industrial design.) This new form of architecture, originating in Europe during the 1920s and named the International Style, accentuated stark functional design. This style utilized inorganic materials, particularly steel and glass. It featured repetitive geometric shapes in a basic asymmetrical plan and cantilevered floors and balconies.

The two most influential practitioners of the International Style were Walter Gropius and Ludwig Mies van der Rohe. The German-born Gropius settled in the United States in 1937, after having founded almost twenty years earlier and then directed in his homeland the Bauhaus, a highly influential school that espoused the integration and coordination of abstract art and industrial design with architecture. A typical Gropius structure is the much-admired American embassy (1960) at Athens. Mies, a later director of the Bauhaus who emigrated from Germany to the United States about the same time that Gropius did, won acclaim for his clear and simple design. His maxim "Less is more" is reflected in the uncluttered look of his steel-and-glass structures. Particularly impressive are his two apartment houses (1951) in Chicago and what is considered his masterpiece, the bronze-covered Seagram Building (1958) in New York City, the latter done in collaboration with the American architect Philip Johnson.

Literature. The aloofness from and cynicism toward the smugly prosperous 1920s on the part of novelists, poets, and playwrights yielded in the 1930s to concern for the problems of a depression-afflicted society.

THE NOVEL. No writer showed greater commitment to portraying the distress of the American people during the Depression than did John Steinbeck. His novel *The Grapes of Wrath* (1939) is a literary landmark of the period. In it he depicts the migration during the 1930s of dispossessed farm families of the drought-ridden midwestern regions to California, where they seek jobs but find themselves cruelly exploited as itinerant agricultural workers. The novel is noted for the restrained sympathy with which Steinbeck treats his characters. Another novelist who arrestingly conveyed social consciousness was John Dos Passos. In his most famous work, the trilogy *U.S.A.* (1930–1936), Dos Passos scans the nation's development during the twentieth century, while praising America's laborers and radical leaders and damning its businessmen and conservative politicians. To achieve his objective he deftly employed innovative literary devices, intertwining with straight narration such elements as biographical sketches, newspaper headlines, and excerpts from popular songs. Naturalist James T. Farrell attained wide recognition with his trilogy *Studs Lonigan* (1932–1935), which fiercely describes social conditions within the Irish Catholic community of Chicago's South Side, focusing on the emotional— and indeed physical—destruction of a young man by his environment. Within the setting of urban-black lower-class life, black author Richard Wright, in his most influential novel, *Native Son* (1940), relates how a youth of the Chicago slums is drawn into and suffers the consequences of a criminal career.

Two great novelists whose writings were not part of the social-consciousness trend were Thomas Wolfe and William Faulkner. Each was uniquely individual. During his short life Wolfe produced four huge novels, all intensely autobiographical. In the first work, *Look Homeward, Angel* (1929), and in its sequel, *Of Time and the River* (1935), the hero grows up in the rural South, attends universities both near home and in New England, settles in New York City to teach and write, and then travels extensively in Europe. Throughout, he exhaustively seeks the meaning of life. Wolfe's prose has been criticized as effusive and disjointed, but it has been admired for a passionately personal expression that often approaches the poetic.

Few American writers of the twentieth century have achieved the honor accorded William Faulkner. A Mississippian, he wrote mostly about the perplexities that beset the South, making his imaginary Yoknapatawpha County a microcosm of the region. He paid particular attention to the antagonism between the declining old aristocratic families and the rising new entrepreneurial ones, and how both groups subjected the blacks. Among his novels are *The Sound and the Fury* (1929), which relates the decay of a once-proud and powerful family, whose members are variously plagued by alcoholism, hypochondria, nymphomania, and idiocy; *As I Lay Dying* (1930), which recounts the death of a woman and the exertions of her husband and children to carry her body home for burial; *Sanctuary* (1931), which deals with murder and rape; and *Absalom, Absalom!* (1936), which treats the failure of whites to establish a just relationship with blacks. Faulkner was a superb craftsman. He handled with extraordinary finesse such literary techniques as symbolism, telling the same story through the perceptions of different characters, and stream of consciousness (presenting a character's manifold thoughts and feelings as a flowing process, without reference to logical discourse or a connected sequence).

POETRY. The absorption with innovative verse forms and language usage that was characteristic of poets of the 1920s gave way in the 1930s to a rekindled regard for content. Although employing the recent technical approaches to their craft, poets for the most part strove for a more sympathetic view of the nation's past glories and present adversities. Stephen Vincent Benét gained fame for his early narrative poem "John Brown's Body" (1928), which patriotically recounts, in strongly marked rhythms, the events of the Civil War. Archibald MacLeish was convinced that a poet should be involved with world affairs and social issues (he was an officeholder in the Franklin D. Roosevelt administration). MacLeish's poetry made a case for political and economic liberalism to such a degree that it was sometimes condemned as propagandistic. His well-known collection of poems *Frescoes for Mr. Rockefeller's City* (1933) criticizes capitalism, rebuking in particular the excesses of those who acquire great wealth.

DRAMA. As the Depression worsened, dramatists showed an increasing propensity to social criticism. Clifford Odets's works epitomized this form of protest. In his play about a New York City taxi drivers' strike, *Waiting for Lefty* (1935), he sought sympathy for working-class strivings.

Three successful dramatists of the period who examined problems more from the individual than the group point of view were Robert Sherwood, Lillian Hellman, and Thornton Wilder. Sherwood's major theme was that a person must act in ways that are free and intuitive rather than prescribed by society's artificial conventions. In *The Petrified Forest* (1935) a fugitive from the law takes over an Arizona desert café and gas station, drawing out the deeply recessed qualities of each captive; one of them sacrifices his life so that a girl can escape her dull and sordid existence. In *Idiot's Delight* (1936) a number of Americans and Europeans at an Italian hotel forget their natural friendliness and become hate-filled nationalists when a world war begins. Lillian Hellman's *The Children's Hour* (1934) is about a pathological child who ruins the lives of two teachers at a girls' boarding school by falsely accusing them of lesbianism. *The Little Foxes* (1939) depicts members of a wealthy southern family in the post–Civil War period who variously lie, steal, and even permit a needless death to satisfy their avarice. Thornton Wilder's masterpiece is *Our Town* (1938), which on the surface depicts ordinary daily living in a small New England community during the early twentieth century. But Wilder suggests that underlying every activity is the sacredness of all human experiences from birth to death. Wilder used a number of innovative nonrealistic devices. For example, in *Our Town* a narrator introduces the characters, philosophizes on much of the action, and even assumes a number of minor roles; also, there is a minimum of scenery and very few stage props.

A highly successful playwrighting team specializing in comedy was that of George S. Kaufman and Moss Hart. The biggest of their many hits was *You Can't Take It with You* (1936), which is about members of an eccentric family, each of whom does what to him or her is most satisfying, oblivious to conformity or social expectations.

Among the most accomplished and popular actors of the 1930s were Katharine Cornell, who in 1931 portrayed the poet Elizabeth Barrett in Rudolf Besier's *The Barretts of Wimpole Street;* Helen Hayes, who in 1935 played the title role in Laurence Housman's *Victoria Regina;* and the husband-and-wife team Alfred Lunt and Lynn Fontanne, who in 1935 appeared in Shakespeare's *The Taming of the Shrew.*

NEWSPAPERS AND MAGAZINES. During the 1930s American journalism largely discarded a long-standing tradition of objective reporting in favor of an analytical coverage of the news. The explosion of news items both domestic (arising out of the continual activity of the New Deal) and international (arising out of military aggression that portended a worldwide war) had a profound effect upon publishers, editors, and reporters. They felt compelled to reconsider their medium's obligation to the public. They became convinced that if newspapers were to truly serve readers, they would have to give them more than the bare facts of an event; they would have to treat the interrelated conditions in which that event occurred.

A development in periodical publishing was the launching of several magazines that presented news events, many of a human-interest nature, through photographs. The most successful of these pictorial news magazines was the weekly *Life,* founded in 1936 by Henry R. Luce; almost as popular was the biweekly *Look,* which appeared the following year.

Music. Both orchestral music organizations and opera companies were able to maintain high standards of performance despite the public's lessening of financial support. Modern dance, which had developed early in the twentieth century, was gaining in popularity. In the field of light music the glittering swing bands reigned.

ORCHESTRAL COMPOSERS AND CONDUCTORS. Two of the most gifted American composers of orchestral music were Roy Harris and Virgil Thomson. Harris often employed the musical forms of the seventeenth century, but with such imaginative technique that the result appears thoroughly twentieth-century American. His output was prolific, including symphonies, among them the highly popular *Third Symphony* (1938); concertos, chamber music; and piano pieces. Thomson used a direct and simple style; many of his works were based on American folk music. He is best known for writing the scores for three documentary motion pictures; from two of these scores he fashioned orchestral suites, including *The Plow that Broke the Plains* (1936), which evokes the abusive exploitation by Americans of their natural resources.

In recognition of the vast opportunities to associate radio with classical music, the National Broadcasting Company in 1937 prevailed upon the inimitable Arturo Toscanini to assume the musical directorship of the NBC Symphony Orchestra, which was being organized with carefully selected virtuoso players. For seventeen years Toscanini led highly acclaimed concerts that were aired from coast to coast.

OPERA. In 1935 Edward Johnson, who had been a leading tenor of the Metropolitan Opera House, began a fifteen-year association with the company as its general manager. He retained the four-year-old series of Saturday-afternoon live broadcasts of operas from the Metropolitan Opera House, an offering which has continued to the present. Johnson directed the engagement in much larger numbers than heretofore of American singers, such as soprano Grace Moore, mezzo-soprano Gladys Swarthout, and baritone Lawrence Tibbett, each of whose repertory was from the Italian and French operas. Highly acclaimed European-born performers in the company were the French soprano Lily Pons, admired for her title role in

Delibes's *Lakmé,* and two who were among the foremost twentieth-century Wagnerian singers—the Norwegian soprano Kirsten Flagstad and the Danish tenor Lauritz Melchior.

MUSICAL THEATER. The leading composers of musicals were Irving Berlin and Cole Porter, each of whom wrote the words to nearly all of his own songs, and Richard Rodgers, who collaborated with lyricist Lorenz Hart. Among Berlin's most successful musicals were *As Thousands Cheer* (1933), which contains the song "Easter Parade," and his outstanding work *Annie Get Your Gun* (1946), starring Ethel Merman and with what became the virtual theme song of the entertainment field, "There's No Business Like Show Business." But more than a composer of musicals, Berlin established himself as the premier American songwriter, with approximately 1000 songs, dozens of which achieved a classic status. His output of melodies and lyrics exhibits an astounding versatility of style. Some of his great creations were "Alexander's Ragtime Band" (1911), which became his first big hit; "A Pretty Girl Is Like a Melody" (1919), which turned into something of a theme song for the Ziegfeld Follies revues during the 1920s; "God Bless America" (1918), which was introduced in 1938 and became almost a second national anthem; and "White Christmas" (1942), which appeared in a film made during World War II, when it seemed to express the nostalgia of American servicemen in African deserts and Asian jungles. Among Cole Porter's most popular musicals were *Gay Divorce* (1932), which contains the song "Night and Day"; *Anything Goes* (1934), with "You're the Top"; *Jubilee* (1935), with "Begin the Beguine"; *Leave It to Me* (1938), with "My Heart Belongs to Daddy"; and his later, greatest work, *Kiss Me, Kate* (1948), starring Alfred Drake and with the song "So in Love." The Porter hallmarks are the arresting quality of his melodies and the wit and debonair elegance of his lyrics, with their ingenious rhymes. Richard Rodgers and Lorenz Hart collaborated on close to thirty musicals, including such popular works as *A Connecticut Yankee* (1927), with the song "Thou Swell"; *On Your Toes* (1936), with "There's a Small Hotel"; *The Boys from Syracuse* (1938), with "Falling in Love with Love"; and *Pal Joey* (1940), with "Bewitched, Bothered and Bewildered." Rodgers brilliantly tailored his melodic style to Hart's always sophisticated, often breezy, and sometimes bitingly cynical lyrics.

MODERN DANCE. During the 1930s a few highly talented performers who had trained at the Denishawn dance company established by Ruth St. Denis and Ted Shawn took modern dance in a new direction, advocating, first, an even greater outpouring of feeling simply displayed, and second, in order to highlight the dance itself, the use of severely simple and somber costuming and staging and minimal musical accompaniment. The most influential of this post-St. Denis group was performer, choreographer, and teacher Martha Graham. She replaced the usual gracefully flowing movements of the dancer's body with sharply angular ones, creating dances that were frequently based on universally significant historical and mythological themes and that were among the most biting works in the field of the performing arts. In 1929 Graham founded her own troupe and then her own school in New York City. She turned them into extraordinarily influential and successful institutions, with the troupe probably conducting more tours than any other modern-dance group. Both the troupe and the school are still operating. Soon, in large measure because of the efforts of Graham and her company, modern dance reached the zenith of its popularity throughout the nation.

In the late 1940s and the 1950s a new group of modern dance choreographers stripped dance down to its barest essentials of pure movement, to a point perhaps never before thought desirable, or even possible. The works they produced were not intended to present a theme, supply a message, or evoke an emotion. Achieving the greatest influence and reputation among the new choreographers was Merce Cunningham, who had trained with Martha Graham and danced in her company for about fifteen years. In 1950 he founded his own company, which has been operating to the present, to give performances and to train dancers and choreographers. The dances he created increasingly were accompanied by the music of the period's avant-garde composers, particularly the highly imaginative John Cage.

SWING. Jazz of the 1920s led to swing of the 1930s. Swing was characterized by a lively insistent beat, the frequent submerging of a basic melody through improvisation of the players, and a collective use of syncopated rhythm. The most striking aspect of the music was a "big" sound, produced by an extensive brass section. Swing was usually arranged for a large commercial dance band. Like perhaps no other popular music before or since, swing was peculiarly suited to being danced to. And always interspersed among the many swing numbers played by the bands were some languorous "sweet" tunes.

Outstanding bandleaders included the superb clarinetist Benjamin David ("Benny") Goodman, who, as a result of his group's captivating arrangements, became known as the "King of Swing"; the trombonist Alton ("Glenn") Miller, whose outfit gave prominence to a strong and distinctive woodwind section; the trombonist Francis ("Tommy") Dorsey, whose group excelled in producing a mellow sound; and Edward ("Duke") Ellington and William ("Count") Basie, each of whom composed for and played piano with his band, using an exhilaratingly simple style. Ellington's "Mood Indigo" (1930) and "Caravan" (1937) were favorite pieces. Basie's most popular composition was "One O'Clock Jump" (1938).

A majority of the swing bands featured vocalists. By far the most popular singer was the bow-tied, emaciated-looking "kid" Francis Albert ("Frank") Sinatra, who was a soloist with the Tommy Dorsey band during the late 1930s and early 1940s. He went on to achieve stardom, becoming an idol of teen-age girls who exhibited their approbation of his talent by squealing with delight, moaning in ecstasy, and even swooning while he performed in his dreamily romantic manner songs such as "I'll Never Smile Again." (Sinatra later enjoyed for many years a rewarding motion-picture acting career.)

Motion Pictures. In the 1930s motion pictures experienced a "golden age" that extended throughout the 1940s and into the early 1950s. For a very small sum millions of people each week would flock to motion-picture theaters to escape, if only for a few hours, from the throes of the Depression.

WIDE APPEAL. In coming to terms with the protracted economic reversal, motion-picture studios were forced to operate within exceedingly low budgets that in many ways cramped the creativity of producers and directors. This led to the issuing of standardized fare—an unbroken succession of motion pictures based on a few popular genres, each type with its own distinctive style, form, and purpose. Nevertheless, many notable films came out of Hollywood. Throughout the nation hundreds of motion-picture "palaces" were built, scores of them in imitation of exotic Moorish architecture. Quickly gaining wide public acceptance were drive-in movie theaters, the first of which opened in 1933 in Camden, New Jersey. To encourage attendance the movie houses offered double features and periodically presented the audience with gifts, such as dishes, glassware, and cutlery. The effect of all this could be seen at the box office. By the last years of the decade approximately 65 percent of the American people were going to the movies every week.

MUSICALS. One of Hollywood's most widely appreciated contributions was the musical, which featured dancing as well as singing. In films such as *Forty-Second Street* (1933) and *Footlight Parade* (1933) most of the singing was done by the boyishly handsome Dick Powell and the perky Ruby Keeler, who executed some sprightly tap-dancing. For those and numerous other musicals Busby Berkeley devised and directed resplendent dance sequences, in which scantily attired pulchritudinous chorus girls arranged themselves into a variety of geometric designs, both at rest and in motion, frequently with the camera taking its shot from high above the set. Fred Astaire brought an unmatched debonair quality to both his singing and dancing. As for the latter, it was absolutely elegant, his entire body moving in astonishingly intricate ways. Among his best-remembered films are *The Gay Divorcee* (1934) and *Top Hat* (1935), in both of which his partner was the charming Ginger Rogers. The impassive baritone Nelson Eddy and the playfully saucy soprano Jeanette MacDonald appeared together in cinematic versions of several popular operettas of an earlier time, including *Naughty Marietta* (1935) and *Rose Marie* (1936). The curly-headed, dimple-cheeked Shirley Temple sang and danced her way to stardom in many films, such as *Little Miss Marker* (1934), becoming perhaps the most celebrated child performer in history. The adolescent Judy Garland had the wide-eyed innocence of a little girl and the clear and powerful voice of a great musical-theater singer, both of which she used to good advantage in a number of films, including *Babes in Arms* (1939), in which her costar was the exuberantly talented Mickey Rooney, and the incomparable *The Wizard of Oz* (1939).

COMEDIES. The invention of sound motion pictures instantaneously changed the nature of screen comedy. Now spoken jokes became as important as sight gags. A new breed of comedians succeeded the funnymen of a few years earlier. None of the new comedians was better received than W. C. Fields. He, of the bulbous nose and rasping voice, was hard-drinking, bragging, pompous, flowery of speech, excruciatingly courtly to the opposite sex, and slightly larcenous. He imprinted this image upon the public

memory in many films, including *You Can't Cheat an Honest Man*
(1939), and *My Little Chickadee* (1940), in which he was the foil
of blond, buxom, swivel-hipped, mockingly seductive Mae West.
The incomparable Marx Brothers appeared in a number of thoroughly zany movies, including *Duck Soup* (1933), *A Night at the
Opera* (1935), and *Room Service* (1938). There was Groucho,
decked out in a swallowtail coat, round steel-rimmed eyeglasses,
painted-on mustache and eyebrows, and a big cigar, loping about in
a stooped manner and delivering with leering glee the most egre-
gious insults, wisecracks, and puns. There was Harpo, outfitted
with a grubby raincoat and a battered top hat upon a curly wig
over a face with a moronic stare, communicating in pantomime and
by a rubber-bulbed horn, chasing after voluptuous women, and
grasping at every opportunity to play the harp. There was Chico,
turned out in a little pointed hat and a tight, ill-fitting jacket,
speaking in a broad Italian accent and playing the piano with his
right hand in the form of a pistol aimed at the keys.

A type of screen comedy emerged that was called "screwball."
Conveying much sophistication (largely through brilliant dialogue)
leavened by some slapstick, screwball comedies showed daily living
as a wonderfully enjoyable madcap experience. Director Frank Ca-
pra brought out a number of screwball comedies, including the
most celebrated ever made, *It Happened One Night* (1934), with
Clark Gable as a news reporter covering the story of a runaway
heiress, played by Claudette Colbert. Other popular films of this
kind were *The Thin Man* (1934), with the suave William Powell
and a calmly collaborating wife Myrna Loy as amateur detectives,
and *Bringing Up Baby* (1938), with Cary Grant as a paleontologist
and Katharine Hepburn as a socialite who became involved with
him.

GANGSTER FILMS. The violent operations of gangs and their rival-
ries during national prohibition formed the basis of the early 1930s
gangster films. Gaining quick fame by portraying gangsters were
Edward G. Robinson, James Cagney, and Humphrey Bogart. Robinson's most memorable performance was in *Little Caesar* (1931),
in which he played a surly hoodlum who determinedly achieved the
status of underworld boss. In *The Public Enemy* (1931) Cagney
depicted a pugnacious criminal, whose end came as a bullet-ridden
corpse dumped on his mother's doorstep. Bogart was a callous killer
in such films as *Angels with Dirty Faces* (1938) and *The Roaring
Twenties* (1939).

HORROR FILMS. *Dracula* (1931), with Bela Lugosi as the blood-sucking vampire, and *Frankenstein* (1931), with Boris Karloff as the synthetic monster, launched not only the horror film as a profitable Hollywood staple but also the careers of these actors as the undisputed masters of screen terror. Other shocking creatures, including cat-people, werewolves, resurrected mummies, and zombies, were introduced to audiences. During the second half of the decade there appeared what seemed like an endless chain of less than artistic reprises of the original horror films.

WESTERNS. The sound-film era witnessed the refining of elements of the western, already firmly established as a classic genre during the silent-film era. Starring in a number of westerns were Gary Cooper and John Wayne, both of whom were markedly true to form as western heroes. Cooper starred in director Cecil B. De Mille's magnificently sprawling *The Plainsman* (1936), and Wayne starred in director John Ford's masterfully gripping *Stagecoach* (1939). For the weekly pleasure of youngsters a host of westerns in the "B" (low-budget) picture category were made in a production-line manner, with such cinematic singing cowboys as Gene Autry and Roy Rogers.

ADVENTURE FILMS. In addition to dispensing the escapism so common to many of the genres during the 1930s, adventure films offered to the audience a glimpse (frequently to some degree distorted) of the culture of other times and other places. Assuming the mantle—and sword—from Douglas Fairbanks, the virile Errol Flynn became *the* swashbuckling hero in numerous "costume" adventure films, such as *Captain Blood* (1935) and *The Adventures of Robin Hood* (1938). In *Mutiny on the Bounty* (1935) Charles Laughton as a ship's commander was corrupted power incarnate. In the popular series of Tarzan films, set in "adventure-filled" Africa, the brawny Johnny Weissmuller, wearing a loincloth for more than a decade and a half, played the title role with such simple conviction that to most people he *was* the king of the jungle.

"MESSAGE" FILMS. An important body of films incorporated pleas for rationality, compassion, and courage in dealing with threatening national issues. *Mr. Smith Goes to Washington* (1939) probed corruption in politics; *Dead End* (1937) examined the breeding of crime in slums; *Fury* (1936) scrutinized the cruel injustice of vigilantism; and *Confessions of a Nazi Spy* (1939) explored the challenge to American democracy from a foreign dictatorship.

"PRESTIGE" FILMS. Biographies and adaptations of literary clas-

sics, mostly novels, formed the core of "prestige" films, which gar-
nered the studio usually only modest financial reward but always
much dignity. The best screen biographies starred either George
Arliss or Paul Muni, both distinguished actors. At the beginning of
the decade Arliss, in his uniquely theatrical style, transformed himself into the English statesman Disraeli, the French philosopher
Voltaire, and the German-Jewish banker Rothschild. With remarkable deftness Muni played the title roles in *The Story of Louis
Pasteur* (1935), *The Life of Émile Zola* (1937), and *Juarez*
(1939), the last with a fine supporting cast that included intense
performers Bette Davis and John Garfield. Among the most successful achievements in adapting novels to the screen were the following: *All Quiet on the Western Front* (1930), starring a thoroughly convincing Lew Ayres; *Grand Hotel* (1932), with a suave
John Barrymore and a soulful Greta Garbo heading a star-filled
cast; *David Copperfield* (1935), authoritatively directed by George
Cukor and with striking characterizations by W. C. Fields and Lio-
nel Barrymore in key Dickensian roles; *The Good Earth* (1937),
with the always accomplished Paul Muni as the central figure of a
Chinese peasant who developed into a rich landowner; *Wuthering
Heights* (1939), sensitively directed by William Wyler and with
Laurence Olivier and Merle Oberon in superb performances as the
Brontëan hero and heroine; and, bringing the decade to a spectacular close, what is regarded as the quintessential Hollywood product,
Gone With the Wind (1939), adapted from Margaret Mitchell's
best-seller, tastefully produced by David O. Selznick, vibrantly directed mainly by Victor Fleming, with an unforgettable musical
score by Max Steiner, and starring what has come to be considered
a "perfect" foursome: Clark Gable, Vivien Leigh, Leslie Howard,
and Olivia de Havilland.

TECHNICOLOR. The most impressive technical advance in filmmaking during the period was Technicolor. Soon after the invention
of motion pictures some movies were produced in color by hand-
tinting the film, frame by frame. During the early twentieth century experiments were conducted employing a two-color (red-and-
green) process, one of the methods using filters on both camera and
projector and the other involving dyes applied to emulsions laid
upon the positive prints. The breakthrough took place in 1932 with
a recently improved form of a process called Technicolor, which
had been invented fifteen years earlier by chemical engineer Her-

bert T. Kalmus. Originally a complex procedure that used three separate negatives, Technicolor now became a simplified three-color (the three primary colors of light—red, green, and blue) process entailing chromatic absorption by a single strip of film having three layers of emulsion sensitive to light plus a filter strip of film that in projecting the motion picture gave accurate natural color in the complete range of the spectrum. In 1935 *Becky Sharp,* based on the Thackeray novel *Vanity Fair,* was presented as the first feature-length production filmed entirely in improved Technicolor. Before long virtually every major motion picture was made in color.

Radio. Like motion pictures, radio experienced a "golden age" in the 1930s; it lasted well into the following decade. During the difficult years of the Depression the entire family could be entertained continually by the purchase of an inexpensive set.

WIDE APPEAL. The number of radios being used increased from approximately 12.5 million in 1930 to about 44 million in 1940, by which time almost 90 percent of the nation's families owned sets and listened to them on the average of a bit over four hours a day. A vast amount of the programming consisted of exceedingly escapist entertainment.

SOAP OPERAS. Much of the morning and early afternoon broadcasting schedule was devoted to serials, dubbed "soap operas" because many of them were sponsored by soap-products companies. Intended for housewives, the daily fifteen-minute segments focused on the anguishing vicissitudes of the human condition. *Ma Perkins* was about a sweet middle-aged woman from a small town who in addition to operating a lumberyard found time to help her neighbors whenever misfortune befell them. In *Just Plain Bill*, set in the Midwest, the main character was a likable barber who had to contend with the ramifications of having married a woman of higher social status. *The Goldbergs* was the story of a New York City Jewish family whose guiding spirit was the warmth-exuding Mama Molly and whose troubles were always small ones. *Our Gal Sunday* portrayed a young woman from a little mining town in Colorado striving to find happiness as the wife of a wealthy, titled Englishman. In *Young Widder Brown* a long tender love affair was carried on between a young widow who ran a tea room and an intern at the nearby hospital. *The Romance of Helen Trent* featured a fashion designer who, after her marriage ended, tried to remake her life and again capture romance.

ADVENTURE SERIALS. Late afternoon and early evening broadcasting contained a host of serials for youngsters. Delighting listeners for years were serials based on well-known comic-strip characters, among the most popular being *Buck Rogers in the Twenty-fifth Century, Dick Tracy, Little Orphan Annie,* and *Superman. Jack Armstrong, The All-American Boy* was about a high-school student who through all sorts of adventures exhibited sterling behavior and a sense of fair play. In *The Lone Ranger* law and order were brought to the western plains through the resourceful efforts of a daring masked rider on a fiery steed named Silver, aided by his faithful Indian companion Tonto.

EVENING FARE. Programming in the evening was directed at the family as a whole. There were situation comedies. They revolved around a few main characters who were present in virtually every episode, each of which had its own story line. The best-known situation comedy of all—indeed the first big hit of the medium—was *Amos 'n' Andy.* It was about two blacks (played by white actors Freeman Gosden and Charles Correll) who owned a taxi service and were much involved in their social fraternal order. Few listeners then found the broad delineation of the characters offensive in its basic attitude toward blacks. Another enduring favorite was *Fibber McGee and Molly* (with the title roles played by the husband-and-wife team Jim and Marian Jordan), in which occurred little domestic crises whose resolutions were helped or hindered by a myriad of visiting neighbors, such as the pompous Mayor La Trivia and the henpecked Wallace Wimple. There were comedians. Among the most popular were the stingy Jack Benny, with his broken-down vintage car and his basement vault for his money; the long-suffering George Burns and scatterbrained Gracie Allen; the giggling Ed Wynn, with his "Perfect Fool" routines; and the caustic-witted Fred Allen, who acquired a gallery of ethnic characters—the punning southern Senator Claghorn, the resourceful Jewish housewife Mrs. Nussbaum, the wily New Englander Titus Moody, and the saturnine Irishman Ajax Cassidy. There were singers. A stellar triumvirate consisted of Bing Crosby, the warbling baritone, whose theme song was "Where the Blue of the Night Meets the Gold of the Day"; Kate Smith, the crystalline mezzo-soprano, whose theme song was "When the Moon Comes over the Mountain"; and Rudy Vallee, the nasal tenor, whose theme song was "My Time Is Your Time."

FM. Radio acquired the capacity to carry the full range of sound reproduction by Edwin Howard Armstrong's invention in 1933 of FM (Frequency Modulation). A method of broadcasting wholly different from the existing AM (Amplitude Modification), FM transmitted static-free signals of high fidelity that in time became a boon to avid listeners of classical music.

Sports. Not until the easing of the Depression during the second half of the 1930s were professional athletics able to attract the great crowds that they had enjoyed in the prosperous 1920s.

BASEBALL. Still retaining its position as by far the most popular spectator sport was baseball. The best-known player was Joseph Paul ("Joe") DiMaggio, who, in his more than fifteen years with the New York Yankees, won fame as one of the greatest outfielders in the history of baseball. Noted primarily for his batting prowess, DiMaggio hit safely in fifty-six consecutive games during a single season (1941), setting a record that has not yet been broken. During the 1930s the Brooklyn Dodgers achieved a unique status. No matter how low or long the slumps the colorfully undaunted players found themselves in, "dem Bums" (as they were affectionately called) could command unfaltering homage from their colorfully undaunted fans. Improved technology in lighting made possible night baseball; the first major-league night game was played in 1935 in Cincinnati.

BOXING. On the whole, professional sports followed a policy of excluding blacks (who established their own teams and leagues). The exception was boxing, which made a black—Joe Louis—the preeminent athlete of the period. Louis won the heavyweight championship in 1937; successfully defended his crown a record twenty-five times, scoring twenty-one knockouts; and retired undefeated in 1949, after holding the title longer than anyone else before or since. He was known and respected as the "Brown Bomber." Grave of expression, Louis would pummel his opponent with rapid two-fisted punches.

TENNIS. During the 1930s tennis was dominated by John Donald ("Don") Budge, the first player to make the sport's grand slam by winning the United States, British, French, and Australian men's singles championships in 1938. The following year he turned professional and won the world professional title.

Chapter 4

THE AFFLUENT PERIOD: 1940–1960

In the decade and a half after World War II the United States achieved a height of prosperity unmatched by that of any other nation in history. Both the war itself and the subsequent Cold War forced American industry to operate at its greatest levels ever, providing the most advanced standard of living experienced at any time. The post–World War II period was one of affluence like that of the decade after World War I. But there the similarity—as important as it is—ends. For during the 1920s Americans looked upon the serious contemporary issues with complacency while engaging in unbridled pleasure–seeking. In the latter half of the 1940s and in the 1950s the knowledge that the many international crises resulting from the Cold War might turn into a nuclear conflict made people sober and anxious.

HISTORICAL BACKGROUND

In 1941 the United States entered World War II on the side of the Allies, headed by Great Britain, France, and Russia, and against the Axis, headed by Germany, Italy, and Japan. American manufacturing, agriculture, labor, and transportation were mobilized to support the armed forces fighting the enemy. Conferences among Allied leaders during the war, followed by the establishment of the United Nations, inspired hope for a lasting peace based on worldwide cooperation. In the postwar period, however, tensions increased between the Western Allies, led by the United States, and the Communist bloc of nations, led by the Soviet Union. In April 1945 Franklin D. Roosevelt died of a massive cerebral hemorrhage.

For Harry S. Truman and then Dwight D. Eisenhower to take on the presidency following Roosevelt, who had performed brilliantly in the office for a dozen years, was exceptionally difficult. Although foreign affairs dominated the Truman and Eisenhower administrations, many important domestic issues—some bitterly controversial—emerged.

World War II. In the 1930s the military aggression of the Axis nations—Nazi Germany, Fascist Italy, and imperialistic Japan—brought war to Europe and Asia, turning the American people from a policy of neutrality to one of aiding victims of that aggression. Despite elaborate neutrality legislation, the Roosevelt administration moved steadily, although at times hesitantly, to prepare the nation for a world war. On December 7, 1941, the United States was brought into the two-year-old World War II as a result of a Japanese attack on Pearl Harbor.

As in World War I, the difficult task of providing people to serve in the armed forces was successfully accomplished. For the second time in less than a quarter of a century, young men were compelled to perform military duty. Popularly called "GIs" (from "government issue"), they did not fail their nation. Modern warfare requires the participation of a nation in its totality. Those who go to meet the enemy must be buttressed materially as well as spiritually by those they leave at home. When the United States entered the war against the Axis powers, it needed to mobilize quickly national resources—manufacturing facilities, food, labor, transportation. To raise the huge sums necessary to pay for the war, the old methods of collecting revenue—taxation and borrowing—had to be refined.

The German conquests in Western Europe, once they got under way, were swift and devastating. Then the German attack upon the Soviet Union quickly brought stunning military success. But the Allied invasions of North Africa and of Italy prepared the way for the 1944 landings in France that began the defeat of Germany. Although the Germans fought stubbornly, their resistance was crushed within a year by Allied military might. The Japanese conquests, like the German, were massive. After the surrender of Germany in May 1945 there came the surrender of Japan in the following September—hastened by the dropping of the atomic bomb.

During World War II the leaders of the principal Allied nations held conferences, where they discussed not only pressing military affairs but also the nature of the peace they desired. Many viewed those wartime meetings as steps in reaching the goal of permanent postwar international cooperation for peace. And many hoped that goal had been attained when in 1945 representatives of fifty nations signed the Charter of the United Nations. In 1952 the permanent headquarters of the world body were established in New York City.

The Cold War. One year after the end of World War II, relations began to deteriorate between the Western Allies, under the general leadership of the United States, and the Communist bloc, which was strictly led by the Soviet Union. According to Winston Churchill's phrase, an "iron curtain" had been dropped by the Soviets between Soviet-controlled Eastern Europe on one side and Western Europe plus the Western Hemisphere on the other. The persistent hostility between the Western and Communist nations known as the Cold War turned into armed conflict in Korea in 1950.

The Quest for Stability at Home. Both Truman and Eisenhower, the former more intently than the latter, worked closely with members of Congress from both parties to bring about reorganization and reform of the government in the direction of greater efficiency. The domestic issue making for the greatest controversy was that of internal subversion. The extent of Communist infiltration into every sector of society was examined and argued. Although Truman's achievements in the sphere of foreign policy were impressive, his accomplishments in the field of domestic affairs—except in the area of government reorganization and reform—were meager. Viewing his victory in the election of 1948 as a directive from the people to devote himself to pressing for the enactment of his proposals for social improvement, Truman proceeded to do so with much vigor but with little success. In his State of the Union Message to Congress in January 1949 he recommended a comprehensive program of social legislation that he regarded as an extension of Roosevelt's New Deal; Truman referred to this program as the Fair Deal. Although the legislative branch rejected significant portions of the Fair Deal, it did pass bills on housing, minimum wages, and the extension of Social Security, which brought about some improvement in the general condition of the American people. As the issue of internal subversion related specifically to the Truman administration, a dispute centered on whether the government was taking strong enough measures against suspected disloyalty. In 1953, after twenty years of Democratic rule, the nation had a Republican chief executive. However, the new president, Dwight D.

Eisenhower, disappointed those conservative members of his party who wanted a frontal attack on the laws of Roosevelt's New Deal and Truman's Fair Deal. The moderates of both major parties accepted the principle that the federal government was responsible for the welfare of its citizens.

SOCIETY

The affluence of the period was all the more startling—and comforting—to the American people since they had just undergone the worst depression in their history. The extensive business failures and massive unemployment of the 1930s were like a bad dream. The nation seemed to be arriving at the point where the desire for all sections of society to get a share of an economic "pie" was to be fulfilled. In addition to the satisfying availability of consumer goods, the swelling affluence was accompanied by the movement to the suburbs, the improved status of blacks, a vast rise in the employment of women, a strengthening of organized labor, an increased governmental commitment to education, and great advances in technology and medicine.

The Effects of Affluence. Unlike the prosperity that characterized the 1920s, the prosperity from 1940 to 1960 proved securely founded, considering the vast outlay of sums to carry on the Cold War and the ever-increasing buying of consumer goods.

The extent of America's affluence could be seen in the statistics of the gross national product (see footnote, p. 70): it increased from about $205 billion in 1940 to about $500 billion in 1960 (a rise of almost 150 percent). Included in the approximately 3 million business firms in 1940 were approximately 413,000 corporations with assets totaling about $320.5 billion; included in the approximately 6.5 million business firms in 1960 were approximately 1,141,000 corporations with assets totaling about $1.2 trillion. It was estimated that within a decade and a half after World War II the 150 largest corporations owned approximately 50 percent of the nation's industrial wealth, which in turn equalled approximately 25 percent of that of the whole world.

Between 1940 and 1960 the number of employed workers increased from about 52.8 million to about 66.7 million. During World War II unemployment was practically nonexistent. In the decade and a half after the war, the rate was minimal, fluctuating between 3 and 5 percent.

With virtually everyone in the labor force having a good-paying job, business firms strove to supply the American people with both essential and nonessential albeit appealing consumer goods. Business firms paid vast amounts of money—by 1960 it was more than $10 billion annually—to advertising agencies (most of which were located on New York City's Madison Avenue) to use their collective imagination to motivate consumers to buy a particular brand of a dizzying array of products.

The Relentlessness of Poverty. And yet amid the affluence of the postwar period there were those who lived in want—whites in areas along the Appalachian mountain range, blacks in urban ghettos throughout the North, Indians on reservations that dotted the Far West, Mexican-Americans in both rural and urban areas of the Southwest, and Puerto Ricans in New York City. In 1960, according to federal-government findings, of the total American population of approximately 180 million perhaps as many as 20 million (about 11 percent) lived at the poverty level.

Suburban Growth and Urban Transformation. A significant social change stemming from postwar affluence was the growth of the suburbs and the concomitant transformation of the urban centers. The movement to the suburbs had an extensive impact on the thought and action of vast numbers of the American people.

STATISTICS. At the end of World War II the United States was predominantly urban. During the next fifteen years the population of the suburbs went from approximately 36 million to approximately 68 million (an increase of close to 100 percent); the population of the central cities went from approximately 52 million to approximately 58 million (an increase of about 12 percent). In the rural areas, the population actually declined, going from about 59 million to about 54 million. But what is just as important regarding the move to the suburbs is that it was made overwhelmingly by whites, drastically changing the racial composition of American cities. At the same time that whites, mostly affluent, were fleeing to the suburbs, poor blacks and poor Hispanic-Americans thronged into the inner cities. By 1960 blacks, who formed about 12 percent of the national population, accounted for approximately 20 percent of the population in over two hundred metropolitan areas. By the end of another decade black Americans constituted about 70 percent of the population of Washington, D.C.; about 55 percent of that of Newark, New Jersey; about 53 percent of Gary, Indiana; and about 50 percent of Atlanta, Georgia. In more than half a dozen major cities, including Detroit and New Orleans, the black population was over 40 percent.

LIFE IN THE SUBURBS. To have one's own home with a bit of lawn on a tree-lined street was a traditional American dream. It was realized by many during the postwar years as a result of such things as the accessibility of inexpensive dwellings (standardized units were made possible by advances in mass-production and pre-fabrication methods); the availability to World War II veterans through federal legislation of long-term mortgage loans at low interest; the opportunity to buy one or more automobiles per family as industrial plants quickly switched from wartime to peacetime operations; and the creation of a vast network of highways. The boom in housing construction was such that by 1960 approximately 25 percent of all the nation's dwelling units had been built during the preceding decade. The majority of American families lived in homes that they owned rather than rented, a situation that had not existed since the beginning of the twentieth century. Quickly following those who fled the cities to settle in the suburbs were business firms and professional groups. Retail establishments came together in shopping malls conveniently located for their affluent suburban customers who found plentiful space to park their automobiles. The most serious charges leveled at the suburbs were their accentuation of racial separation and what seemed to many the dull uniformity of areas whose residents tended to conform to the values and practices of a self-contained community.

The Coordination of Federal Social Programs. In 1947 President Truman's proposal for the establishment of a department of welfare was defeated by a coalition of congressional conservatives. A few years later, during the Eisenhower administration, the legislative branch took positive action. In 1953 Congress created the Department of Health, Education, and Welfare, to be headed by a cabinet member. The new department was established to consolidate and supervise the various government agencies that dealt with the people's health, education, and social and economic welfare.

Extension of Social Security. During the Truman and Eisenhower administrations Social Security was extended to provide greater benefits. In 1950 the Social Security Act was amended to extend coverage to new groups of wage earners, to provide pensions for some who were self-employed, and to increase benefits to retired workers. Four years later Congress amended the Social Security Act to provide coverage to new occupational groups, including farmers and state and local government employees, and to increase the amount of pensions. In 1956 the Social Security Act was extended to cover new vocational groups, such as physicians and those in the armed services. Also, the eligibility age for receiving pensions was lowered for women to sixty-two and the eligibility age for receiving disability benefits was lowered to fifty. Two years later further amendments provided for a substantial increase in benefits to those receiving old-age, survivor's, and disability assistance.

Internal Subversion. As in the post–World War I era, the United States in the years following World War II was convulsed by fear of widespread Communist infiltration. In the latter period, however, there was greater justification for belief in the existence of Communist subversion, prompting the people to be more receptive to drastic measures against anyone suspected of it.

In 1947 Truman issued an executive order inaugurating a comprehensive investigation of the loyalty of all federal employees. By the end of the probe, which lasted four years, over 3 million government employees had been cleared, approximately 2000 had resigned, and 212 had been dismissed on the basis of a reasonable doubt as to their loyalty. Further, in what were described as "sensitive" areas of government, Truman consented to the dismissal of persons who were deemed not disloyal but—for one reason or another —security risks. The execution of Truman's loyalty probe was severe and thorough. However, this did not prevent the Republican party from exploiting the issue of Communists in government through allegations that the Truman administration was too "soft" on Communist infiltrators.

TRIALS AND CONVICTIONS. In 1948 Whittaker Chambers, an editor of *Time* magazine, while giving evidence regarding a Communist cell to which he had belonged in the 1930s, named as a fellow member Alger Hiss, a former State Department official. Admitting to having been a messenger for the Soviet espionage system, Chambers asserted that Hiss had passed on to him State Department classified documents. Hiss denied this charge under oath before a federal grand jury. After Chambers produced evidence to corroborate his charge, Hiss was found guilty of perjury and sentenced to five years in prison.

With the public alarmed by the Hiss case, another episode took place that lent some credence to wild charges of Communist infiltration. In 1940 Klaus Fuchs, a naturalized British physicist engaged in atomic research during World War II, confessed that he had supplied the Soviet Union with data on making the atomic bomb. Fuchs provided information that led to the arrest of his accomplices in the United States. Julius Rosenberg, a civilian employee in the United States Army Signal Corps during World War II, and his wife Ethel were arrested and tried for passing information on atomic weapons, as well as standard military equipment, to Soviet agents. The Rosenbergs were found guilty, and executed in 1953.

The Alien Registration Act of 1940, which was called the Smith Act after its congressional sponsor, among other things declared it illegal to advocate the overthrow of the United States government by force or to belong to a group dedicated to that end. Put aside during World War II when the United States and the Soviet Union were allied against a common enemy, the act was revived during the postwar period of American-Soviet tensions. In 1949 a dozen leaders of the American Communist party, including national chairman William Foster and national secretary Eugene Dennis, were indicted for violating the Smith Act provisions on subversive activities. Because of ill health Foster did not go on trial, but the eleven others were tried, found guilty, and sent to prison.

FURTHER RESTRICTIONS ON "SUBVERSIVES." Determined to strike at Communism even harder, Congress in 1950 overrode Truman's veto to pass the Internal Security Act. Known as the McCarran Act after its sponsor, Democratic Senator Pat McCarran of Nevada, it required the registration of Communist and Communist-front organizations, compelled the internment of Communists during declared national emergencies, and prohibited the employment of Communists in defense work. The McCarran Act also contained a provision forbidding immigration to the United States of anyone who had been a member of a totalitarian organization. This was amended in 1951 to permit exceptions for those who had been forced to belong to such groups.

In 1952 Congress passed over Truman's veto an act sponsored by Senator McCarran and Republican Representative Francis E. Walter of Pennsylvania that revised immigration and naturalization statutes. The McCarran-Walter Act retained from the Quota Act of 1924 the quota system that favored immigration from northern and western European countries but repealed the Quota Act's prohibition of immigration and naturalization of people from Asia. The new act gave preferential treatment to would-be immigrants who possessed occupational skills deemed useful to American society or the economy and to relatives of American citizens. It barred entry into the United States of anyone who had been a member of a Communist or Communist-front organization, and it provided for the deportation of any immigrant or naturalized citizen who, once in the United States, participated in a Communist or Communist-front organization.

McCarthyism. There were many politicians who exploited the deep anti-Communist feeling in the nation, but no one did so with such vehemence and initial success as Republican Senator Joseph R. McCarthy of Wisconsin. Because of his activities his name entered the English language; the term "McCarthyism" soon came to denote the making of indiscriminate and unsubstantiated charges of subversive activities.

McCarthy first achieved national prominence when he charged in a speech delivered in 1950 in West Virginia that he had in his possession a list of "card-carrying" Communists in the State Department. But he was never able to prove his case. Over the next few years he alleged that a number of government agencies were infiltrated by Communists, Communist sympathizers, and "security risks." Anyone who took issue with him he characterized as disloyal or at best obtuse. He charged with treasonable conduct such persons as General George C. Marshall and Secretary of State Dean Acheson.

In 1954 the Army accused McCarthy of seeking preferential treatment for an assistant who had been drafted. McCarthy, who chaired both the Senate Committee on Government Operations and its permanent Subcommittee on Investigations, countered that the Army was trying to embarrass him for his investigations of spying at Fort Monmouth, New Jersey, Army Signal Corps facilities. From April to June 1954 televised hearings were held on the two sets of charges. In many confrontations with Army counsel Joseph B. Welch, McCarthy's bullying methods were revealed to an estimated 20 million American viewers, with the result that the senator's reputation among his supporters was severely damaged.

The television exposure of McCarthy's long-standing methods convinced the Senate to take action. In December 1954, by a vote of 67 to 22, it decided to "condemn" his conduct as "unbecoming a member of the United States Senate." His influence was precipitately destroyed.

Civil Rights. During the 1940s and 1950s a major domestic issue was that of extending equality of public treatment to black Americans. This matter divided the nation along predominantly sectional lines. In their efforts to broaden the application of civil rights, Democratic President Harry Truman was supported by many Republicans and opposed by most southern Democrats and Republican President Dwight D. Eisenhower was supported by many northern Democrats. Encouraged by the basic sympathy of the Truman and Eisenhower administrations, blacks became increasingly more active in attempting to improve their status.

PRESIDENTIAL ACTION. In 1946 President Truman appointed a Committee on Civil Rights, which made a number of recommendations, including the establishment of a permanent commission to enforce fair employment practices; the denial of federal subsidies to health, education, and housing facilities that practiced racial discrimination; the prohibition of segregation in interstate transportation facilities; and the designation of lynching as a federal crime. In 1948 Truman urgently requested Congress to pass legislation embodying these proposals. When Congress failed to do so, Truman issued an executive order against racial segregation in all government departments and another abolishing it in the armed services. After his upset victory in the presidential election of 1948, Truman appealed to Congress to enact measures based on the civil rights planks of the platform he had campaigned on. But the conservative wing of his own party blocked the proposed legislation. Disappointed and discouraged, Truman again resorted to the only course open to him to achieve some limited gains—executive action. For example, in 1951 he appointed the first black judge in the federal court system, and in 1951 he appointed a committee to oversee the awarding of federal defense contracts and to bar contracts to companies that practiced racial discrimination in employment.

Brown v. *Board of Education of Topeka.* By the middle of the twentieth century most public schools in the South were racially segregated by state or local laws, whereas in the North a number of public schools were segregated because of custom or neighborhood housing patterns. On May 17, 1954, the Supreme Court handed down a momentous decision that reversed the Court's earlier position in the *Plessy* v. *Ferguson* case of 1896. The *Brown* v. *Board of*

Education of Topeka case involved a Kansas law requiring segregated classrooms in the public elementary and secondary schools. In this case the Court held unanimously that segregation in the public schools was unconstitutional. The justices declared that maintenance of "separate but equal" school facilities for blacks (the practice in seventeen states) was a denial of the Fourteenth Amendment's guarantee of equal protection of the laws. Writing the Court's opinion, Chief Justice Earl Warren stated that separating black children from others solely because of their race "generates a feeling of inferiority as to their status in a community that may affect their hearts and minds in a way unlikely ever to be undone" and therefore concluded that "separate educational facilities are inherently unequal." In 1955 the Supreme Court ordered that the desegregation of public schools should proceed "with all deliberate speed."

THE MONTGOMERY BUS BOYCOTT. In December 1955 Rosa Parks, a Montgomery, Alabama, black woman, refused to give up her seat on a bus to a white man and was arrested. The black community thereupon decided to call a boycott of the buses as a protest against segregated seating on public transportation. Car pools among blacks were organized. Under the skillful leadership of the Reverend Dr. Martin Luther King, Jr., a black Baptist minister, the boycott was extraordinarily successful. Enduring intense hostility from many whites, the black community persevered month after month. In November 1956 the Supreme Court declared segregated seating in local transportation unconstitutional. Soon thereafter Montgomery blacks began using the city buses once more—and sat where they pleased. The Montgomery bus boycott had become the first direct community action by blacks to achieve national prominence.

CONFRONTATION IN LITTLE ROCK. Implicit in the *Brown* v. *Board of Education of Topeka* decision was the Supreme Court's understanding that desegregation would require careful planning over a considerable period of time. The Eisenhower administration encouraged the states to work out their own plans. At hundreds of southern schools integration was accomplished peacefully. But there were scattered incidents of violent opposition, the most prominent occurring in Little Rock, Arkansas. In September 1957 the Board of Education of Little Rock was prepared to admit to one of the city's high schools nine carefully selected black students. Governor Orval Faubus of Arkansas, insisting that violence would erupt if the students were admitted, used the Arkansas National Guard to bar them from the school building. President Eisenhower declared that Faubus's action violated the law of the nation. Obeying a federal court injunction, Faubus withdrew the National Guard. When a taunting mob prevented the black students from going into the high school, Eisenhower responded by ordering federal troops to Little Rock. During the entire academic year of 1957–1958 the troops protected the black students.

THE CIVIL RIGHTS ACTS OF 1957 AND 1960. Influenced both by the ruling of the Supreme Court for school desegregation and by the increasing activism of blacks to improve their condition, Congress passed a civil rights act—the first since the Reconstruction period. After long and hard debate, during which many conservative white southern legislators voiced strenuous objections, Congress passed the Civil Rights Act of 1957, which created the Civil Rights Commission, composed of six members. The commission was empowered to investigate the denial of voting rights and the violation of the equal protection of the laws and to make recommendations for new legislation as it saw the need. The attorney general was authorized to obtain court orders to secure the right to vote anywhere in the nation.

After the Civil Rights Commission appointed by President Eisenhower under the 1957 act declared that the act was in itself ineffectual in protecting the voting rights of blacks, Congress passed the Civil Rights Act of 1960, which empowered federal judges to appoint referees to assist blacks in registering and voting. Further, in order to halt a recent spate of bombings of buildings, such as churches and schools used by blacks, the act made it a federal crime to transport explosives across a state line in order to bomb a building or to cross a state line in order to escape prosecution for having bombed a building.

The Employment of Women. During World War II approximately 260,000 women enlisted for noncombatant duty in all branches of the armed forces. In the Army they were popularly known as WACs (Women's Army Corps) and in the Navy, WAVEs (Women Appointed for Voluntary Emergency Service). But women made their greatest contribution to the war effort by serving in nonmilitary capacities.

The critical need for labor resulting from the nation's wartime

production efforts led to the hiring of women in such numbers that
their long-standing rise in participation in the job market skyrocketed. During the war the employment of women increased from
about 12 million to more than 18 million; by its end women made
up approximately 35 percent of the labor force. And of the women
hired during the war, about 65 percent remained at work after it
was over. Just as significant is the fact that women performed exceedingly well in jobs, such as truck driving and riveting, that had
hitherto been denied them as being beyond their physical strength.
Of the married women who went to work during the postwar period
the vast majority did so not out of a desire to pursue a career but to
help their husbands pay for the increasing number of appealing
consumer goods available in an affluent society. By 1960 more than
40 percent of women were employed, totaling approximately 22
million, about 33 percent of the nation's labor force. Compared
with men, women were poorly paid; the idea of equal pay for equal
work was not prevalent.

The Labor Movement. When the United States entered World
War II it needed to mobilize quickly all national resources, including labor. After the war an epidemic of strikes brought about widespread antilabor feeling that culminated in the enactment of legislation by a conservative Republican-controlled Congress to curb
"unfair" labor practices. To strengthen its position, the two largest
factions of a long-split organized labor reunited. But labor still
faced many difficulties.

WARTIME MOBILIZATION OF LABOR. During World War II the
War Manpower Commission handled the task of apportioning the
work of approximately 50 million men and about 20 million women
in the labor force. Although the activities of workers were more
strictly supervised by the government than at any other time in the
nation's history, American laborers escaped the kind of regimenta-
tion experienced by workers of most other countries at war. American workers were spurred to great efforts. Their record of output
from 1942 to 1945 surpassed by far any previous record for a comparable period. At the same time, average weekly earnings rose
from approximately twenty-five dollars to about forty-five dollars,
while the length of the workweek increased from approximately
thirty-eight to about forty-five hours.

MANAGEMENT-LABOR UNREST. In the immediate postwar period
relations between management and labor were troubled. As is usu-

ally the case, war had caused inflation. When wages lagged behind spiraling prices, workers demanded wage increases and turned to the strike to compel employers to meet their demands. In 1946 close to 1.75 million persons were on strike. Both the United States Steel and the General Motors corporations were struck by the unions for months. A strike by maritime workers closed the nation's ports for two weeks. A strike of railroad workers was cut short when President Truman threatened to have the government seize and operate the railroads. When the United Mine Workers went on strike against the bituminous coal mine companies, Truman seized the mines. The government retained control of the mines after some operators rejected a contract that had been negotiated between the union and government representatives. John L. Lewis, president of the United Mine Workers, then called on the bituminous coal miners to strike again, this time against government operation of the mines. Lewis soon ordered the miners to resume work while the Supreme Court wrestled with the legal issues. The decision was in favor of the government, and Lewis agreed to a compromise contract with the mine owners.

THE TAFT-HARTLEY ACT. In an attempt to reduce management-labor disputes and to curb what the conservative Congress believed were "unfair" labor practices, the legislative branch in 1947 passed the Labor-Management Relations Act over President Truman's veto. Commonly referred to as the Taft-Hartley Act after its two Republican sponsors, Senator Robert A. Taft of Ohio and Representative Fred A. Hartley, Jr., of New Jersey, the measure, in amending and to an extent superseding the National Labor Relations Act of 1935, removed some restrictions upon management and added a number of restrictions upon organized labor. Specifically, the Taft-Hartley Act (1) prohibited the closed shop; (2) permitted employers to sue unions for breaking contracts or for damages incurred by a strike; (3) required employers and unions to give sixty days' notice of a decision to modify or terminate a contract; (4) authorized the federal government to take legal action to delay for eighty days a strike that threatened public health or safety; (5) required unions to divulge their financial statements; (6) forbade unions to make contributions to political campaigns; (7) prohibited the paying of union dues by the "check-off" system;* (8) compelled

*A method whereby the employer collects dues for the union from the workers' pay.

union leaders to sign oaths that they were not members of the Communist party; (9) declared illegal the secondary boycott* and a strike over a jurisdictional dispute.†

Unions assailed the Taft-Hartley Act as a "slave-labor" measure. However, by making organized labor feel a vulnerability it had not recently experienced, the act had the effect of unifying labor. In the following years President Truman repeatedly urged Congress to repeal—or at least modify—the Taft-Hartley Act, but without success.

THE FORMATION OF THE AFL-CIO. As one reaction to the widespread hostility toward it, organized labor assumed a united stand by bringing to an end the two decades of rivalry between the American Federation of Labor and the Congress of Industrial Organizations. In 1955, after years of discussion, the two groups merged under the name of the American Federation of Labor and the Congress of Industrial Organizations (AFL-CIO) into a powerful approximately 15-million-member body. Assuming the presidency of the AFL-CIO was George Meany, who had been the head of the AFL; becoming the vice-president in control of the program of organizing, where appropriate, workers along industrial lines was Walter Reuther, who had been the leader of the CIO.

The new organization still faced quite serious difficulties within the labor movement. The long-standing and bitter controversy over the value of craft unionism as opposed to industrial unionism still rankled among many members of the organization's two components. Further, approximately 2 million organized laborers, including the railroad workers and the miners, were still not affiliated with the AFL-CIO, preferring to belong to their totally independent unions. In addition, about 50 million workers throughout the nation (more than 75 percent of the total labor force) were not in unions at all. The AFL-CIO undertook to organize unaffiliated workers, a massive task not only because of the sheer numbers to be contacted but also because of the increasing prosperity of the late 1950s, which gave workers a notably higher standard of living and thus made the benefits of joining a union seem less substantial.

Education. The vast economic and social changes that occurred

---

*A boycott of an employer in order to induce him to bring pressure upon another employer to come to terms with his workers.

† A dispute involving two or more unions over which one has the right to exclusive control over certain work.

during the period impelled many Americans to reexamine the goals of education, causing school administrators and teachers to redesign both curriculums and instruction methods. Having a particular impact on the direction of education were the notable Soviet achievements in space exploration.

ELEMENTARY EDUCATION. With the return to normal family life after the end of World War II, the birthrate began a long and marked rise, presenting challenges to the field of elementary education. The postwar "baby boom" required a massive effort to prepare additional teachers and to construct more classroom buildings. Enrollment in elementary schools increased by more than 1 million each year during the 1950s, reaching approximately 30.3 million by 1960. During the 1940s and 1950s elementary education increasingly came under attack as having become inadequate at its task. Most of the critics declared the cause to be what they considered the pernicious influence of John Dewey's philosophy. In fact, many teachers had misinterpreted Dewey's aims and misused his methodology. The critics endeavored to achieve a quick and full return to the arduous learning of the traditional academic disciplines.

SECONDARY EDUCATION. Enrollment in secondary schools increased from about 6.8 million in 1940 to about 10.2 million in 1960. In the latter year approximately 85 percent of the nation's adolescents were in high school, a remarkable figure compared with that of approximately 10 percent in high school at the turn of the century.

HIGHER EDUCATION. In 1940 the number enrolled in American colleges and universities was approximately 1.5 million; in 1960 it was approximately 3.6 million. The sharp increase is easy to understand. During World War II millions of young Americans performing military duty saw that the best opportunities in the services went to those who had formal education. After the war the colleges and universities were deluged with former servicemen eager to make up for lost time. They were assisted in this aim with extensive financing provided by the federal "GI Bill." By and large, the veterans were sensitive to the value of higher education, conscientious in pursuit of their studies, and, according to both administrators and professors, performed admirably. Of course, the sudden and enormous rise in college and university enrollments placed an unprecedented burden on the institutions to provide adequate classroom and housing accommodations for their students.

THE NATIONAL DEFENSE EDUCATION ACT. In 1957 the Soviet Union launched the first unmanned spacecraft (Sputnik) that escaped the gravity of earth. Appalled at being beaten in the competition for space exploration, the American people immediately heaped blame on their educational system on all levels. Demands were made for strengthening the entire range of American education, especially the mathematics and science curriculums. In 1958 Congress passed the National Defense Education Act, which, among other things, provided funds for (1) long-term, low-interest loans to college students, with half the loan to be canceled for those who after graduating taught in elementary or secondary schools for at least five years; (2) fellowships for graduate students who agreed to enter college or university teaching; (3) matching grants with state governments to public schools for the purchase of textbooks and laboratory equipment to improve the teaching of mathematics, science, and modern languages.

Religion. Perhaps it was the concomitant anxieties of World War II and the Cold War that influenced many Americans to recommit themselves to organized religious bodies. From 1940 to 1960 membership in churches and synagogues increased substantially. One manifestation of the surge in religious awakening was a tide of revivalism.

PROTESTANTISM. Membership in Protestant churches rose from about 40 million in 1940 to about 63.5 million in 1960. Two significant Protestant developments were the merging of bodies within a denomination and coalition among the various denominations, reversing the trend of extreme denominationalism which had long dominated that wing of American Christianity. For example, a group of Methodist bodies merged to form a united Methodist church; a number of Presbyterian bodies merged into a united Presbyterian church; and a group of Lutheran bodies merged into a united Lutheran church. As for interdenominational alliance, the National Council of the Churches of Christ in the United States, comprising twenty-six Protestant denominations plus four Eastern Orthodox bodies, was founded in 1950. The most famous Protestant revivalist was the Reverend William F. ("Billy") Graham. An evangelist of markedly persuasive eloquence, Graham conducted highly successful preaching crusades not only throughout the United States but also in many foreign nations and on every continent.

ROMAN CATHOLICISM. In relative membership growth Roman

Catholicism surpassed Protestantism. The number of its adherents rose from about 21.4 million in 1940 to about 42.1 million in 1960. The most prominent expounder of Roman Catholic views on the moral and social issues then facing the American people was Bishop Fulton J. Sheen. Through a weekly television program, *Life Is Worth Living,* he gained an enormous following with his earnestness, charm, and wit.

JUDAISM. Membership in the three bodies of Judaism—Orthodox, Conservative, Reform—rose from approximately 3 million in 1940 to approximately 5.4 million in 1960. Many of the children of the Jewish immigrants of the late nineteenth and early twentieth centuries, in their desire to become thoroughly Americanized, had become less than dedicated to the religious practices of their forebears, although they had retained the moral principles of their religion. However, the next generation, in part because of reaction to the Holocaust—the killing of approximately 6 million Jews by the Nazi regime—and in part because of dissatisfaction with a blandly homogeneous American society, sought identity in a recommitment to the rituals and traditions of their ancestral faith.

Technology. If the United States had any "secret weapon" during the early years of World War II, it was the marvelous efficiency of its transportation facilities, notably the railroads and airplanes. Wartime needs not only led to the development of the atomic bomb but also spurred rapid advances in electronics, which became the most important technological development of the 1940s and 1950s. By 1960 electronics was the nation's fourth largest—and fastest-growing—industry, with sales totaling close to $13 billion. As for the automobile, production soared after the war.

THE RAILROADS. During World War II the government did not assume control of the railroads and operate the lines as a unified system, as it had during World War I. However, the railroad operators and employees, working with the Office of Defense Transportation, carried unprecedented numbers of arms and equipment. In 1942 the railroads transported 40 percent more passengers and 30 percent more freight than they had the previous year. (This was done with 20,000 fewer locomotives and 600,000 fewer freight cars than they had possessed during World War I.)

THE AIRPLANE. The commercial airlines, although subordinating their activities to World War II needs, managed to keep many of their normal schedules. Virtually all airplane construction by private firms was for military purposes. Within a year after the Pearl Harbor attack the nation produced about 49,000 airplanes. In 1943 the output was over 5500 airplanes a month, compared with approximately 200 a month in 1939.

THE ATOMIC BOMB. Through the cooperative efforts of scientists from many Allied nations and of a number who had fled from Nazi-controlled nations the atomic bomb was perfected. The American physicist J. Robert Oppenheimer directed the Los Alamos laboratory, where the bomb was designed and constructed. Making particularly significant contributions were three physicists who were refugees from Nazi-dominated Europe: the German Albert Einstein, the Italian Enrico Fermi, and the Dane Niels Bohr. The atomic bomb that was developed was the most devastating weapon that the world had ever seen. On August 6, 1945, American airmen dropped the first such bomb on Hiroshima. Approximately 180,000 people were killed or wounded. Three days later a second bomb was dropped, this time on Nagasaki. There were 80,000 immediate casualties. Both cities were virtually obliterated.

THE COMPUTER. In 1944 Harvard University engineering professor Howard Acken developed the first digital* computer, the operation of which was controlled by mechanical and electrical apparatus. Two years later research engineers at the University of Pennsylvania made the first totally electronic digital computer, whose circuits were controlled by vacuum tubes. In 1950 computers were introduced for business use. The machines manufactured for the rest of the decade were still controlled by vacuum tubes and were able to perform thousands of calculations a second. (They were superseded early in the 1960s by computers controlled by transistors and able to perform approximately 1 million calculations a second.) In 1955 the number of computers in use in the United States was about 300; by 1970 the number had increased to about 100,000. Virtually every sector of life found a use for computers. With them, for example, manufacturers regulated the machines that produced goods, including food and clothing; wholesale and retail businesses kept account of sales and payments; banks registered deposits and withdrawals; hotels and airlines processed reservations; educational institutions maintained the academic records of their students.

* Treating information in the form of words or solving problems expressed in words by converting the material into numbers and then calculating those numbers.

THE TRANSISTOR. In 1947 three physicists at the Bell Telephone Laboratories—John Bardeen, Walter H. Brattain, and William Schockley—invented the transistor. The device was enormously valuable, serving the same purpose as, but being vastly superior to, the vacuum tube. The transistor presented much less bulk and much less weight than did a vacuum tube of identical implementation. Further, the transistor, unlike the vacuum tube, needed no warming up; it ran on considerably less power while generating a minimal amount of heat; and it was less sensitive to physical impact. With the use of transistors, electronic items could be made attractively convenient for the consumer; for example, a radio that could be carried in a pocket and a television set that could be moved easily from one room to another.

THE AUTOMOBILE. Car sales in the United States plummeted to a low of about 1.1 million in 1932, when the effects of the Great Depression were at their worst, but thereafter began to rise steadily, reaching about 4.8 million in 1939. Automobile production was negligible during World War II, but spurted after the war to fulfill the public's desire, unsatisfied for four years, for new cars. During the late 1940s and the 1950s car sales averaged about 5.8 million annually. And the automobiles were longer, wider, heavier, equipped with mightier engines, and filled with a greater complement of technical refinements and decorative embellishments than ever before. In vastly increasing numbers, purchasers selected vehicles with automatic transmission, power steering, and power brakes. In styling, manufacturers tried to outdo one another in providing products with such adornments as many gradations of a single color or even of a two-color scheme of body paint from which to choose, a surfeit of chromium trimming, and tailfins of extravagant sizes and shapes.

Medicine. A natural result of the postwar affluence was the ease with which Americans could pay for recently developed medical preparations and techniques. This made for a notable gain in health, perhaps the best index of which was a rise in life expectancy from 62.9 years in 1940 to 69.7 in 1960. A component of the great strides in medicine was the use of an extensive and varied group of "wonder drugs" called antibiotics. Penicillin was discovered by British bacteriologist Alexander Fleming in 1928. It was not until a decade later, however, that the drug was proved useful in the treatment of a host of diseases, most effectively in combating scarlet fever, syphillis and gonorrhea, and most types of pneumonia. The value of penicillin was an impetus to scientists to pursue an investigation for other antibiotics. The result was the discovery in the 1940s of several different antibiotics, including streptomycin, which is particularly useful in controlling tuberculosis, and tetracycline, which is helpful in controlling whooping cough and stomach infections.

The urgent medical needs concomitant with World War II produced within a few years breakthroughs that ordinarily might have taken decades to achieve in the prevention and treatment of illness and the care of wounds. Improvements in surgical techniques were a direct result of the experience gained from operations on hundreds of thousands of wounded servicemen. Intensified research on the preservation of blood for care of the wounded led to the production of blood plasma and the establishment of blood banks.

The insecticide DDT (which is the popular designation taken from the first letters of each of the three parts of its complex scientific name) is a substance whose value was recognized in 1939 through the research of the Swiss chemist Paul Müller. It was first used by United States military forces during World War II in an attempt to eliminate typhus on the European front, particularly in Italy, and malaria on the Pacific front. However, some years later it became increasingly clear that the indiscriminate use of DDT and other insecticides had a seriously adverse effect upon the balance of nature by destroying large numbers of insects, such as honeybees, that are directly useful to human beings, in addition to those constituting much of the food supply of several of the higher forms of animal life.

In 1953 the American Jonas Salk announced his development of a vaccine against poliomyelitis. After two years of extensive testing of the vaccine a vast immunization program throughout the nation was undertaken.

CULTURE

The affluence of the postwar period significantly aided the flourishing of art, literature, and music. With the advent of television a revolution occurred in the fields of both entertainment and communication. A notable development in sports was the breaking of the barrier against participation by blacks.

Art. The most significant new developments in American art were the emergence of the first major movement in painting that consciously rejected the imitation of a European style and the entering of sculpture into a stage of modernity.

PAINTING. During the mid-1940s and the 1950s many American painters turned from social criticism to a new movement called "abstract expressionism." In this style traditional subject matter, such as the human body, still life, a rural scene, that had previously occupied the attention of painters was of little or no concern. Within a basic structure of nonrepresentational intent, the focus was upon such things as the utilization of space, of dimension (a huge canvas was often preferred), of surface texture (such as the distinctiveness of the brushstrokes), and of the interrelationship of colors. Abstract expressionism is sometimes referred to as "action painting" because of the speed, energy, spontaneity, and emotional ardor involved in applying the paint to the canvas; it is sometimes referred to as the New York School because the leading abstract expressionists worked in Manhattan. Abstract expressionism was the first major movement in American painting whose practitioners emphatically declined to imitate a European style. Indeed, the abstract expressionists affected the trend of painting outside the United States, exerting such influence that the painting center of the world shifted from Paris to New York City.

The members of the abstract expressionist school exhibited a broad diversity of styles. Jackson Pollock is acknowledged as the theoretician of the movement, and his work is considered to be its epitome. He created the "drip" technique, in which onto a large canvas placed on the floor liquid paint is dribbled from a can, stick, or brush, or sometimes poured or even flung from a can, or occasionally viscous paint is applied directly from the tube. Using this method, Pollock produced works consisting of whirling and criss-crossing lines of pigment that form a complicated and turbulent network. A typical painting is *Autumn Rhythm* (1950). Other leaders of the movement were Willem de Kooning and Mark Rothko. The Dutch-born de Kooning used sweeping, almost savage brushstrokes to produce bold shapes of extremely intense color. He achieved his greatest popular success with an extensive series of paintings, done during the early 1950s and later during the 1960s, entitled *Woman*, in which, contrary to his usual style, the subject matter is discernible. Rothko's works are characterized by a huge canvas filled with two or three blurry-edged rectangles of intense color arranged beside each other and floating on a background of intense color.

Realism was by no means completely gone from American painting. The most-acclaimed exponent of this genre was Andrew Wyeth. His works, many of them depicting people and places around his winter home in rural Pennsylvania and his summer home in coastal Maine, are executed with meticulous detail and often convey a feeling of deep loneliness. His best-known work, *Christina's World* (1948), portrays a lame and thin-armed woman creeping through a field toward an old house.

Interestingly, the height of the abstract expressionist movement coincided with the enormous popularity of Anna Mary Robertson ("Grandma") Moses and Norman Rockwell. The octogenarian Grandma Moses was the most famous American practitioner of the centuries-old tradition of primitive art (a genre in which works characterized by simple directness, two-dimensional flatness, and homeliness are executed by self-taught painters). Moses, who spent her life on farms, usually showed, in a cheerful and sentimental fashion, people engaged in various farm chores and pastimes. Rockwell was the most successful illustrator of his time, concentrating on the creation of winsome vignettes, often having a humorous tinge, that sentimentalized small-town America. Although art critics maintained that his works lacked social consciousness and subtlety, most praised him for his painstaking and skillful execution, shown in an abundance of consistently high-quality detail. He was appreciated by the public for his magazine covers, particularly the more than three hundred that he produced for the *Saturday Evening Post* during an approximately half a century association with that periodical.

SCULPTURE. In sculpture the decades-old commitment to realism was challenged by Alexander Calder, who achieved fame with the creation of two types of abstract metal construction: the mobile and the stabile. Mobiles, hanging from the ceiling and consisting of colored pieces of various shapes that are meticulously balanced and connected by wires, are set in motion by an air current or the human touch. Larger and heavier mobiles, whose pieces are connected by rods, are turned by electric motors. Stabiles are similar in appearance to mobiles, but they stand on the floor and the components are stationary.

PHOTOGRAPHY. Furthering and solidifying the approximately

twenty-five-year-old movement of photography as an art form was Edward Steichen. As director of the photography department of the Museum of Modern Art, he organized the 1955 exhibition Family of Man, which had as its theme the oneness of humankind and is widely considered the most important photographic display ever presented. Steichen was himself a great master of the medium; his works are strikingly imaginative in their incorporation of detail and use of light and dark.

ARCHITECTURE. Some architects of the period repudiated the shunning of ornamentation associated with the International Style. Their resistance was based on the conviction that recent commercial buildings with their starkly austere rectangular shapes presented an unappealing sameness. Eero Saarinen and Edward Durrell Stone were among leading architects who asserted that although a building should benefit from the functional design and structural materials (such as glass) of contemporary architecture, it ought, through ornamental expression, to possess its own unique appearance. Many of the structures of the Finnish-born Saarinen are noted for their undulating lines and widely extending curves, which give them a warmth that seems lacking in the International Style. Included among his many well-known designs are the auditorium (1955) and chapel (1955) at the Massachusetts Institute of Technology; the Dulles International Airport Terminal (1963), outside Washington, D.C.; and Gateway Arch (1966) in St. Louis, Missouri, a 630-foot-high stainless-steel arch that symbolizes the city as gateway to the West. In mid-career Stone turned from the International Style to develop a romantic style that eventually became ornately decorative and was widely condemned by a large segment of architectural authorities. A distinguishing feature of his buildings is the use of an elaborate concrete grillwork as the facade. Among his famous works are the American embassy (1958) at New Delhi, India, and the John F. Kennedy Center for the Performing Arts (1971) in Washington, D.C.

Literature. During the 1940s and 1950s American novelists, poets, and playwrights continued to use established forms and techniques, but the playwrights seemed to do so with more notable creativity than did the novelists and poets.

THE NOVEL. The post–World War II generation of novelists leaned toward realism and naturalism in the honed form achieved during the two preceding decades. But in the view of many literary critics, the newcomers' clarity of goal and skill of style did not come up to those of the eminent novelists of the 1920s and 1930s.

Among the most acclaimed postwar writers were Norman Mailer, J. D. (Jerome David) Salinger, and Truman Capote. There was, naturally, a spate of novels about World War II, perhaps the finest of which was Mailer's *The Naked and the Dead* (1948). This smoothly crafted work is a close study of a small unit of American soldiers of widely varying social, educational, and ethnic backgrounds and personalities; it reveals how each in turn responds to the confrontations of combat. Salinger made his mark with *The Catcher in the Rye* (1951), in which he depicts the frustrating attempts of an adolescent boy to defy the hypocrisy that pervades a society controlled by adults. Salinger uncannily captured not only the mind and heart but also the speech patterns of a rebellious teenager. For many years the work enjoyed an enormous popularity with high-school and college students. Unlike other significant postwar novelists, Truman Capote did not show an affinity for realism and naturalism. His works focus on a world filled with fantasy and inhabited largely, although not exclusively, by grotesque persons. His novel *Other Voices, Other Rooms* (1948) is concerned with a boy's search for a father he has never known; in the process he matures by coming to grips with a number of physically and psychologically abnormal individuals.

POETRY. Three major poets of the 1940s and 1950s were William Carlos Williams, W. H. (Wystan Hugh) Auden, and Marianne Moore. Williams, who was a physician from Rutherford, New Jersey, in idiomatic language scrutinizes unemotionally the diverse existences of the American people. His most celebrated work is *Paterson* (1946–1958), a five-volume poem that deals with the ordinary daily activities and the historical events in that northern New Jersey manufacturing town, as a means to "explaining" society in the twentieth century. The British-born Auden settled in the United States in 1939, soon becoming a citizen. His verse, which shows extraordinary technical proficiency, treats in simple and vigorous language a broad range of contemporary issues. Unlike Williams and Auden, Moore did not feel compelled to deal with political or social matters. Her poetry, which covers a wide variety of subjects and is often quite dispassionate in tone, earned distinction for its wit and keen images.

DRAMA. The great Eugene O'Neill had spent the 1930s concentrating on a cycle of plays, many of them autobiographical, most of which were not staged until the 1950s. *The Iceman Cometh* (1946), widely regarded as his finest work, deals with an annual visitor to a saloon (a role identified with Jason Robards, Jr., who played it with extraordinary impact), who is convinced that by killing his wife he has released her from her illusions and burdens. Thus propelled, he engages in destructive and ultimately unsuccessful efforts to persuade the saloon's drunken habitués to give up their own illusions and return to the outside world. *Long Day's Journey into Night* (1956), produced three years after O'Neill's death, is a compelling treatment of the intense love-hate relationships among four family members (patterned after O'Neill's parents, older brother, and himself): a miserly Irish-born actor-father, a drug-addicted mother, a cynical and alcoholic older son, and a consumptive younger son who hopes to become a writer.

Thomas Lanier ("Tennessee") Williams and Arthur Miller emerged to form along with O'Neill a triumvirate of the nation's finest playwrights. The prolific Williams was noted for an extensive use of deep symbolism and for a keen and poetic dialogue. A native of the South, he set many of his plays in that region, frequently depicting highly sensitive individuals (usually women) who retreated into self-delusion and memories in order to avoid what seemed certain doom from their current condition. His most successful plays were *The Glass Menagerie* (1945) and *A Streetcar Named Desire* (1947). *The Glass Menagerie* is about a fluttery widow in reduced circumstances (a role in which Laurette Taylor gave a legendary performance) who tries to find a suitor for her lame and painfully shy daughter. Like the mother, who has reveries of a time when she was a southern belle, the daughter inhabits a world of make-believe—in her case, a collection of little glass animals. *A Streetcar Named Desire* deals with a woman from an aristocratic but now decadent southern family, who is outwardly elegantly fastidious but inwardly nymphomaniacally neurotic. Her virile and crude brother-in-law of Eastern European immigrant stock (stunningly played in the original cast by Marlon Brando), aware of her true nature and incensed by her pretensions, rapes her, thus precipitating her complete mental breakdown.

Although Arthur Miller's position in the theater is less exalted than that of Williams, it is a highly important one. Miller's style was clear-cut; it avoided symbolism, portrayed "ordinary" individuals, produced simple and direct dialogue, and placed the story in an average American middle-class home. *Death of a Salesman* (1949) is his masterpiece. It is the study of an aging traveling salesman (a part movingly and convincingly played originally by Lee J. Cobb) who, having always extolled material achievements, commits suicide when he finally realizes that not only has he failed in that regard, but that his two sons have become weak and ineffectual.

NEWSPAPERS AND MAGAZINES. American newspaper and magazine (and radio) correspondents covered World War II in an exemplary manner. Their performance won widespread respect as the finest and most comprehensive wartime reporting ever achieved. Thirty-seven correspondents were killed during the war, including the highly admired newspaperman Ernest Taylor ("Ernie") Pyle, who had followed the typical American soldier through the ordeals of fighting both in Europe and in the Pacific. The late 1940s and the 1950s saw an acceleration of the trend begun in the 1930s toward analytical coverage of the news. This was evidenced in the popularity and influence of such columnists as Walter Lippmann, whose incisive writing on domestic politics and foreign affairs for the *New York Herald Tribune* was carried by many other newspapers, and Drew Pearson, whose Washington, D.C.–based syndicated column frequently exposed the misconduct of government officials. The movement from urban to suburban areas had an influence on journalism. Since the suburban newspapers were able to cater to the interest of their readership in local affairs, metropolitan dailies felt the need to compete by broadening their coverage of a wider geographic area, often by instituting sections devoted to the news and advertising of individual suburban communities.

A striking move in periodical publishing was the reversal of the 1930s trend of producing general-interest magazines somewhat to the detriment of those that served a special-interest readership. Undoubtedly the most successful special-interest magazine was *TV Guide*, which appeared as a weekly in 1953. It comprehensively listed the television programs of the week and in addition included several articles on various television personalities. Within half a dozen years the circulation was approximately 6.5 million; by a decade later it had more than doubled. Another successful special-interest magazine was the monthly *Playboy*, founded in 1953 by Hugh Hefner. With such popular features as the centerfold of beautiful and provocative nude females and ultra-frank interviews with celebrities, the circulation by 1960 reached more than 1 million and by 1970 more than 5 million. The monthly *Sports Illustrated* appeared in 1954 as one more in an impressive collection of influential magazines published by the organization established by Henry R. Luce and his associates; it soon became almost indispensable reading matter for the nation's sports enthusiasts.

THE PAPERBACK REVOLUTION. Undoubtedly the major development in the field of publishing in the twentieth century was—after a number of earlier efforts by many—the successful marketing of softcover books. In 1939 Robert D. de Graff and three associates in conjunction with the Simon and Schuster publishing firm put in department stores and on newsstands in New York City pocket-size paperbound reprints of the hardcover editions of ten best-selling books, with a price of twenty-five cents each. Within three months about 500,000 copies were sold. A veritable revolution had been wrought. At last, persons with limited means could possess both literary classics and the works of contemporary writers. By the end of the 1950s approximately 350 million paperbacks were being purchased annually.

Music. The quality of both the composition and performance of orchestral music and opera during the postwar period equaled or surpassed that of the immediately preceding decades. The musical theater was revolutionized through a new conception of coordinating all the elements of a production. Country and western music gained steadily in popularity.

ORCHESTRAL COMPOSERS AND CONDUCTORS. The foremost composers of orchestral music were Aaron Copland, Walter Piston, and Roger Sessions. Copland's compositions frequently incorporated American folk tunes, as with the ballets *Billy the Kid* (1938) and *Appalachian Spring* (1944). Two of his most acclaimed works are the spirited orchestral suite *El Salón México* (1936) and the majestic *Third Symphony* (1946). Piston imaginatively fused dissonant harmonies and jazz rhythms with the traditional classical musical forms, producing a large body of intellectually stimulating works, including two widely esteemed symphonies, the third (1947) and the sixth (1955), and the popular orchestral ballet suite *The Incredible Flutist* (1938). Sessions's music is vastly more complex than that of Copland or Piston. He virtually shunned melody in favor of intricate harmonic and rhythmic patterns, arranging his material without reference to a single key or tonal center. Among his works were symphonies, concertos, and chamber music—all masterfully intricate and vigorous.

The permanent conductor of the New York Philharmonic Symphony Orchestra during the late 1940s was the German-born Bruno Walter, who was noted for the languorous tempos and heavy lyricism that he extracted from his musicians. In 1958 Leonard Bernstein was chosen the New York Philharmonic's first music director; for eleven years he held the post with distinction, conducting with an inimitable verve. Bernstein also turned his impressive musical talent to composing, producing well-received classical orchestral works, such as the *Jeremiah Symphony* (1942) and the orchestral ballet suite *Fancy Free* (1944), as well as musicals, including the long-standing favorite *West Side Story* (1957). The Boston Symphony Orchestra was led during the 1950s by the Frenchman Charles Münch, who achieved fame for his interpretations of twentieth-century French composers. In 1938 the Philadelphia Orchestra selected as its principal conductor the Hungarian-born Eugene Ormandy. During a tenure of more than forty years he became well known for creating a uniquely sumptuous orchestral sound eminently suited to the works of the nineteenth-century romantic masters. Two other distinguished companies, the Chicago Symphony Orchestra and the Cleveland Orchestra, were led by Hungarian-born gifted precisionists, the former company by Fritz Reiner and the latter by George Szell.

CONCERT VIRTUOSOS. During the 1940s and 1950s there were four virtuosos, two pianists and two violinists, who reached their full musical maturity and dominated concert playing, winning plaudits wherever they performed. Three of the four emigrated from Eastern Europe to the United States, eventually becoming American citizens. The Russian-born pianist Vladimir Horowitz enthralled his listeners with a remarkable technical ability. The Polish-born pianist Arthur Rubinstein pursued a spectacular career that astoundingly lasted for more than seventy-five years. He earned notable success with the sonorous tones he could create from the nineteenth-century romantic compositions, particularly those of Chopin. Considered by most critics the greatest twentieth-century violinist, the Russian-born Jascha Heifetz was unmatched as a technician of the instrument. He undertook to introduce the works of many contemporary composers. The violinist Yehudi Menuhin won enthusiastic appreciation not only for his fresh interpretation of established concertos but also for resurrecting little-known but worthy ones.

OPERA. The most important twentieth-century composer of American operas was the Italian-born Gian-Carlo Menotti. Among his highly successful works were *The Medium* (1946), about a spiritualist who feels that a mute associate is attempting to drive her mad; *Amahl and the Night Visitors* (1951), the first opera composed for television, about the Three Wise Men, who, in seeking out the Christ Child, come upon a crippled boy who offers his own gift to the infant Jesus; and *The Saint of Bleecker Street* (1954), about a mystically religious young woman, whose brother is torn between personal devotion to her and revulsion at her beliefs. In addition to composing the music, Menotti wrote the libretti for and directed his operas, giving them a notable unity of mood. He impressively employed a wide variety of both subject matter and musical forms. Some of his stories are realistic, others romantic; some of his arias are dissonant, others melodious.

In 1950 the Austrian-born Rudolf Bing became general manager of the Metropolitan Opera House. During a distinguished twenty-two-year tenure he raised to even greater heights the company's high artistic standards. Bing's accomplishments were many and varied. He infused vigor into the company's repertory by encouraging new interpretations of roles, new stage procedures, and new set designs; he obtained the services of theatrical directors to put on certain productions; he engaged the company's first black singer, the much-acclaimed contralto Marian Anderson. Outstanding Metropolitan Opera tenors during the 1950s were Jan Peerce and Richard Tucker; both excelled in the works of Puccini and Verdi. Two European sopranos, the Italian Renata Tebaldi and the Swede Birgit Nillson, won praise for their vocal interpretations, the former in the Italian repertory and the latter in the Wagnerian.

MUSICAL THEATER. In the 1940s a revolution in American musical theater was effected by the team of composer Richard Rodgers and lyricist Oscar Hammerstein II. In 1942, shortly before the death of Lorenz Hart, his lyricist for twenty-five years, Rodgers began his collaboration with Hammerstein, who had worked with composers Rudolf Friml, Sigmund Romberg, and Jerome Kern in the 1920s. In contrast with Hart's somewhat sardonic lyrics, Hammerstein's were romantic and optimistic, although they were just as meticulously crafted in terms of construction and rhyming. Rodgers and Hammerstein endowed musical theater with a new stature through their harmonious coordination of dialogue, music, lyrics, and dance in the treatment of serious plots. All this was evidenced in their first show together—the towering *Oklahoma!* (1943), which is acknowledged to be *the* American musical. *Oklahoma!*, which starred Alfred Drake, features the unforgettable songs, "Oh, What a Beautiful Mornin'," "The Surrey with the Fringe on Top," and "People Will Say We're in Love." Ballet choreographer Agnes De Mille created the dances, which were acclaimed for their marvelous imaginativeness. In her contribution to *Oklahoma!* De Mille not only revolutionized the style of dance in musicals but also, in using dance to advance the plot, played a significant role in bringing about a basic change in musical theater itself. Other monumental hits by Rodgers and Hammerstein include *Carousel* (1945), starring John Raitt and with the song "You'll Never Walk Alone"; *South Pacific* (1949), starring Mary Martin and Ezio Pinza, with "Some Enchanted Evening"; *The King and I* (1951), starring Gertrude Lawrence and Yul Brynner, with "Getting to Know You"; and *The Sound of Music* (1959), starring Mary Martin, with "Do Re Mi."

The achievement of Rodgers and Hammerstein in creating a well-integrated musical encouraged others to attempt the same. In this manner the new team of composer Frederick Loewe and lyricist Alan Jay Lerner produced their two greatest works, *My Fair Lady* (1956), starring Rex Harrison and Julie Andrews and with the songs "I've Grown Accustomed to Her Face" and "I Could Have Danced All Night," and *Camelot* (1960), starring Richard Burton and Julie Andrews and with the song "If Ever I Would Leave You."

COUNTRY AND WESTERN MUSIC. The origin of country music is in the Southeast and that of western music is in the Southwest and West. Both styles have their roots in the folk songs and ballads of the early English and Scottish settlers in the southern colonies. Both developed over a long period with melodies and lyrics reflecting rural life of the regions. The styles are very similar, each depending on the guitar, banjo, and fiddle (a bowed string instrument resembling the violin) for its distinctive sound. The lyrics focused largely on tribulations such as unrequited love and the economic hardships of poor whites in the rural areas, and in later decades also in the urban areas, of the South, Southwest, and West. During the 1920s the two styles were increasingly mingled. In the 1940s the music, for long appreciated only by a regional audience, began to attract nationwide attention. The growing popularity was due in large part to the talent of singer Jimmie Rodgers, who, during a short career that ended with his death in 1933, recorded many traditional songs as well as a large number of new ones that he himself had composed. Rodgers's influence greatly helped to establish country and western music as a respected part of American culture.

LONG-PLAYING (LP) DISCS. One of the most important developments in twentieth-century music was the introduction, in 1948, of the long-playing microgroove phonograph record, recently invented by a team of research engineers headed by Peter Carl Goldmark. The new nonbreakable plastic disc, which was turned at a speed of 33⅓ revolutions per minute, played for almost twenty-five minutes on one side, as compared with less than five minutes on one side of the then-standard relatively heavy, breakable shellac disc, which was turned at 78 revolutions per minute. Getting onto a single LP disc a body of music that had heretofore required five discs meant that within two decades virtually the entire repertory of both classical and light music appeared in compact form on phonograph records, offering listeners a vastly expanded content to enjoy.

Motion Pictures. Early in the 1950s, because of intense competition from the new and vigorously growing television industry, attendance at motion pictures began a steep and fast decline, from which it was never able to rebound. However, there was a select group of directors whose creativity secured them a place in motion-picture annals; there was a small group of stars whose popularity remained relatively constant; and there was a large number of motion pictures, including some of high quality, still being produced.

DIRECTORS. Of the many fine directors of the period, three achieved particular eminence—the traditionalist John Ford, the technician Alfred Hitchcock, and the experimentalist Orson Welles.

During an approximately fifty-year career, Ford made close to two hundred films. His works are characterized by their commitment to traditional values of European and American society as well as by a hauntingly beautiful sparseness of style when dealing with human emotions. Although Ford was especially noted for directing westerns, such as *Stagecoach* (1939), that brilliantly captured the locale's nuances, he made significant contributions to a wide variety of genres, bringing forth such classics as *The Informer* (1935), *The Grapes of Wrath* (1940), and *How Green Was My Valley* (1941).

The British-born Hitchcock's forte was the "thriller"; he made more than two dozen, achieving the utmost in suspense with such remarkable technical skill and style that the director and the genre became inseparably linked in the public mind. From the most ordinary actions or objects of daily life, Hitchcock extracted an extraordinary—usually evil—aspect of them to evoke a stark and unsettling image. Among his most popular works were the British-made *The 39 Steps* (1935) and *The Lady Vanishes* (1938), *Rebecca* (1940), *Notorious* (1946), *Strangers on a Train* (1951), *North by Northwest* (1959), and *Psycho* (1960).

Welles ranks with the very top creative directors in motion-picture history. After a few years of both directing for and acting on the stage and radio (in which he created a nationwide stir with the broadcast of a script, based on a work by H. G. Wells, about a Martian invasion of earth, done with such realism that it appeared to be actually happening), Welles went to Hollywood to channel his talents into filmmaking. His first work was *Citizen Kane* (1941), which is considered by virtually all critics one of the very greatest motion pictures ever made. It was a work that Welles co-wrote the screenplay for, directed, starred in, and produced. *Citizen Kane* was a withering probe of the career and personality of a wealthy and powerful newspaper publisher, loosely based on William Randolph Hearst. Technically and stylistically it was an exemplary work, encompassing devices, of which most were old and a few new. But all the techniques—including flashbacks, close-ups, montages, deep-focus scenes, novel camera angles, combinations of excessively bright and subdued lighting, striking group arrangements of performers, and overlapping conversations—were brilliantly executed in a fresh, virtuoso-like manner. Welles directed a few other highly regarded films, including *The Magnificent Ambersons* (1942), *Lady from Shanghai* (1948), and *Touch of Evil* (1958), the first of which he did the off-camera narration for and the latter two of which he acted in. Besides directing, Welles performed to critical acclaim in several motion pictures directed by others.

DISNEY PRODUCTIONS The body of widely beloved animated cartoons of Walter Elias ("Walt") Disney occupies a special niche in the history of filmmaking. In 1928 Disney drew what came to be the most famous cartoon character ever created, Mickey Mouse, introduced in a black-and-white short film, *Steamboat Willie,* which was also Disney's first venture into sound. In 1932 he produced the first Technicolor cartoon. Soon after the appearance of Mickey Mouse, Disney gave up the actual drawing of cartoons himself and devoted himself to overseeing a large staff, who produced delightfully clever animated cartoons that presented many other characters, including the irrepressible Donald Duck.

In 1938 Disney released the first feature-length animated cartoon—*Snow White and the Seven Dwarfs.* It was an instant smash hit. This was followed by other popular full-length cartoons, such as *Pinocchio* (1940); *Fantasia* (1940), a highly experimental work comprising a series of animated cartoons, which were visual interpretations of classical music representing a diverse group of composers, including Bach, Tchaikovsky, and Stravinsky, being performed by the Philadelphia Orchestra under the direction of Leopold Stokowski; *Dumbo* (1941); *Alice in Wonderland* (1951); and *Peter Pan* (1953). Beginning in the early 1950s the Disney studio produced in addition to animated cartoons a host of adventure films, such as *Davy Crockett, King of the Wild Frontier* (1955), and nature documentaries, such as *The Living Desert* (1953). (Always a person of many and varied inventive ideas and unerring business acumen, Disney in 1955 opened Disneyland, a sprawling amusement park near Los Angeles, California, that has continued to attract crowds of tourists; in 1971, five years after Disney's death, another such amusement park, Disney World, was opened near Orlando, Florida.)

STARS There were a few stars who had started in films in the late 1920s or the 1930s, reached the heights of their popularity during the 1940s and 1950s and retained beyond that period, indeed to the ends of their careers, the enduring loyalty of the moviegoing public. They were known not only by the vast majority of Americans but also by tens of millions of people all over the world.

Clark Gable, the prototype of the ruggedly handsome and brash "he-man," was referred to as the "King"—an eloquent testimony to his standing as *the* screen idol. Humphrey Bogart was hard and cynical in almost every role; yet, if the part required it, he could at the same time convey integrity. Spencer Tracy, who achieved distinction for his "natural" acting, often depicted gruff characters; the portrayals were enhanced by his ever-developing craggy facial features. The rawboned Gary Cooper played to perfection the soft-spoken but courageous hero, usually hailing from the western plains. So too did an equally rawboned John Wayne. The diminutive James Cagney frequently was either the mean-spirited gangster or the feisty "little guy" who "made it" against all odds. No one on the screen could evoke better than Henry Fonda the decent and idealistic small-town American. The tall and loose-jointed James Stewart endeared himself to audiences with his drawl and modest bearing. Cary Grant was elegant and urbane in a host of sophisticated comedies.

Among the female stars, four had exceptionally durable box-office attraction. The dark-haired Joan Crawford was a handsome rather than a beautiful woman, who often depicted a strong-willed, intelligent type. Bette Davis, who could convey the entire range of human emotions with her big and expressive eyes, filled the screen with a particular radiance. Having a hint of a lisp and a trace of a German accent, Marlene Dietrich was often cast as a seductive and mysterious woman who lured men into compromising or even perilous situations. Katharine Hepburn achieved fame with her patrician appearance (including high cheekbones that became part of her trademark) and performances based upon a strong intelligence and wit. She formed a team with Spencer Tracy, and together they made nine films remembered for their fast-paced humor and sophistication.

Three of the biggest new stars to emerge were Marilyn Monroe, Elizabeth Taylor, and Marlon Brando. Monroe was one of the top sex symbols in motion-picture history. In addition to swiveling the hips of her curvaceous body, she excelled in the art of fluttering her lashes, keeping her eyes half closed, holding her mouth half open, and speaking in breathy tones—a total image ever so sexy. But underneath it all there was talent enough, particularly for comedy, to satisfy audiences. Taylor was a dark-haired, violet-eyed, full-mouthed woman of unsurpassed beauty who frequently chose roles that would display her ability to portray fiery temperament. Brando, of "open" countenance and superb physique, with a mumbling way of speaking and a "natural" manner, was regarded by many as the best American film actor of his time.

MUSICALS. Hollywood retained its reputation, for which it was justly famed, of making far better musicals than those of any other nation's film industry. It was during the 1940s and 1950s that this type of production was most lavishly—but tastefully—crafted.

Meet Me in St. Louis (1944), directed by Vincente Minnelli, who was noted for his skill with musical films, and starring Judy Garland, was about a middle-class family living in St. Louis at the time (1903) of that city's World's Fair. Minnelli directed and Gene Kelly choreographed and starred in *An American in Paris* (1951), which dealt with an American serviceman who after World War II remained in Paris to pursue a career as a painter—and found love. *Singin' in the Rain* (1952), which Kelly co-directed and starred in, spoofed the film industry of the late 1920s as it struggled to change over from silent to sound motion pictures.

WESTERNS. The outstanding westerns of the period were *High Noon* (1952) and *Shane* (1953). In the former film an about-to-retire sheriff, portrayed by Gary Cooper, chose with apprehension but determination to confront four desperadoes after the fearful townspeople had reneged on their promise of aid. In the latter film Alan Ladd played an ex-gunfighter who had taken work with a homesteading family, whose young son came to idolize him; he reluctantly used his renounced skill to shoot to death a hired killer who was preying upon settlers.

WAR FILMS. The public fully expected that the motion-picture industry would respond to the armed conflict that engulfed the world in the first half of the 1940s by bringing forth a number of patriotic war films. The filmmakers did so. Among the productions were four that became classics of the genre. *Casablanca* (1942), with memorable characterizations by Humphrey Bogart and Ingrid Bergman plus those by a first-rate supporting cast, was a study of individuals of various nationalities and political loyalties thrown together in the war-torn Moroccan city. *Mrs. Miniver* (1942), starring Greer Garson and Walter Pidgeon, dealt with an "average" British family responding to wartime tribulations. *The Best Years of Our Lives* (1946), regarded as the finest of a long list of distinguished films from producer Samuel Goldwyn and with Fredric March in a major role, probed how three former servicemen attempted under difficult circumstances to resume a life interrupted by war. *The Bridge on the River Kwai* (1957), starring William Holden and the Briton Alec Guinness, devastatingly examined ramifications of the bitter confrontation between two strong-willed professional military officers, one the head of a Japanese prisoner-of-war camp in Southeast Asia and the other the commander of the incarcerated British troops.

ADVENTURE FILMS. As they had previously done, adventure films dispensed escapism through a look at past eras and different locales. In the late 1950s, however, the productions began to be more carefully researched and therefore more culturally accurate. *Ben-Hur* (1959), with Charlton Heston playing the title role, was a treatment of Palestine at the time of Christ; the production's eleven-minute-long chariot race was one of the finest action sequences in film history. *Lawrence of Arabia* (1962), with the Irishman Peter O'Toole in the title role, dealt with the experiences of the British soldier-adventurer T. E. Lawrence as he attempted to enlist the Arabs on the side of the Allied nations in World War I.

"MESSAGE" FILMS. The motion-picture industry continued the forthright treatment of various social injustices, a theme that had been handled with such commitment in the 1930s. *Gentleman's Agreement* (1947), with Gregory Peck in the leading role, examined the invidious effects of anti-Semitism in society. *On the Waterfront* (1954), with Marlon Brando as the central figure, explored the rampant corruption in the New York City local of the longshoremen's union. But the 1940s and 1950s also saw added to this genre something new—films that dealt with human illness, both physical and mental. *The Lost Weekend* (1945), starring Ray Milland, scrutinized the physical, emotional, and social impairment of an alcoholic. *The Snake Pit* (1948), starring Olivia de Havilland, examined the appalling conditions in some mental institutions.

ADAPTATIONS OF NOVELS. The studios had always been particularly proud of their films based on novels, although such productions rarely yielded high financial returns. Three of the period's very best screen adaptations of well-respected novels were director John Ford's *The Grapes of Wrath* (1940), with Henry Fonda as the John Steinbeck hero; director Orson Welles's *The Magnificent Ambersons* (1942), taken from Booth Tarkington's minor classic about the decline of a wealthy American family in changing times; and *All the King's Men* (1949), a faithful transfer to the screen of Robert Penn Warren's work about an American demagogue.

WIDE-SCREEN AND THREE-DIMENSIONAL INNOVATIONS. As a way of countering the threat of television, the film industry introduced new technology to heighten viewing enjoyment. Among the numerous innovations, which included such devices as piping in powerfully augmented stereophonic sound and wafting in smells suitable to the particular sections of the film being shown, were a few wide-screen processes and one three-dimensional process.

The first of the new devices was Cinerama, a wide-screen system introduced in 1952. An illusion of depth was accomplished by using a huge, sweeping, wide-angle screen to receive a blended three-panel image, each third of which had been taken by a separate camera and was cast by a separate projector. Most of Cinerama's offerings were travelogues; the producers seemed to have an irrestistible urge for eye-catching and even stomach-churning effects, as in a memorable segment of film that was shot from the perspective of a rider on a roller coaster

Another wide-screen system was Cinemascope, which achieved a sensation of depth in an image by projecting it onto a screen more than twice as wide as it was high, effected by using a distorted wide-angle lens on the camera, thus producing on the film a horizontally compressed image, which was then stretched out by a counteracting lens on the projector. Cinemascope was first used in 1953 in *The Robe*, a biblical spectacle that became a great financial success.

In 1952 3-D (three-dimensional cinematography) burst upon the nation. The inaugural motion picture was *Bwana Devil*, which had as its locale an Africa replete with ferocious wildlife. To view a 3-D production at the movie houses the patrons were issued disposable cardboard-framed spectacles with cellophane lenses, one red and the other green, which merged the two images, laid one on top of the other, that had been shot by two separate cameras and then cast onto the screen by two projectors; one projector was fitted out with a special "right-eye" lens and the other a special "left-eye" lens, and a viewer's lens-covered right eye picked up only the image cast by the "right-eye" projector and the lens-covered left eye the image cast by the "left-eye"projector. All this produced a three-dimensional effect, and the filmmakers made sure that, with regularity, things both animate and inanimate would "leap out" from the screen at the startled viewers.

Eventually deemed by both film critics and fans to be no substitute for a regular well-directed and well-acted motion picture, none of the technical innovations continued to be used for more than a few years.

Television. A revolution in the presentation of entertainment and the transmittal of information was wrought by television—a revolution perhaps even more profound than that brought about earlier by motion pictures and radio.

BEGINNINGS. Inventors in various nations played a role in the development of television. One of the earliest was the Englishman William Crookes, who in 1878 made a simple cathode-ray tube, an improved version of which is a basic element in the relaying of television signals. Six years later the German Paul Nikow invented a mechanical scanning disc that gave a recognizable reproduction of a subject. In 1923 the Russian-American Vladimir Kosma Zworykin patented the iconoscope, an electronic tube that converts light rays into electric signals that can then be changed into television waves. In 1930 the American Philo T. Farnsworth produced an electronic scanning system. That same year the National Broadcasting Company began operating an experimental television station in New York City. Franklin D. Roosevelt became the first president to appear on television when he opened the New York World's Fair in 1939. During World War II commercial television production was halted as part of the effort to manufacture war items. Within a year after the war, the medium swept the country with phenomenal force.

WIDE APPEAL. The number of families that owned television sets increased from approximately 15,000 in 1946 to close to 4 million in 1950 to more than 30 million in 1953 to close to 46 million in 1960. By the middle of the 1950s about 65 percent of the nation's homes contained sets, and by the decade's end about 90 percent did. In 1960, in a home having at least one set, viewing was done on an average of approximately five hours a day.

VARIETY SHOWS. With elements such as guest stars who could now be seen as well as heard, sight gags, attractive dancers in chorus lines, and lavish costumes and sets, the variety show was a "natural" for the new medium. The first big hit of television was in this genre—*Texaco Star Theater* with comedian Milton Berle as master of ceremonies. Soon becoming known as "Mr. Television", Berle, dressed in outlandish costumes, featured boisterous comedy routines with much mugging and slapstick and one-line jokes. Vastly more sophisticated was *Your Show of Shows* starring the brilliantly humorous Sid Caesar, aided by the talented Imogene Coca. Although the program had attractive singing-and-dancing regulars and drew big-name guest stars, the highlights were the exceedingly original comedic episodes, consisting of sketches or pantomimes on such themes as the vagaries of married life and the follies of current political affairs, and satires on motion-picture classics. The *Ed Sullivan Show* (originally entitled *Toast of the Town*) was a top favorite with television viewers for almost a quarter of a century. On stage stiff of movement and stilted of speech, former newspaper columnist Sullivan as host nevertheless seemed to possess an unfailing intuition for preparing a varied entertainment package that would please a large audience. For example, on the same telecast, there might be a Shakespearean monologue delivered by a distinguished actor along with a troupe of versatile acrobats engaging in outrageously zany antics.

SITUATION COMEDIES. Of the hundreds of situation comedies that have been on television since the beginning, the most popular was *I Love Lucy* with the inspired clown Lucille Ball. On the program, which was an amiable parody on married life, Ball played a young wife with a fertile imagination for scatterbrained schemes and Desi Arnaz played her Cuban-born bandleader-husband who was unbelievably patient. Another longtime favorite was *The Honeymooners*, starring the ingeniously talented pair Jackie Gleason and Art Carney. Gleason portrayed a "know-it-all" New York City bus driver continually—and unsuccessfully—seeking through impractical projects to better his financial lot, and Carney portrayed his best friend, a sewer worker, who genially but ineptly abetted him.

ADVENTURE SERIALS. Evening telecasting included a multitude of adventure serials, mostly westerns and police dramas. To a much greater extent than motion-picture westerns had been, television westerns were designed for an adult audience. So popular did the westerns become that by 1960 an average of four per evening appeared on the television screen, each very much like the others in characters and plots. The two biggest favorites were *Gunsmoke* and *Bonanza*. *Gunsmoke* was set in Dodge City, Kansas, during the years after the Civil War and had typical western, but more sharply etched main characters: the courageous and resolute marshal, played by James Arness; the trusted deputy-sidekick; a ladyfriend (the relationship was, of course, platonic) with a "heart of gold"; and a lovable old "doc." *Bonanza*, set outside Virginia City, Nevada, during the Civil War period, was about a wealthy ranch-owning widower, played by Lorne Greene, who had three sons, each by a different wife and distinct from the others in appearance, temperament, and ambitions. Although it depicted a fair amount of riding and shooting, the program was different from the usual television westerns in its focus on individuals, on specific problems the main characters faced, and on the effect of those problems on their inter-relationships. The indisputable top police drama was *Dragnet* with Jack Webb as star, director, and sometimes scriptwriter. Winning fame for its realism, the serial portrayed the grueling work of police detectives in a large city. (Delivered in an unemotional tone, the principal character's laconic phrases when he questioned a wit-ness—such as "Just the facts, ma'am"—became a speech fad.)

SOAP OPERAS. A large portion of morning and early afternoon telecasting was given over to daily half-hour segments of soap op-eras. Like those of radio, the television soap operas were aimed at housewives and focused on life's problems. *As the World Turns*, set in the Midwest, was about the interaction between two close-knit families. One family lived in modest circumstances, and its mem-bers were loving toward one another. The other family was wealthy and powerful, and its members had to contend with a multitude of troubles, many of which they brought on themselves. *The Edge of Night* portrayed two small-town law partners who while thwarting criminals had to deal with a host of crises, mostly of a romantic nature, facing them, their families, and their friends. *The Guiding Light* was the story of a German-American family that was able to resist successfully adversities by solidly standing together. In *Love of Life* the main characters were two sisters who were in perpetual conflict because of their antipodal views of life, the one being altru-istic and concerned with morality and the other being selfish in her quest for personal happiness. *Search for Tomorrow* featured a young widow who in addition to caring for her child found time to help her many relatives and friends when they were in need. All these soap operas have flourished to the present.

CHILDREN'S SHOWS. From the outset television producers real-ized that the segment of the population most eager for and appre-ciative of their offerings in the morning, afternoon, and early eve-ning would be children. The first successful children's program was the *Howdy Doody Show* with Bob ("Buffalo Bob") Smith, his snub-nosed, jug-eared, freckle-cheeked puppet Howdy Doody, and the mute clown Clarabell cavorting to the great delight of the "pea-nut gallery," which consisted of an onstage stand holding a sam-pling of the program's young devotees. *Kukla, Fran and Ollie* was a trio comprising the woman Fran Allison and the puppets, shrewd bulbous-nosed clown Kukla and gentle snaggletoothed dragon Ollie (both were supplied movement and voice by Burr Tillstrom). The three engaged in appealing banter and song. Of a more educational nature and directed toward preschool children were *Captain Kangaroo* with the soft-spoken whimsical patter of Bob Keeshan, which has continued to be shown, and *Ding Dong School* with Dr. Frances ("Miss Frances")Horwich, the benevolent, school-bell-clanging teacher. *Disneyland* (later *Walt Disney Presents*) offered an assortment of animated cartoons, real-live adventure films, and nature documentaries, some of them produced specifically for television while others had been made previously for motion-picture theaters. Premiered in 1954 and still running, the show has become the longest-lasting offering in prime-time programming in television history.

TALK SHOWS. In the mid-1950s about 80 percent of those who owned television sets regularly stayed up until past midnight watching them. The most popular type of program presented late at night was the talk show; of this genre by far the most successful was *The Tonight Show*, which went through a number of changes of host, regular cast, and format. The first host, Steve Allen, developed a potpourri of, among other things, playing the piano, chatting with a wide variety of guest celebrities, going into the audience to banter with a few of its members, and doing remotes (portions of a program originating outside the studio). A few months after Allen left the show, Jack Paar became host. He retained some elements of the program, but it was on being an interviewer of guests that he concentrated—and in that capacity he was incomparable. A brilliant conversationalist with celebrities, he exuded incisiveness, wit, and frequently, high emotionalism.

QUIZ SHOWS. Enjoying constant and widespread appeal among television audiences were the quiz shows. Steadfastly popular was *What's My Line?* with moderator John Daly and a panel comprising regular members actress Arlene Francis, newspaper columnist Dorothy Kilgallen, and publisher Bennett Cerf, and a guest panelist. By asking a contestant questions that could be answered only "yes" or "no," the panelists would attempt to determine what the individual did for a living, an invariably novel occupation. In *You Bet Your Life* quizmaster Groucho Marx would elicit howls of delight from the audience with his mildly insulting side remarks during his interviews with the team of contestants before the quiz game, in which the contestants would bet money on their ability to answer correctly questions within a category selected by them.

In 1955 *The $64,000 Question* premiered. The first of the "big-money" quiz shows, it was an immediate hit. On this program (based on radio's more modest *The $64 Question*) a contestant could ultimately win the sum in the show's title by answering correctly a series of increasingly difficult questions on the topic about which he or she claimed superior knowledge. To give a contestant the fullest opportunity to concentrate and to prevent the person from hearing answers that might be yelled by members of the studio audience, one attempting to answer the higher-value questions was placed in an onstage soundproof "isolation booth." But in 1958 the "big-money" quiz-show craze came to a sudden end in scandal. A former contestant on one of the programs publicly declared that they were rigged by "feeding" correct answers to the more engaging contestants.

LIVE DRAMA. By the early 1950s many more live dramas were being presented each year on the television screen than on the stages of New York City theaters. Among the best of the dramatic series were *Kraft Television Theatre*, *Goodyear TV Playhouse*, *Philco TV Playhouse*, *Playhouse 90*, and *Studio One*. Most television presentations were of well-known plays or of adaptations of novels or short stories, but several were of original scripts written by new dramatists.

Some of the most-acclaimed of the original television dramas were Paddy Chayefsky's *Marty*, which is about a desolate butcher from the Bronx who finds solace in the companionship of a plain and shy woman as lonely as he; Rod Serling's *Requiem for a Heavyweight*, a study of a played-out boxer who is faced with engaging in degrading activities in order to survive, bringing about painful relationships with his manager, his trainer and a woman social worker; and Reginald Rose's *Twelve Angry Men*, which shows how one juror with reasonable doubts eventually persuades the other eleven to change their votes to "not guilty" in the case of a youth on trial for the murder of his father.

Beginning in the late 1950s, with the invention of video tape, the presentation of live dramas rapidly gave way to the presentation of taped productions; one result of this changeover was loss of spontaneity. Subsequently the taping of dramas was superseded by the motion-picture filming of them, which process made for a much higher quality of likeness.

NEWS AND PUBLIC AFFAIRS. Leaders in the television industry soon began to tap the potential of their medium in news and public-affairs coverage, which became more and more effective as the technology improved. As it related to dealing with the institution of the American presidency, for example, there occurred the following "firsts" in telecasting: in 1949 of inaugural ceremonies; in 1952, in an extensive way, of the national conventions of the two major political parties; in 1955 (through the use of motion-picture film) of a presidential press conference; in 1960 of campaign debates. (In 1963 a zenith was reached when for three days the networks stopped all regularly scheduled programming, telecasting only material associated with President John F. Kennedy's assassination and funeral.) The televising live in 1951 of the hearings conducted by a Senate subcommittee, chaired by Democratic Senator Estes Kefauver of Tennessee, on the investigation of crime in the nation and in 1954 of the hearings on charges leveled at each other by Republican Senator Joseph R. McCarthy of Wisconsin and the United States Army drew millions of viewers.

Two highly regarded weekly public-affairs programs were *Face the Nation* and *Meet the Press*, on both of which a panel of print and television reporters questioned leading public figures, most often in government or politics, usually American but occasionally foreign. They have continued to be telecast to the present. Among the most respected of the news analysts and nightly news program anchormen were the trust-evoking Walter Cronkite, the team of the "solid" Chester R. ("Chet") Huntley and the whimsically witty David Brinkley, and—in a class by himself—Edward R. Murrow. Having distinguished himself with his radio broadcasts from London as a correspondent during World War II, Murrow further enhanced his reputation when he became a dynamic news commentator on television. He served as both producer of and narrator of the vivid and provocative weekly *See It Now*, a documentary series in which were treated important, often controversial, issues relating both to the United States and to the rest of the world, and he served as both producer of and interviewer on the lighter weekly *Person to Person*, on which celebrities were visited in their homes.

SPORTS EVENTS. The large number of spectators who flocked to stadiums to see college and professional sports events in the 1940s and 1950s were "joined" by an even larger number of spectators who watched the contests on television screens. One professional sport that was well served by the medium's coverage was baseball. The first televised major-league baseball game was played in 1939 between the Brooklyn Dodgers and the Cincinnati Reds; the first televised World Series was that of 1947 between the Brooklyn Dodgers and the New York Yankees. In the early years of television, boxing contests were featured twice (in some areas three times) a week. The first televised heavyweight championship boxing match was held in 1946 between titleholder Joe Louis and contender Billy Conn. As the sport soon became a victim of overexposure, its promoters decided to show heavyweight-championship fights solely on closed-circuit television in theaters. In large measure because of aggressive recruiting of many outstanding former college players, professional football became a major telecast spectator sport. The first televised professional football game was played in 1939 between the Brooklyn Dodgers and the Philadelphia Eagles. (Almost three decades later the very first Super Bowl football game, which was played in 1967 between the Green Bay Packers and the Kansas City Chiefs, was televised; all subsequent Super Bowl contests to the present have been covered by television, evolving into the medium's top annual professional sports event.)

SPECIALS. During the early 1950s part of a regular evening's telecasting was sometimes superseded by the presentation of a new type of show, often musically based, first called the "spectacular" and later the "special." The genre was characterized by a single showing and by a greater length than that of the usual type of daily or weekly program. The period's most-acclaimed special was telecast in 1953 simultaneously by two major networks to honor the Ford Motor Company on the fiftieth anniversary of its founding. The highlight of the lavishly produced show was a duet by musical-theater stars Mary Martin and Ethel Merman, who while seated on stools on a bare stage sang in their inimitably exciting styles a medley of more than twenty-five popular songs.

FILMS. The early reaction of the motion-picture industry to television was utter indifference. Since recent productions of the film studios were not made available for showing on home screens, the television networks resorted to presenting older films, some of them silent, that were acquired from film libraries or were independently owned, in addition to more recent foreign motion pictures. By the end of the 1950s, however, the American motion-picture industry had completely reversed its attitude, welcoming the opportunity to realize a profit by selling its productions to the television networks.

SPORTS. One of the most significant developments in athletics during the 1940s and 1950s was the breaking down of the long-standing bar against hiring blacks, a situation prompted by the civil rights movement.

BASEBALL. A changing racial attitude was most notable in baseball, the professional sport in which the racial restriction had been strongest. The barrier was broken in the major leagues in 1947, when Jack Roosevelt ("Jackie") Robinson was hired by the Brooklyn Dodgers, through the resolute efforts of general manager Branch Rickey. The following year half a dozen black players were on major-league teams. Robinson as second baseman with the Brooklyn Dodgers set batting and fielding records and won fame for his base-running.

Two of the greatest hitters during the 1940s and 1950s—indeed of all time—were Stanley Frank ("Stan") Musial and Theodore Samuel ("Ted") Williams. Musial, an excellent outfielder and first-baseman for the St. Louis Cardinals, set a record for the most base hits in his league. Williams was an outfielder with the Boston Red Sox. During a career that was interrupted twice by military service, first in World War II and then in the Korean War, the powerful left-hander hit a total of 521 home runs and had a lifetime batting average of .344. Willie Howard Mays, Jr., was an early black star in the major leagues. A centerfielder for the New York Giants for almost twenty years, he was the epitome of the "complete" baseball player, excelling in all aspects of the sport—hitting, catching, throwing, and running. Mays finished his career with a total of 660 home runs in regular-season major-league play, putting him in third place in that category of records.

Charles Dillon ("Casey") Stengel was not only one of America's greatest baseball managers but also perhaps the sport's most colorful personality, known particularly for his interview replies replete with outrageously funny tortured syntax. Managing a number of teams over a more than thirty-year career that ended in the mid-1960s, Stengel attained his most notable achievements with the New York Yankees, including the leading of that club to a sensational winning of five consecutive World Series.

BOXING. After the great Joe Louis retired undefeated in 1949, the heavyweight crown passed on to half a dozen others over the next decade. The most outstanding of Louis's successors were Rocky Marciano and Floyd Patterson. The hard-punching Marciano won the title in 1952 and, having successfully defended it six times, retired undefeated. In 1956 Patterson became at the age of twenty-one the youngest person to win the heavyweight championship. After losing the title in 1959, having successfully defended it four times, Patterson became in 1960 the first person to regain the heavyweight crown.

TENNIS. In the 1940s and 1950s the game had its first Hispanic-American star, Richard Alonzo ("Pancho") Gonzales, who won the United States men's singles championship in 1948 and 1949. Turning professional soon thereafter, Gonzales became the United States professional champion in 1954. He retained the title each year except one until 1961, when he retired from competition. In 1957 Althea Gibson became the first black to capture the United States women's singles championship, also winning the British that same year. In 1958 she again took both titles.

GOLF. The player who dominated professional golf during the 1940s and 1950s was the slightly-built William Benjamin ("Ben") Hogan. A year after winning the United States Open championship in 1948, he was so severely injured in an automobile accident that the end of his career seemed certain. But he made a spectacular comeback, winning the United States Open in 1950, the United States Open and the Master's in 1951, and the United States Open and the Master's and the British Open in 1953. The powerful-driving Samuel Jackson ("Sam") Snead was another outstanding professional golfer. Between 1946 and 1954 he won the Master's title three times and the British Open title once. Mildred ("Babe") Didrikson Zaharias is considered the best woman golfer of all time. In 1946 she won the United States Amateur women's title and in 1947 she became the first American to win the British. Later in 1947 she turned professional and won the United States Open women's title three times during the next seven years before dying of cancer in her early forties. More than a superb golfer, Zaharias is acknowledged as America's greatest all-around woman athlete. In the 1932 Olympic games she established two world records in the track and field events. Among the many sports in which she participated— and often excelled—were baseball, boxing, football, basketball (she was twice elected to the All-America women's team), and tennis.

Chapter 5

THE TURBULENT ERA: 1960–1980— AND BEYOND

The period 1960–1980 wrought a revolution in the life of the American people in many respects as profound as had the War for Independence and the Civil War. It was one of the most turbulent eras in the nation's history. Americans were subject to the disillusioning Vietnam War, the horrendous Watergate political scandal, the unrestrained demands of oil-exporting nations, and soaring inflation. And yet the turmoil that diminished the nation and caused pessimism among its people had ultimately a beneficial sobering— indeed maturing—effect. Through all the disturbance there were positive social strides. Blacks, Hispanic-Americans, and women, among other groups, achieved astounding gains in status. In technology, the American exploration of space was an accomplishment of which the people were enormously proud. Through all the disturbance notable cultural advances took place.

HISTORICAL BACKGROUND

In 1961 the elderly and staid Republican Dwight D. Eisenhower vacated the White House for the young and vigorous Democrat John F. Kennedy, who attempted to implement the goals of what he referred to as the New Frontier. In November 1963, while on a political trip in Texas, Kennedy was assassinated. He was succeeded by Vice-President Lyndon B. Johnson. In seeking to become president in his own right, Johnson spoke of achieving what he called the Great Society.

The election of 1968 enabled the Republicans to secure the presidential office for the first time in eight years. The new chief executive, Richard M. Nixon, achieved notable successes in foreign affairs. But his administration came to a crashing end in the greatest political scandal in the nation's history—the Watergate affair. Appointed vice-president upon the resignation of Vice-President Spiro T. Agnew and then elevated to the highest office in the land by the resignation of President Nixon, Gerald R. Ford basically continued Nixon's policies.

Narrowly achieving success over Ford in the election of 1976, the liberally inclined Democratic Jimmy Carter (his legal name was James Earl Carter, Jr., but he had discarded it long ago), was unable to realize the domestic program his administration had evolved. In foreign policy, it was in relating to the Middle East that Carter ironically both won his most exhilarating victory and met his most humiliating defeat.

Throughout the course of his campaign preceding the election of 1980 the victorious Republican presidential candidate, ultraconservative Ronald Reagan, assailed the belief that had remained virtually an article of faith to one degree or another since Franklin D. Roosevelt's New Deal: that the federal government was responsible for the social welfare of its citizens.

The New Frontier. From the beginning, the Kennedy administration captivated the American people with its distinctive verve. In accepting the presidential nomination Kennedy stated that Americans faced many domestic and foreign challenges constituting what he called a New Frontier. As the geographic frontier of the past had afforded Americans many opportunities, this spiritual New Frontier offered them opportunities to effect economic and social reforms at home and to exercise moral and humane leadership abroad. After his inauguration, Kennedy failed to persuade Congress to accept the domestic program that he regarded as essential for improving the general condition of the American people. His proposals for aid to education, medical care for the aged, and a department of urban affairs were all defeated by the coalition of Republicans and southern Democrats that had existed since the late 1930s. The coalition received help from various special-interest groups. As for civil rights, Kennedy, who had previously shown little interest in the trying status of the blacks, as president became more and more committed to their struggle for equality.

The Great Society. After Kennedy was assassinated, Lyndon B. Johnson assumed the presidential office and firmly guided the nation. In a number of addresses beginning in mid-1964 and culminating in his State of the Union Message to Congress in January 1965 President Johnson outlined the goals he cherished for the nation—goals that would bring about what he referred to as the Great Society. Johnson asserted that the federal government should assume a role more commanding than it had ever before played in improving the quality of American life. In the Great Society no one would suffer from poverty, controllable diseases, lack of education, or racial injustice. The Great Society was to some extent achieved after Congress approved a program capable of being implemented in a practical way. During the Johnson administration the civil rights movement reached its climax.

Continuance of the Cold War. The foreign policy of the Kennedy and Johnson administrations was controlled by the same factor that had regulated the diplomacy of the Truman and Eisenhower administrations—the Cold War. The conflict between the Western and Communist nations forced Kennedy and Johnson to couple hardheadedness with the moral idealism that they said they would bring to American foreign policy. American-Soviet tensions were fierce. Kennedy expended massive energy to prevent Soviet challenges to the United States, both in Latin America and Europe, from erupting into armed conflict. On the other hand, Johnson led the nation deeper and deeper into the fighting between the Communist and anti-Communist forces in Vietnam.

The Nixon Administration. The trend of many domestic policies supported by the John F. Kennedy and Lyndon B. Johnson administrations was turned back by the Richard M. Nixon administration. Nixon vetoed a number of bills relating to health and education and impounded funds already appropriated by Congress for economic and social programs of which he disapproved. He disappointed those who desired more progress in the enforcement of civil rights legislation, particularly in school desegregation. A severe setback in the economy bedeviled the Nixon administration. Despite his lack of success in solving domestic problems, particularly that of the economy, Nixon was easily reelected in 1972, primarily because his Democratic opponent, Senator George S. McGovern of South Dakota, was unable to inspire confidence in his judgment.

President Nixon's major concern in foreign affairs was the Vietnam War. After implementing a phased removal of American military forces from South Vietnam, he negotiated a cease-fire agreement with the government of North Vietnam. In other aspects of foreign policy, the Nixon administration engaged in détente* with the two leading Communist nations, the Soviet Union and the People's Republic of China, and through its mediation efforts after a brief Arab-Israeli war assisted in the creation of United Nations-sponsored buffer zones in the Middle East.

Soon after Nixon had begun his second term his reputation plunged as the Watergate affair unfolded, revealing unprecedented corruption at the highest level of the executive branch. On August 9, 1974, Nixon resigned; he was the first American president to do so.

Ford and a Post-Watergate Nation. As the first chief executive after the Watergate scandal, Gerald R. Ford cleansed the air of schemery. He sought the advice of people of divergent views from many sectors of society; he established frequent consultation with members of Congress; he instituted press conferences on a regular basis—all practices that his predecessor had allowed to lapse. He quickly put an end to the pervading nationwide bitterness and to the governmental impotence that characterized the last stages of the Nixon administration. Although Ford's character and style were far different from Nixon's, he retained many of Nixon's staff members and continued practically all of his policies, both domestic and foreign. Possessing little experience in foreign affairs, Ford permitted Secretary of State Henry A. Kissinger to take the lead in this field.

The Carter Administration. In the election of 1976 Jimmy Carter wrested the presidency from Ford, thus signaling the conclusion of the Nixon era in American politics. Carter continued with even greater resolve than Ford's the effort to end the "imperial" presidency that had reached its peak during the Nixon tenure. If the executive and legislative branches of the federal government, both now controlled by the same party for the first time in eight years, had worked together effectively, a period of significant social progress could have resulted. But this was not to be the case. Carter was never able to establish a sound working relationship with Congress, and he acquired a reputation for being somewhat vacillating, if not

*An easing or relaxation of strained relations and political tensions between nations.

in establishing domestic and foreign policies at least in choosing the methods for implementing them. The domestic issue on which the Carter administration expended the most effort was that of an economy significantly affected by inflation.

Carter continued the basic foreign policy established by Nixon, including the pursuit of an easing of strained relations and political tensions with the Soviet Union and Communist China. He achieved a personal diplomatic triumph by serving skillfully as mediator in the difficult negotiations between Israel and Egypt that resulted in a peace treaty between the two longtime bitter enemies. But the United States suffered frustrating grief when, as part of a revolution in Iran, there occurred the takeover of its embassy and the holding of fifty-two of its citizens as hostages for 444 days.

As the election of 1980 approached, and Carter decided to seek reelection, he appeared to be more concerned about a threat to his nomination from the left wing of the Democratic party than about accommodating himself to the economic and social needs of the American people.

Reagan and a New Direction. The election to the presidency of Republican Ronald Reagan in 1980 marked the beginning of a new era in American politics. In his vigorous criticism of the number and expense of the various social welfare programs and of the power of the regulatory agencies, the new unabashedly conservative president conveyed the image of one who wanted desperately to turn the nation away from "big" government to an embracing of the previous laissez-faire system. He immediately launched a frontal attack on the many laws implementing social welfare passed during the previous two decades, especially those of Johnson's Great Society.

The major domestic issue faced by the Reagan administration was that of the economy, which was wracked simultaneously by both inflation and recession. Of the two scourges, the president decided that it was the former that needed to be cured first. The devastating effect on people's income of having to pay so much for the necessities of life produced the worst economic slump since the Great Depression of the 1930s. The high unemployment rate made the recession the most serious one in over four decades.

In foreign affairs, the Reagan administration, while not completely abandoning the recent position of pursuing détente with the Soviet Union, showed an inclination to take a harder line in its dealings with that nation. Further, the Reagan administration vigorously advocated a considerable increase in the defense budget in order to strengthen the nation's security in an unsettled world.

SOCIETY

The attitude of Americans during this period tended to be fearfully apprehensive. They agonized over the wrenchingly divisive Vietnam War; they experienced a disheartening loss of confidence in government and of respect for public officials as they witnessed the unfolding of a political scandal that resulted in the near-paralysis and then the total destruction of a presidential administration; in their dependence upon petroleum, they became seemingly helpless captives of an association of oil-exporting nations patently unrestrained in their quest for wealth and power; they suffered cruelly from the devastating effect upon their lives of soaring inflation.

The most obvious social development was that of the astounding gains in status by blacks, Hispanic-Americans, and women. But there were other elements in the period's social ferment that had far-reaching and long-lasting effects on the nation: the structure and values of the family experienced profound changes; young people rejected established principles of social conduct; the elderly effectively banded together to obtain accommodation for their special needs; the sexual conduct of large numbers of people underwent a revolution. Educational institutions and religious bodies were not only influenced by the social movements of the period, but themselves became very much a part of those changes. In technology, the penetration of space by the United States was a triumph second to none in the history of science—and adventure.

The Population. In 1980 the population of the United States was approximately 226.5 million—an increase from that at the beginning of the century of about 200 percent. Of the total number, 173.7 million (76.7 percent) were non-Hispanic whites; 26.5 million (11.7 percent) were blacks; 14.6 million (6.4 percent) were Hispanic-Americans; 1.1 million were American Indians; 3.5 million were Asians, mostly Chinese and Japanese. Hispanic-Americans formed the nation's fastest-growing minority group during the 1970s at 2.2 percent annually, compared, for example, with 1.3 percent for blacks.

The Growth of Rural Areas and Small Towns. During the 1970s there was a marked reversal of long-continued migration patterns within the United States. For the first time in more than a century and a half, rural areas and small towns grew faster than did cities. During the 1960s, with people in large numbers still moving away from the nation's rural areas and small towns, the population of the nonmetropolitan areas increased by about 4.4 percent whereas that of the metropolitan areas increased by about 17 percent. During the 1970s, however, the population of the rural areas and small towns increased by about 15.4 percent (from approximately 54.4 million to approximately 62.8 million) whereas that of the metropolitan areas increased by about only 9.1 percent (from approximately 148.8 million to approximately 162.4 million). But the people who left the urban areas did not generally move to farms. The trend of a steady percentage decline in the number who worked on farms, begun in the last quarter of the nineteenth century, continued; by 1980 farm workers constituted 2.7 percent of the population. The migration of large numbers of people to the rural areas and small towns resulted from, among other things, the convenience of commuting over long distances by private automobile or public transportation, the relocation of business firms and industrial plants, and the development of retirement communities. The greatest rise in population in both rural and urban areas during the decade took place in the South, with an increase of 18.6 percent, and in the Far West, with a spectacular increase of 26.5 percent.

The Family. The "typical" American family of the first half of the twentieth century—with the father as undisputed head and sole economic support, the mother as housekeeper and child nurturer, and the several offspring as dutiful respecters of their parents—was no more. By 1980 only 7 percent of the nation's families fitted that pattern. Largely as a result of the women's rights movement of the 1960s a new relationship between men and women developed, effecting profound changes in the structure and values of the family itself. Of the married women who worked, most did so to add to their spouses' incomes to be better able to meet family expenses, especially during the accelerating inflation of the late 1970s. But there were now other compelling reasons for a woman to seek employment, including a fervent disinclination to be "tied down" to household chores, a desire for the social and intellectual stimulation from pursuing a career, and a realization of the worth of establishing herself in a particular line of work before her children grew up and left home. As a result of changing social attitudes, divorce laws were liberalized in state after state, so that married partners dissatisfied with the relationship were able to obtain a divorce that in earlier years would have been denied them. By the 1970s certain basic trends within the family structure were clearly in evidence: the average number of children in a family had decreased from three or four to one or two; the portion of employed married women with children in school had reached approximately 55 percent; the divorce rate had increased by more than 100 percent, with 38 percent of all first marriages being dissolved; the proportion of children who lived in a home with only one parent had reached approximately 35 percent; the percentage of households in which a woman was the head had risen by about 35 percent.

Youth and the Counterculture. Concomitant with, and obviously influenced by, the various political and social movements of the 1960s, including opposition to the Vietnam War, the struggle by blacks for equality of public treatment, and the drive by women for the removal of discrimination against them in all aspects of life, was a youth movement that came to be known as the counterculture. Throughout the nation hundreds of thousands, if not millions, of young people, most from a white middle-class background, blatantly showed their disdain for and hostility to such long-standing tenets of established American society as the respect for parental, religious, and governmental authority; the value of education; the importance of striving for economic security; the benefits deriving from technological developments; and the worth of continent sexual behavior. Young men and women by the tens of thousands left school or quit their jobs; adopted unkempt clothing, including the ubiquitous faded and torn jeans; took to wearing long ungroomed hair; used drugs; became immersed in rock music; flocked to live together in a totally unstructured fashion in certain sections of some cities, such as the East Village of New York City and the Haight-Ashbury area of San Francisco, or in communes in the mountainous regions of the Northeast or the deserts of the Southwest. These youth were known as hippies (a term derived from the phrase "to be hip" in jazz vocabulary, meaning to be knowledgeable about current situations).

Many of those young people who felt deeply their alienation from the so-called Establishment but nevertheless remained in attendance at institutions of higher education became dedicated activists. The Students for a Democratic Society, founded in 1959 by Al Haber and Tom Hayden, had its first major base at the University of Michigan. Within three years chapters of the organization on numerous campuses were agitating against research being conducted by faculty and staff for the war effort in Vietnam under the sponsorship of the Department of Defense; against the recruiting of graduating students for jobs with the chemical firm that manufactured the napalm that was a component of the incendiary bombs and flamethrowers used by American troops in Vietnam; and against the Reserve Officers' Training Corps, an on-campus organization that prepared students to become military officers. In 1964 at the University of California at Berkeley the members of the Free Speech Movement on two occasions took over an administration building, refusing to leave until their demand for the right to voice their opinions on current issues was respected. In 1968 at Columbia University a number of militant student factions took over five buildings; occupied the office of the president, for whose belongings they showed no respect; seized three administrators, whom they held as hostages for a day; and after being removed by policemen, pressured the institution into suspending classes for the rest of the semester. By 1970 hundreds of thousands of students were among the millions of Americans who had participated in many rallies against the continuation of the war in Vietnam. Some student protesters publicly burned draft cards and raided draft-board offices, where they destroyed records.

Among the demonstrations throughout the nation against the government's military policy were many on college and university campuses. In one demonstration, in May 1970 at Kent State University in Ohio, students were fired upon by members of the Ohio National Guard and four were killed. Hundreds of other campuses experienced uprisings; there were demonstrations, confrontations between students and administrators, and building takeovers at such institutions as Harvard, Yale, and Cornell universities. And yet at the approximately 2500 other colleges and universities throughout the nation, although students made demands, relative peace and stability prevailed.

Senior Citizens. The steady increase in life expectancy that had been continuing since the beginning of the twentieth century had a considerable effect upon many facets of society during the 1970s.

By 1980 approximately 25 million Americans were sixty-five years of age or older. Referred to as "senior citizens," they successfully used their strength as a special-interest group, relying on their cause's strong appeal to the collective conscience of younger people and on their power as a voting bloc. For example, the age at which the vast majority of Americans had traditionally retired was sixty-five. Congress in 1978 passed an act that made the legal mandatory retirement age seventy. Understandably, many younger Americans were vexed by the possibility that the older people who chose to remain employed would prevent many younger people either from being hired or from being promoted. On the local and state levels, there was for the elderly the reduction of such things as the price of admission to motion-picture theaters and museums, the fares on public transportation, and the rate of taxation on their homes. Home-construction firms played an important role in serving the elderly by developing, mostly in mild-weather regions, such as Florida and the Southwest, "retirement villages" that served the needs of older people in housing, shopping facilities, leisure activities, and medical care.

Crisis in Social Security. During the Kennedy administration Social Security was again extended. In 1961 Congress amended the Social Security Act to provide such benefits as aid to the children of unemployed workers and retirement funds, although in reduced amounts, to all covered workers who chose to leave their jobs at the age of sixty-two rather than at sixty-five. However, by the 1980s a crisis impended regarding the solvency of the Social Security system, since for many years larger sums had been paid to its beneficiaries than had been put in by wage earners enrolled in the system who were not yet drawing benefits. Thus in order to prevent Social Security from running out of funds, many proposals were offered to get the system back on a stable financial course. Although the methods that would eventually be adopted were not yet certain, the movement to somehow strengthen Social Security gathered momentum.

A New Sexual Morality. The 1960s and 1970s saw a revolution in the sexual beliefs and practices of Americans. Giving impetus to this basic change were published findings of researchers into human sexual behavior. In the previous two decades Indiana University professor Alfred C. Kinsey and his associates, after a comprehensive investigation of sexual conduct, which included extensive carefully controlled, confidential interviews with thousands of people of various backgrounds, wrote *Sexual Behavior in the Human Male* (1948) and *Sexual Behavior in the Human Female* (1953), both of which provided factual support for the existence of widespread premarital and extramarital intercourse and of sexual practices that had long been considered by the vast majority of society to be "unnatural" and perhaps even sinful. The books of the sex-research team of William H. Masters and Virginia E. Johnson, *Human Sexual Response* (1966) and *Human Sexual Inadequacy* (1970), both focusing on the physiology of sexual behavior, challenged long-held beliefs.

The use by women of the newly developed birth-control pills, which proved highly effective in preventing conception, contributed to participation by more people in premarital and extramarital intercourse. The health facilities of many colleges and universities dispensed contraceptive devices to single as well as married female students. Many unmarried mothers made no effort to conceal their status from the community. Young couples tried "living together" before deciding whether or not to get married. Numbers of married couples engaged in what soon came to be called "swinging," the exchange of partners for sexual activity by two or more married couples. Responding to the freer attitudes regarding sexual conduct, tens of thousands of male and female homosexuals who, often out of a real concern for job security, had heretofore kept secret their sexual orientation, openly declared themselves to be "gay," the word that was increasingly coming into use to designate a homosexual individual or condition. In 1970 in New York City homosexuals formed the Gay Liberation Front to contend militantly for the removal of the many and varied kinds of discrimination to which they had been for so long subjected.

Of course, the new sexual morality was reflected in literature in terms of the candid description of sexual acts and the use of explicit language. The theater, motion pictures, and television presented, in addition to explicit language, nudity and even physical contact for sexual purposes (the extent of these portrayals varied according to the accessibility of the medium to youngsters). Those who desired stronger fare were able to avail themselves of the offerings of the pornographic book stores (in 1980 there were approximately 20,000 throughout the United States) and of the pornographic movie houses (in 1980 there were about 800). Yet there were those Americans—such as adherents to the Moral Majority, a politically oriented, ultraconservative religious organization founded in 1979 and headed by Baptist minister Jerry Falwell—who rejected the new sexual conduct as destructive of the foundations of society and fought such conduct vigorously but with little success.

The Black Revolution. Although in the 1950s measurable progress had been made toward school integration and safeguarding the right to vote, blacks became increasingly forceful in their efforts to put an end to their "second-class citizenship." Early in 1960 a new direction in the civil rights movement was started that soon came to be called the Black Revolution. An unprecedented upsurge in black activism, it reached its climax within several years.

SIT-INS. Throughout the South black college students began to defy local laws and customs of racial segregation. The form of their protest was based on the principle of nonviolent resistance that the Reverend Dr. Martin Luther King, Jr., had expounded since the 1955–1956 successful Montgomery bus boycott. On February 1, 1960, four black students from the Agricultural and Technical College of North Carolina in Greensboro sat at a nearby Woolworth's variety store "whites-only" lunch counter, requested service, and refused to leave when they were denied it. The use of the sit-in was taken over by many college students, both black and white, and it spread quickly throughout the South. The young people received a great deal of moral and financial support from such civil rights organizations as the National Association for the Advancement of Colored People (NAACP), directed by Roy Wilkins; the Southern Christian Leadership Conference (SCLC), under King; and the Congress of Racial Equality (CORE), led by James Farmer. In April 1960 at Shaw University in North Carolina the Student Non-Violent Coordinating Committee (SNCC) was formed to bring into concerted action the efforts of the sit-in demonstrators. During 1960–1961 eating facilities were desegregated in scores of southern towns and cities. By 1962 approximately 75,000 students had made use of the sit-in. The sit-ins prompted kneel-ins at churches, read-ins at libraries, and wade-ins at beaches. Segregation as a way of life in the South was slowly disappearing.

FREEDOM RIDES. In May 1961 CORE began a campaign against the "whites-only" facilities of bus terminals in the South. An integrated group known as Freedom Riders set out by bus from Washington, D.C., to New Orleans to test the observance of the recent federal integration orders. The Freedom Riders were attacked by hostile mobs at several stops, with a number of serious incidents occurring in Alabama. Since the bus-company drivers would not subject themselves to further danger, the Freedom Riders were compelled to complete their trip by airplane. Soon more Freedom Riders took to buses throughout the South. In September 1961 the Interstate Commerce Commission, in response to a request by the Justice Department, issued an order prohibiting segregation on buses and in terminals used in interstate commerce. Not long afterward railroads and airlines voluntarily desegregated all their facilities.

DESEGREGATION OF UNIVERSITIES. Beginning in the 1950s a small number of black students were admitted to some white colleges and universities in the South. But black Americans were dissatisfied with the slow pace of this desegregation. In September 1962 James Meredith, a black Air Force veteran, obtained a federal court order that he be admitted to the University of Mississippi. But when he attempted to enroll, he repeatedly found his way barred, on two occasions by Governor Ross Barnett. Finally Meredith was accompanied to the campus by several hundred armed federal marshals. President Kennedy, in a television address, implored all those affected by the situation to comply with the law. But to no avail. Rioting by students and townspeople erupted on the campus. Two persons were killed and scores were injured. Kennedy then ordered federal troops into the area, and calm was restored. The troops protected Meredith first as he enrolled and then as he pursued his studies until his graduation at the end of the academic year. A repetition of the Mississippi incident threatened to occur at the University of Alabama. In June 1963 Governor George C. Wallace of Alabama personally barred the way of two black students when they tried to enroll for the summer session. But the governor immediately backed down when President Kennedy federalized units of the Alabama National Guard and dispatched them to the campus.

MASS DEMONSTRATIONS. A new level in the demand by blacks for equality of treatment became evident in the spring of 1963 when they held mass demonstrations throughout the South. City after city felt the demand for a complete end to segregation in all public facilities, including schools, libraries, stores, and restaurants. Many black leaders, following the philosophy of Dr. King, advocated to their followers the use of persistent pressure for civil rights by non-violent methods, such as petitions, boycotts, sit-ins, and orderly street demonstrations. However, nonviolent protests, in the North as well as the South, degenerated into violent clashes between blacks and their white sympathizers on the one hand and police authorities who claimed they were complying with local laws on the other. The nation's attention was drawn to Birmingham, Alabama, where King himself was leading mass demonstrations to effect desegregation. In May 1963 there was violence in Birmingham as the police resorted to the use of high-pressure fire hoses, electric cattle prods, and dogs against the demonstrators. Soon, however, leaders of the black and white communities reached agreement on a desegregation plan. But in September violence erupted once more in Birmingham; a bomb was thrown into a black church and killed four girls attending a Sunday-school class.

THE MARCH ON WASHINGTON. Believing that black protests could be better served if they were moved off the streets and into the courts, President Kennedy in June 1963 submitted to Congress a civil rights bill. The proposed legislation prohibited a number of common discriminatory practices and granted the Civil Rights Division of the Department of Justice increased authority to deal with instances of discrimination. Conservative white southern members of Congress began to block the measure. In August 1963, while legislators were debating the bill, black civil rights leaders organized the "March on Washington for Jobs and Freedom" to dramatize the need for such a measure. The civil rights groups received notable support from numerous service, religious, and labor organizations. More than 200,000 people (about 60,000 of them white) took part in the largest demonstration ever to take place in the nation's capital. The participants proceeded in orderly fashion from the Washington Monument to the Lincoln Memorial, where they listened to speeches by such prominent black leaders as longtime civil rights activist and head of the Brotherhood of Sleeping Car Porters A. Philip Randolph, executive secretary of the NAACP Roy Wilkins, and Dr. King. Among the whites who spoke was the head of the United Automobile Workers of America, Walter Reuther. In a memorable addresss King described his "dream" that his children might one day live in a nation where they would be judged not "by the color of their skin but by the content of their character."

THE TWENTY-FOURTH AMENDMENT. Since the end of the nineteenth century, as one method of keeping blacks from voting, many southern states had adopted the poll tax. The result was that poor blacks—as well as poor whites—were kept from participating in elections. By 1960 five southern states still retained the poll tax. Passed by Congress in 1962 and ratified in 1964, the Twenty-fourth Amendment to the Constitution prohibited the poll tax as a requirement for voting in federal elections.

THE CIVIL RIGHTS ACT OF 1964. Largely as a result of pressure from President Johnson, a filibuster by conservative southern senators was finally overcome and Congress in 1964 passed a new civil rights act. The measure, among other things, (1) strengthened voting-rights protection; (2) prohibited discrimination in places of "public accommodation," such as stores, restaurants, hotels, and theaters; (3) required the federal government to withdraw financial assistance from any state or local program permitting discrimination in its operation; (4) authorized the attorney general to institute suits to desegregate schools; (5) established the Equal Employment Opportunity Commission to foster compliance with the law forbidding discriminatory practices by employers and labor unions.

CONFRONTATION IN SELMA. It was soon evident that the Civil Rights Act of 1964 would be effective only if the American people carried out its provisions in good faith. Crucial in the minds of many blacks was the issue concerning registration of voters. The act specifically forbade election officials to apply standards to black voting applicants that differed from those applied to white applicants. In 1965 Selma, Alabama, a community where black voters were few (approximately 350) in proportion to blacks who were of voting age (about 15,000), was chosen as a place to test the willingness of state and local officials to abide by the federal law. Voter registration among blacks was ferociously opposed by many whites, led by the county sheriff, who readily ordered the use of whips and clubs against demonstrators for black rights. What happened was a travesty, arousing Americans to the brutal ways in which the right to assemble, the right to petition, and the right to register were being denied to white citizens as well as black. The killing of a black civil rights worker and then of a white one, a young minister from the North, attracted nationwide attention.

THE VOTING RIGHTS ACT OF 1965. The events at Selma spurred President Johnson to address the Congress in March 1965 as he submitted legislation which he believed would give the federal government power to ensure nondiscriminatory procedures in all elections—federal, state, and local. The measure was necessary, the president insisted, in order to enforce the Fifteenth Amendment to the Constitution, which ninety-five years before had conferred on blacks the right to vote. Congress responded positively and a new civil rights act was signed into law in August 1965. It contained the following provisions: (1) literacy tests were to be suspended in any county where less than 50 percent of the population eligible by age to vote was registered or had cast ballots in 1964 (five southern states and portions of two others were affected by this); (2) federal examiners would be dispatched to register prospective voters in any county practicing voting discrimination; (3) the attorney general was empowered to institute suits against the use of poll taxes (four southern states were affected by this).

MODERATE ORGANIZATIONS AND LEADERS. There was disagreement among the major black organizations and their leaders, especially after 1965, concerning the strategy to use in the battle for equal treatment for blacks. The NAACP employed a variety of methods, such as lobbying and educational programs, but concentrated on legal action in the courts and consistently rejected the use of violence. Roy Wilkins, the organization's executive secretary, ably presented the views of the moderates. The National Urban League had A. Whitney Young as its executive director. Young was an articulate spokesman for vigorous but nonviolent black community action. Established in 1957, the SCLC sought to end segregation in the use of public facilities and to end discrimination in employment and in voting. The founding president of SCLC, Dr. King, had difficulty reconciling his nonviolent methods with the demands of those blacks who advocated force to get results. In April 1968 King was assassinated in Memphis, Tennessee. His death deepened the sense of bitterness and hostility among all blacks, whether moderate or militant.

MILITANT ORGANIZATIONS AND LEADERS. The Black Muslims, whose organization, the Nation of Islam, was founded in 1930, continued into the 1960s as a religious body that declaimed the inherent superiority of the black over the white race and advocated the complete separation of the two. Although Elijah Muhammad was the revered spiritual leader of the Black Muslims, his most prominent follower, the ardent Malcolm X, was the body's leading spokesman. In the mid-1960s both CORE and SNCC became radicalized. Founded in 1942 by James Farmer, CORE, which had always encouraged the membership of whites, sought through nonviolent means to do away with racial discrimination. In 1966 Farmer resigned as head of CORE, and under such leaders as Roy Innes the organization became increasingly separatist in philosophy. By 1967 SNCC had renounced its original commitment to nonviolent methods and begun to force white members out of the organization. The fiery Stokely Carmichael, the new chairman of SNCC, popularized the slogan "Black Power," which the moderate NAACP, National Urban League, and SCLC rejected as hate-fomenting. The Black Panther Party for Self-Defense was founded in California in 1966 by Huey Newton and Bobby Seale. Its most articulate spokesman was Eldridge Cleaver. The Black Panthers advocated that blacks arm themselves in preparation for the direct violent confrontation with whites that they believed was certain to occur in the struggle for black liberation. As the years went by there were numerous violent encounters between the Black Panthers and the police. Emerging during the mid-1960s as a forceful intellectual leader in the black nationalist movement was the author LeRoi Jones, who assumed the African name Imamu Amiri Baraka.

URBAN GHETTOS. Significant in the black fight for an improved status was the fact that most black Americans had moved into the cities. By the mid-1960s close to 70 percent were living in metropolitan areas. Although they shared on a small scale in the national prosperity, their income level steadily fell behind that of white city dwellers. Because of their separation from whites through neighborhood housing patterns, schools that black children attended were segregated, not by law but in reality. A powerful theme running through all black objectives in the 1960s was the desire to break out of the ghetto's restrictions. Each summer from 1964 to 1967 riots erupted in the black sections of many cities, predominantly in the North. At times looting and gun battles between blacks and police were rampant in the streets. Of the approximately fifty affected cities, those that suffered the most severe violence were Newark, Detroit, and Los Angeles. When the destruction finally came to an end, hundreds of people had been injured and scores had been killed.

A DIVIDED NATION. President Johnson appointed a biracial and bipartisan eleven-member Advisory Commission on Civil Disorders, headed by former governor Otto Kerner of Illinois. The commission's unanimous report, issued in 1968, declared that the primary cause of the riots was the intolerable economic, social, and psychological conditions of urban blacks as a result of widespread and long-standing white racism. The report went on to state that some of the disturbances had been accentuated by the inefficiency of local police and of the National Guard units called in to help restore order. "Our nation is moving toward two societies, one black and one white—separate and unequal, " the commission concluded.

RETRENCHMENT—WITH HOPE. Republican presidents Nixon, Ford, and Reagan sought the base of their support from middle-class Americans who had grown weary of "big government"—what Nixon called the "silent majority." To those people the Nixon, Ford, and Reagan administrations represented a turning back of governmental activism, particularly in the areas of civil rights and social welfare. Also, in their attempts to bring about the entry of the notably conservative Democratic white voters of the South into the Republican party, Nixon, Ford, and Reagan embraced what came to be called during the Nixon tenure the "southern strategy." That combination of pursuits resulted in a lessened concern of the executive branch for implementation of civil rights measures. For example, each of the three presidents advocated the passage of legislation prohibiting the busing of students solely for the purpose of achieving racial integration in the schools. (Democratic President Carter, however, did make vigorous efforts to ensure the full application of civil rights laws.) But there was still hope among the civil rights activists. During the 1960s and 1970s blacks had made considerable gains in status—politically, economically, and socially. Symbolic of the new pride of race was that in high schools and colleges across the nation black students emphasized the importance of their heritage by insisting on and having adopted courses in black history and culture. And, as never before, black Americans fought for and won acceptance by white Americans.

The Continuing Plight of the Indians. With the arrival of white people from the European continent centuries ago the Indians began suffering at their hands. For the past several decades their particular problems were poverty, inadequate education, and unemployment. In the 1960s the Indians exhibited a resurgence of militancy.

TRENDS IN GOVERNMENT POLICY. The philosophy underlying

both the Dawes Act and the Burke Act that Indians should completely adapt to white American society was reversed in 1933 when Indian Commissioner John Collier began to stress government interest in a revival of tribal arts and crafts. In 1934 Congress passed the Wheeler-Howard Act, fostering the efforts of tribes to govern themselves and to preserve their customs and traditions. Individuals could still seek a place outside the reservation, but tribal Indians were encouraged to cherish their heritage.

INDIAN SELF-RELIANCE. In 1966 the Bureau of Indian Affairs began to allow tribal councils greater independence and authority and also began implementing plans to improve the education of Indian youth. Many Indian tribes showed a militancy rivaling that of many blacks. By the early 1970s most Indian leaders were determined that the affairs of the tribal Indians should be controlled not by the government but by the Indians themselves. Further, throughout the nation tribes began developing many highly successful business enterprises on their reservations, engaging in such ventures as coal and oil production, small-articles manufacturing, and tourism. In 1980 about 65 percent of the 1.1 million Indians lived on one of the nation's 260 reservations. For most of them the primary decision was an individual choice between life on the reservation and entrance into the larger society dominated by whites.

The Cause of Hispanic-Americans. The long and hard struggle by blacks for equality of public treatment had a deep influence upon another group that was the victim of prejudice—Hispanic-Americans.

MEXICAN-AMERICANS. By far the largest group of Hispanic-Americans comprised those of Mexican background; by 1980 there were approximately 8.1 million, the vast majority of whom lived in the Southwest. In Los Angeles, the largest city in California and the second largest city in the nation, there were about 815,000 Mexican-Americans, constituting about 27.5 percent of the population. Until the mid-1960s, in the Southwest Mexican-Americans were the last to be employed in good times and the first to be dismissed in bad times. And when they worked, their pay was generally lower than that of others who performed the same jobs. Mexican-Americans were also subjected to discrimination in housing.

In the mid-1960s Mexican-Americans, who as a group had tended to refrain from drawing attention to their economic and social condition, began to organize. They strove to acquire all those elements—good education, well-paying jobs, decent housing—that constitute having "arrived" in American society. Important to the movement was the emphasis on the worth and beauty of Mexican-American culture. Militant members of the movement called themselves Chicanos (probably derived from *Mexicano,* the Spanish word for "Mexican"). The best-known Chicano was Cesar Chavez, who left social work to become a labor organizer in California and the Southwest among farm workers, many of whom were Mexican-Americans. In 1981 Henry Cisneros became the first Mexican-American to be elected mayor of a large city—San Antonio, Texas.

PUERTO RICANS. According to the 1898 treaty ending the Spanish-American War, the United States acquired Puerto Rico from Spain. In 1917 Congress passed the Jones Act, conferring American citizenship upon all Puerto Ricans. In 1952 President Harry S. Truman signed a joint resolution of Congress which approved a new constitution drafted by the islanders themselves, under which Puerto Rico became voluntarily associated with the United States as a commonwealth.*

During the 1950s the government of Puerto Rico made a concerted effort, with aid from the United States, to develop production of agricultural commodities other than its principal crop, sugar, and to promote the growth of industry. It was hoped that such a policy would provide economic support for social and cultural opportunities, including a better school system, for the island's people. As a result of the new economic program the Puerto Ricans' income rose significantly in the 1950s. Nevertheless, their standard of living was far below that of Americans in the continental United States. Consequently, Puerto Ricans, as was their right as American citizens, began to move freely to the mainland, settling for the most part in and near New York City. By 1980 approximately 1.2 million Puerto Ricans lived in New York City itself, constituting approximately 18 percent of the population. As with every migrating group that had preceded them, they experienced culture shock and were subjected to various forms of discrimination. And as with every other migrating group, the Puerto Ricans took the initiative in order to achieve full equality. By establishing self-help organizations such as Aspira (meaning, in Spanish, "aspire") they sought to acquire, among other things, better employment and good housing. They

---

*A colony that achieves a self-governing, autonomous status but remains associated in a loose political federation with its former ruling power.

were particularly concerned with the establishment of bilingual and bicultural educational programs for Puerto Rican and other Hispanic-American students.

CUBANS. As a result of the Spanish-American War, Cuba was given full independence from Spain but eventually came under an American influence that was in reality control. Before the United States withdrew the armed forces that had been sent to Cuba during the war, it compelled the newly established island republic to accept conditions that made it dependent upon—while not an actual possession of—the United States. In the following decades the United States engaged in military intervention and economic penetration of the Caribbean nation.

In 1959 Fidel Castro seized power in Cuba and established himself as premier. He soon used repressive measures against his countrymen, grew more and more virulently anti-American, and turned to the Soviet Union for economic and military support. Affairs between Cuba and the United States rapidly deteriorated to the point where the United States severed diplomatic relations. In 1961 anti-Castro Cuban refugees, who had been secretly trained and equipped by the United States Central Intelligence Agency, launched an invasion of their nation at Bahía de Cochinos (Bay of Pigs), an operation that ended in utter failure.

During the 1960s and 1970s hundreds of thousands of Cubans emigrated to the United States, choosing to be uprooted from their homeland because of its totalitarian regime. By 1980 approximately 900,000 Cubans, the majority of whom were refugees, lived in the United States and were concentrated largely in Florida. About 500,000 Cubans were settled in the Miami metropolitan area, constituting about 35 percent of the population. Cherishing and retaining their Hispanic traditions and language while cautious about assimilating into the "anglo" way of life, the Cubans transformed Miami into a thriving bilingual and bicultural urban center.

Women's Liberation. The term "women's liberation" (familiarly shortened to "women's lib") was applied to a surge of activity during the 1960s and 1970s in the women's rights movement, which had started in the nineteenth century and achieved a major goal with the granting of the suffrage to women in 1920.

OBJECTIVES. The basic objectives of the new feminists were full legal equality with men and the removal of economic and social discrimination between the sexes. Given high priority among their specific aims were abortion without charge for any woman who requested it and the establishment of government-supported child-care centers.

NATIONAL ORGANIZATION FOR WOMEN. Particularly active leaders of the women's liberation movement were writers Betty Friedan and Gloria Steinem, and Bella Abzug and Shirley Chisholm, both New York City Democratic congressional representatives. To a large degree the movement was decentralized, with little conventional organizational makeup. Nevertheless, there were some organizations created for the women's liberation cause. The largest and most influential was the National Organization for Women (NOW), formed in 1966 largely through the efforts of Friedan, whose widely read book *Feminine Mystique* (1962) analyzed how society had assigned women the role of unthinking followers of men. NOW concentrated on legal and political action to achieve its goals. In 1975 factional disputes hurt the women's liberation movement. Friedan and a dozen other leading members of NOW formed a splinter organization named Womensurge, asserting that NOW had become too radical in its philosophy and tactics and was thereby alienating many women.

THE EQUAL RIGHTS AMENDMENT. The women's liberation movement influenced Congress to pass in 1972 the proposed Equal Rights Amendment to the Constitution, which declared that "equality of rights under the law shall not be denied or abridged on account of sex." But ratification was not achieved; within the ten-year deadline the proposed amendment won the approval of only thirty-five state legislatures, three short of the number required for it to be incorporated into the Constitution.

CADETS AT THE SERVICE ACADEMIES. By 1980 virtually every field of employment that had heretofore been largely closed to women was now open to them, including those of police work and fire fighting. A striking indication that the women's rights movement had achieved a large measure of success was apparent when in 1980 the Army, Navy, Air Force, and Coast Guard academies— the once-undisputed bastions of male ambience—graduated women cadets, 227 out of classes totaling 2638.

Environmentalism. During the 1960s and 1970s environmentalist groups came into being. Vociferously pointing out that the nation was in grave danger of using up or poisoning its natural resources, they criticized what they considered the "soft" posture of the federal and state governments on the use of land for industrial purposes and on the production of nuclear energy. They focused on such specific issues as water pollution and automobile emission standards. The environmentalists found even greater fault with the Reagan administration than they had with the immediate previous ones, for it boldly declared its intention of loosening many of the recently adopted federal regulations protecting the environment. The argument for this position was that while the environmentalist endeavor was an important one, it must not be permitted to affect adversely the nation's economic growth, in particular the development of energy.

The Energy Crisis. During the 1960s and 1970s approximately 75 percent of the energy used by the United States came from petroleum and natural gas. The American people were troubled by the spiraling cost of both gasoline and fuel oil and of natural gas; the increase caused constant economic hardship, for most Americans had to drive automobiles and virtually all Americans had to heat their homes.

THE ORGANIZATION OF PETROLEUM EXPORTING COUNTRIES. During the 1970s the United States got almost 50 percent of its petroleum from foreign sources. An energy crisis resulted because of the price levels established by the Organization of Petroleum Exporting Countries, most of whose members were Arab nations. In the United States the average price of a gallon of regular gasoline went from about sixty-five cents in 1975 to about $1.30 in 1980—an increase of approximately 100 percent! During those years fuel oil went from about thirty-five cents to about $1.00 a gallon—an increase of approximately 200 percent!

DEPARTMENT OF ENERGY. Americans wanted strong action from their government. Responding to President Carter's declaration that combating the problem in energy was "the moral equivalent of war," in 1977 Congress established the Department of Energy, which was authorized to develop the policies and to supervise the programs of the federal government in the field of energy.

PLANS TO ALLEVIATE THE PROBLEM. Believing that the federal government should decrease its participation as much as possible in the field of energy and allow the American petroleum and natural-gas companies to have greater latitude than heretofore, President Reagan announced his desire to dismantle the Department of Energy and permit some of its functions to be performed by other agencies of the federal government. To help alleviate the energy crisis, in 1981 the president by executive decree removed the government regulations on the price of domestic oil and natural gas, thus permitting a rise in the cost of both. His purpose was twofold: first, to reduce the consumption of those two high-demand, dwindling commodities, and, second, to stimulate a search for additional sources by the American oil and natural-gas firms. Opposed to the president's plan, yet unable to agree among themselves, the Democratic leaders in Congress, the lower house of which their party controlled, failed to formulate an acceptable counterproposal.

Meanwhile, the striving went on toward the goal of less dependency on petroleum both through the conservation of energy and through the utilization of alternative sources of energy: electric batteries for running automobiles; the "old standby" coal (there was enough to last approximately three hundred years at the current rate of use), with the problem of pollutants released into the atmosphere by its burning; wind power; solar power; and nuclear power, with the dangers of the possible escape from nuclear plants of substances harmful to animal and plant life, of explosions of nuclear reactors, and of radioactive waste that could not be safely disposed of and might remain active for thousands of years.

Inflation. Undoubtedly the most serious domestic concern during the latter half of the 1970s and beyond was the economy. The nation was suffering from a continuing inflation. From an already high rate of 9 percent at the beginning of 1975 the rate of inflation reached 13.2 percent by the end of 1980. The devastating effect on people's income of having to pay so much more for the necessities of life produced the worst economic crisis since the Great Depression of the 1930s. Particularly hurt were the elderly trying to get along on fixed incomes, consisting of Social Security plus perhaps a pension, with increases in cost of living far outstripping their means to pay for them.

In order to combat inflation, President Reagan, immediately upon taking office, advocated such measures as a sharp reduction in government spending and a decrease in taxes. But at the same time that he assaulted as inflationary a plan of government spending to create jobs for many of the almost 8 million workers (more than 7 percent of the total labor force) who were unemployed, he approved certain programs that either directly or indirectly raised prices. For example, his energy conservation plan was based in part on the imposition of higher costs for petroleum products.

Early in 1981 the president recommended to Congress an anti-inflation program that included both a sharp reduction in government spending, which affected many long-standing social programs, and a substantial lowering of the personal income tax, which provided for a 25 percent decrease over the following three years, across the board for all income groups. Initially, a majority of the members in both houses of Congress, including virtually all Republicans and a large number of conservative Democrats, supported his plan. By the fall of 1982 the scourge of inflation abated somewhat; the rate had decreased to 5.9 percent. But the affliction of unemployment continued; out of work were over 11 million people (more than 10 percent of the total labor force), making for the highest rate of joblessness since the Great Depression.

The Labor Movement. During the first six decades or so of the twentieth century organized labor achieved many gains through carefully developed and vigorously implemented programs. But during the 1960s and 1970s, although labor continued to win increased benefits, it faced serious challenges.

IMPROVED WORKING CONDITIONS. Throughout the twentieth century American laborers by effective organization improved their lot in many ways, including, for example, the shortening of the hours of work. In 1900 a ten-hour workday and a six-day workweek were the norm; in 1940 an eight-hour workday and a six-day workweek; in 1980 an eight-hour workday and a five-day workweek. But more was achieved than that. By 1980 most workers were being given ten paid holidays a year, whereas in 1940 most had received five and in 1900 none. Also, by 1980 most workers were being given a two-week vacation with pay each year, whereas in 1940 most had received one week without pay and in 1900 no vacation time.

MEMBERSHIP GAINS. In terms of membership there were some important gains during the 1960s and 1970s. The recently formed United Farm Workers, many of whose members toiled in California and the Southwest, after much bitter confrontation with large agricultural producers, finally won recognition to represent farm laborers. The union achieved for its members far more satisfactory working conditions. White-collar employees, who had always been disinclined to join unions, regarding such an affiliation as a mark of lesser social status, were prompted to reconsider their attitude in view of increasing automation of office work. By 1980 close to 15 percent of the nation's white-collar workers had become union members. But the most telling gain in unionization was among government employees. During the 1960s the federal government took a position in favor of its employees unionizing. By the mid-1970s practically all state and local governments permitted their employees to organize and bargain collectively. For example, by 1980 about 570,000 public-school teachers belonged to the American Federation of Teachers, an affiliate of the AFL-CIO, and about 1.7 million belonged to the National Education Association, which, although it considered itself a professional group, conducted itself very much like a union; for example, its chapters resorted to strikes.

RECRUITING UNAFFILIATED WORKERS. As the 1970s drew to a close the AFL-CIO had to come to grips with the challenge of recruiting still unaffiliated workers. Between 1955, when the AFL-CIO was formed, and 1980 the nation's total labor force increased from about 68 million to about 104 million, but the portion in unions decreased from 34 percent to 22 percent. As for the AFL-CIO itself, in 1955 the organization had about 16 million members (21 percent of the labor force), whereas in 1980 it had about 13.6 million members (13 percent of the labor force). Further, in 1980 a combined total of approximately 3.8 million organized laborers composed the membership of two independent unions, the International Brotherhood of Teamsters and the United Automobile Workers of America, the former having been expelled from the AFL-CIO in 1957 for alleged wrongdoing and the latter having severed itself from the AFL-CIO in 1968 because of a dispute over policies and programs. However, influenced by a concern for increasing the role of labor through unified action during a period of economic difficulties, in 1981 the United Automobile Workers of America, with its approximately 1.2 million members, rejoined the AFL-CIO.

DEVELOPING A NEW LEADERSHIP. Tough and stubborn, George Meany as president of the AFL-CIO held together the 111 separate and autonomous unions that formed the AFL-CIO in the late 1970s. He and his close associates fought hard and successfully for labor's traditional principal aims: higher wages, shorter hours, and safe and sanitary working conditions. But critics, both in and out of the labor movement, maintained that the leadership of the AFL-CIO was hidebound and uncreative. In 1979 the frail octogenarian Meany resigned the organization's presidency and was succeeded by Lane Kirkland, who, although he was considered as philosophically conservative as Meany, showed much imaginativeness and flexibility.

Education In the United States education had always been influenced by the social setting of the period, but during the 1960s and 1970s this was particularly true.

ELEMENTARY EDUCATION. From 1960 to 1980 enrollment in elementary schools decreased from about 30.3 million to about 27.6 million. The movement begun in the 1940s and 1950s for a return to focusing on the mastery of traditional academic disciplines continued unabated during the 1960s and 1970s. The cause was served by recently developed educational technology. Many schools used a programmed form of teaching. In this method a pupil absorbs a body of information or solves a problem at his own pace by answering questions posed by a machine equipped to inform the user whether or not each answer is correct. A number of schools tried instructing by closed-circuit television, in which a "master" teacher can communicate with pupils in different classrooms in one or more buildings in a school system or even in more than one system.

SECONDARY EDUCATION. In 1960 the number enrolled in secondary schools was approximately 10.2 million; in 1980 it was approximately 14.5 million. In the former year about 63 percent of high-school students graduated; in the latter year about 86 percent did so. The insistence by many for a return to a full concentration on the learning of the traditional disciplines was directed at the administrators and teachers of the secondary schools as it was at those of the elementary schools. And as in elementary education, technological equipment was employed as a means to achieve this goal in secondary education. But a situation that hindered the movement prevailed in the high school. The foment that had occurred on college and university campuses during the 1960s reached the high schools by the 1970s. And because the high-school students, younger and not as sophisticated as the college and university students, responded in a less mature manner to the social tumult, the disquiet at the secondary level was perhaps even more distressing. In school after school across the nation the students made increasing demands for greater latitude in the pursuit of their studies and for fewer personal restrictions, such as in language and attire. It was not long before this restiveness turned into a nightmarish scene in inner-city schools. The smoldering hostility between blacks on the one hand and Hispanic-Americans or whites on the other led to frequent confrontations, with severe bodily injury and destruction of property being by no means uncommon. But what was perhaps even more striking during the early 1970s was that in a majority of the high schools in middle- and upper-middle-class, virtually entirely white, rural and suburban areas confrontations occurred between students and school authorities.

HIGHER EDUCATION. Enrollment in colleges and universities increased from about 3.6 million in 1960 to about 6.1 million in 1980. The confrontational activities and violence on American campuses during the 1960s, which halted almost precipitately with the fall 1970 semester, had significant consequences. There were deep negative ramifications. Perhaps most important, academic standards had been impaired. In an effort to return the campuses to peace and stability, administrators and professors catered to the demands of their students to such a degree that they found themselves becoming embarrassingly untrue to what they had always believed to be the integral methods and goals of higher education. For example, course requirements were made less rigorous, often with term papers discontinued and fewer or even no examinations given; grades were inflated, with "B" replacing "C" as the average; and courses were added to the curriculum that were deemed "relevant" for modern society but lacked the traditional body of knowledge to be studied. And yet from the campus unrest there was a positive legacy too. As a result of their demands, students, traditionally denied any meaningful role in the running of the institutions, were now given an opportunity to exert influence in such vital aspects as the appointment, promotion, and retention or dismissal of administrators and faculty members and the development of curriculum. Also, chiefly but not solely as a result of student demands, courses on the history and culture of blacks and other minority groups and on women were developed. Further, blacks, Hispanic-Americans, and other minority groups, and women were admitted in ever-larger numbers to colleges and universities, including Ivy League institutions, that had always had overwhelmingly white, entirely male student bodies. Too, the implementation of what came to be known as "affirmative-action" programs increased greatly the proportion of blacks and other minority groups and women in college and university administrations and on faculties.

THE ELEMENTARY AND SECONDARY SCHOOL EDUCATION ACT.

The Kennedy administration proposed federal aid to education, which would include financial assistance for constructing school buildings, increasing teachers' salaries, and granting scholarships. The proposal failed in Congress, largely because of the administration's inability to come to terms with the demand by Roman Catholic church leaders that parochial schools as well as public schools be given aid. This controversy was settled during the Johnson administration when in 1965 Congress passed the Elementary and Secondary School Education Act, whereby students in elementary and secondary schools, including parochial and other private ones, received governmental assistance indirectly through loans and grants to their schools.

DEPARTMENT OF EDUCATION. Upon the recommendation of President Carter, in 1980 Congress created from the Department of Health, Education, and Welfare two separate departments—the Department of Health and Human Resources and the Department of Education, whose heads would both be cabinet members. The Department of Education was authorized to administer programs for the improvement of education. Appointed by President Carter as the first secretary of education was Shirley M. Hufstedler, who had served with distinction as a federal judge. President Reagan, who believed that the federal government should decrease its role in education and let the state and local governments have greater autonomy than in the recent past, declared his intention either to abolish the department and allow some of its responsibilities to be absorbed by other federal agencies or to replace the department with an agency at less than cabinet level.

Religion. During the 1960s and 1970s there was a halt in the tremendous increase in church and synagogue membership that had taken place during the 1940s and 1950s, although approximately 65 percent of the American people were affiliated with organized religious bodies. Nevertheless, despite a leveling off in membership, vast changes—some of them revolutionary—occurred within Protestantism and Roman Catholicism (particularly the latter) and Judaism.

PARTICIPATION BY RELIGIOUS LEADERS IN SOCIAL CAUSES. Organized religious bodies were very much affected by the social ferment of the period. Feeling a deep moral obligation, large numbers of ministers, priests and nuns, and rabbis played a leading role in such causes of the period as the struggle by blacks and other minority groups against discrimination, the women's liberation movement, the battle against poverty, the environmental crusade, and the opposition to the Vietnam War.

PROTESTANTISM. From 1960 to 1980 membership in Protestant churches rose from approximately 63.5 million to approximately 70 million. The tide of Protestant revivalism of the post–World War II period was repeated with notable vigor during the mid-1970s. Although a few denominations, such as the Presbyterian church, had ordained women for some time, as a direct response to the women's liberation movement other denominations—notably the Episcopal church—took the still-bold action of admitting women to the ministry. As it had during the 1940s and 1950s, Protestantism continued increasingly to merge bodies within a denomination and to unify among the various denominations during the 1960s and 1970s. But what was even more heartening to liberally inclined religious Americans was the fast-developing ecumenical spirit between Protestantism and Roman Catholicism. The long-standing hostility between the two wings of Christianity in the United States (as in the rest of the world) was dissipated as continual dialogue that focused on the many similarities of dogma went on.

ROMAN CATHOLICISM. Membership in the Roman Catholic church rose from about 42.1 million in 1960 to about 50 million in 1980. During 1962–1965 there was held in Rome the Second Vatican Council, a large-scale meeting of Catholic church leaders convened by the charismatic and reform-minded Pope John XXIII to examine what the organization and doctrines of the church should be in the modern world. Catholicism in the United States felt an immediate and deep impact from the far-reaching and liberal promulgations of the Second Vatican Council. Those statements gave the bishops a greater role in governing the church; modernized the life-styles of priests and nuns; increased the participation of the laity in religious services (the vernacular, or native language of a region, was now to be used in place of Latin) and other affairs of the church; advocated the coming together of Roman Catholic, Protestant, and Eastern Orthodox bodies (the last of which comprised approximately 4 million members in the United States) for the unity of Christianity; and expressed respect for non-Christian religions and condemned any kind of discrimination, particularly anti-Semitism.

JUDAISM. Membership in Jewish congregations increased from

1960 to 1980 from about 5.4 million to about 5.8 million. Of the three bodies of the faith, the basic attitudes of the long-standing orthodox branch underwent no significant changes, but that of the more recently formed Conservative and Reform branches underwent substantial changes. Orthodox Judaism, however, largely through attracting many young adherents, experienced a resurgence of power and influence within Jewry. Perhaps the most notable development in Conservative Judaism was the new role of women. Increasingly, Conservative congregations permitted women to participate in the conduct of services and to hold lay offices, including the position of president. And, increasingly, along with boys, who at the age of thirteen formally assumed religious duties and responsibilities through an initiatory ceremony called the *bar mitzvah,* so too did girls at about the same age take on theirs through the *bat mitzvah* ceremony. In the Reform branch of the faith, the change in status of women was quite similar to that in the Conservative. Further, in some Reform congregations women even served as ordained rabbis. But another notable significant development in Reform Judaism was the reinstitution of the observance of many rituals and traditions that had long been abandoned. In many congregations, for example, Hebrew was returned to the liturgy, the yarmulke and prayer shawl were worn once more during services, and the old ceremony of the *bar mitzvah* (and the new *bat mitzvah*) was again performed.

ASIAN FAITHS. As part of their repudiation of the various elements of established American society, many young people turned away from the Christianity and Judaism of the Western world and affiliated with Asian faiths. Of those, the most visible was the Hare Krishna sect, in which shaven-headed, saffron-robed adherents danced and chanted in the streets as part of their homage to Krishna, a Hindu god.

Technology: Space Exploration. Spurred by competition between the United States and the Soviet Union, the exploration of space proceeded at a rapid rate. Each nation sent many spacecraft around the earth, around the sun, to the moon, and to the other planets.

ORBITING THE EARTH. In 1957 the Soviet Union launched the first unmanned spacecraft that escaped the gravity of the earth. In 1958 the United States followed suit. Three years later humans themselves began to travel in space. The first to do so was Soviet cosmonaut Yuri A. Gagarin, who on April 12, 1961, made a single orbit around the earth. The following month American astronaut Alan B. Shepard, Jr., rocketed 115 miles into space. In 1962 John H. Glenn, Jr., became the first American to orbit the earth, doing so three times. In 1965 Virgil I. ("Gus") Grissom and John Watts Young circled the earth three times in a two-person space capsule, which they were able to maneuver from one type of orbit to another. By 1970 the two nations had sent approximately 25,000 unmanned satellites into orbit, of which almost 500 were still circling the earth a decade later.

LANDING ON THE MOON. The American project to land a person on the moon was called Project Apollo. In January 1967 a fire aboard the *Apollo 1* spacecraft on its launching pad at Cape Kennedy, Florida, took the lives of Grissom, Edward H. White, and Roger Chaffee. There was intense national grief, and a long delay in plans for the lunar project. But in December 1968 the *Apollo 8* carried three valiant men—Frank Borman, James A. Lovell, Jr., and William Anders—on a fantastic journey. During 147 hours their spacecraft traveled approximately 240,000 miles from the earth to the moon, orbited the moon ten times, and returned to the earth, dropping into the Pacific Ocean.

On July 20, 1969, the ultimate goal of Project Apollo was achieved. Watched on television by hundreds of millions of people all over the earth, astronaut Neil A. Armstrong stepped onto the moon. "That's one small step for [a] man, one giant leap for mankind," he said. Armstrong and his two fellow astronauts, Edwin E. ("Buzz") Aldrin, Jr., and Michael Collins, brought back from the moon's surface data of immense scientific value. Between July 1969 and December 1972 there were five more landings on the moon. The last flight in Project Apollo was made by Eugene Cernan, Harrison Schmitt, and Ron Evans. Cernan and Schmitt roamed over miles of the lunar surface in a specially constructed jeeplike vehicle.

INTERNATIONAL COOPERATION. In July 1975 American astronauts Thomas P. Stafford, Donald K. Slayton, and Vance D. Brand in their Apollo spaceship and Soviet cosmonauts Aleksei A. Leonov and Valery N. Kubasov in their Soyuz spaceship united their crafts; then two of the Americans entered the Soyuz spaceship and met face to face with the Soviets. This event was the dramatic result of the agreement by the American president and the Soviet Communist party general secretary to have their nations cooperate in space exploration.

REACHING OTHER PLANETS. In October 1975 two Soviet robot crafts *Venera 9* and *10* made landings on Venus (the second body in space to be "visited" by humans) and relayed photographs back to earth before being quickly ruined by Venus's considerable heat and atmospheric pressure.

On July 20, 1976, seven years to the day after a person first walked on the moon, the American robot craft *Viking 1* landed on Mars. This was the culmination of an eleven-month voyage to a planet approximately 230 million miles from the earth. *Viking 1* and the identical *Viking 2*, which landed six weeks later, transmitted photographs of a reddish rock-strewn plain. The two robot crafts were equipped to conduct a number of scientific experiments. They measured such meteorological conditions as atmospheric pressure, temperature, and wind velocity. But the greatest achievement was that *Viking 1* and *2* scooped up Martian soil and poured it into their miniature biological laboratories to analyze it for evidence of life. Scientists refrained from concluding whether the experiments indicated that life did or did not exist on Mars; the crafts detected no organisms, yet gathered evidence that chemical processes related to life on earth occurred also on Mars. Since Mars had for so long intrigued people both as an object of scientific investigation and as a focus of science fiction (besides being the planet other than earth where life had been believed most possible), this landing was particularly significant in space exploration.

In March 1979 the American spacecraft *Voyager 1*, and in July 1979 the identical *Voyager 2*, both of which had been launched in 1977, passed within about 400,000 miles of the solar system's largest planet, Jupiter, transmitting an enormous amount of data and stunning photographs of the planet and the five largest of its fourteen satellites, or moons, all of which was of great value to scientists. After passing Jupiter, *Voyager 1* went on to explore the second largest planet, Saturn, and its environs in November 1980, and *Voyager 2* did the same in August 1981. *Voyager 2*, if its components continued to function, would reach Uranus, approximately 1.8 billion miles from earth, in 1986, and perhaps even Neptune, approximately 2.8 billion miles from earth, in 1989. In September 1979, after almost six and a half years and more than 2 billion miles of a circuitous journey, *Pioneer 11* became the first American spacecraft to take measurements of Saturn, providing important data on such things as its density, temperature, and magnetic field.

It also photographed the planet's spectacular rings in more revealing detail and from different angles than had been seen through earthbound telescopes. Thus by 1980 only three planets of the solar system—Uranus, Neptune, and Pluto—had yet to be reconnoitered by spacecraft from earth.

SHUTTLING. In April 1981 American astronauts John Watts Young and Robert L. Crippen cruised for three days in the reusable winged and wheeled shuttle spacecraft *Columbia* and then returned to earth in a "soft" landing, a feat that augured the making of routine commuter trips in space.

Technology: Land and Air Transportation. Because of the difficult economic conditions and the changing social circumstances of the late 1970s and the early 1980s, the automobile, airline, and railroad industries all suffered traumatic experiences, with many enterprises even facing the stark issue of survival.

THE AUTOMOBILE. By 1980 over 125 million cars were on the roads—something like one vehicle for every two persons in the nation. Astoundingly, one out of every six employed Americans earned a living directly or indirectly because of automobiles. In addition to those who worked in the car manufacturing plants, there were, for example, workers in the industries that supplied the raw materials that went into the vehicles, such as steel, rubber, and glass, or that made components of the vehicles, such as batteries and spark plugs; those who worked for the petroleum companies; those who worked in service stations; and those who worked in road construction and repair.

In the 1960s and 1970s the American automobile industry faced two major crises. During the 1960s there was a growing reaction against what seemed to some the automobile industry's emphasis on selling superpowerful vehicles with exorbitant ornamentation, with little apparent concern for safety features. The leading exponent of this position was Ralph Nader, whose widely read book *Unsafe at Any Speed* (1965) condemned the automakers for paying little attention to safety standards and advocated a more carefully conceived and executed automobile design. As a result of the disclosures by Nader and others, in 1966 Congress passed the National Traffic and Motor Vehicle Safety Act, which required a comprehensive group of strict safety standards to be imposed on all vehicles produced from 1968 on. Soon installed were such devices as seat belts, concave steering wheels made of relatively soft material atop steering columns that would collapse under strong impact from the driver, and padded dashboards containing no sharp or pointed edges or protuberances. Over the next several years the car manufacturers found themselves recalling vehicles to repair or replace prospectively faulty parts. The most notable recall incident, which occurred during the late 1960s, involved a particular make produced by one company—more than 6.5 million cars—that had possibly defective engine mounts. The recalling zenith was reached during the first half of 1972 when, incredibly, the industry recalled more than 7 million automobiles—many more than it had sold during the same period! (Nader, who turned his attention to the improper practices in other fields of industry and commerce and earned a reputation as the nation's foremost consumer advocate, later established The Center for the Study of Responsive Law, which exposed abuses in business, focusing on evidence of laxity in fully complying with the provisions of federal regulatory legislation that had been passed in the public interest.)

The crisis—a wrenching one indeed—faced by the American automobile industry during the 1970s was the result of the stiff competition from the European and the Japanese car manufacturers. The situation stemmed from the energy pinch, in which the cost of gasoline skyrocketed because of the ever-rising prices demanded by the Organization of Petroleum Exporting Countries. In past decades the price of gasoline in the United States was relatively low compared with the exceedingly high price in practically all other industrialized nations because most of what those nations needed had to be brought in from foreign sources. Consequently, compared with the automobiles produced in the United States, those produced in other nations were smaller and their engines were more fuel-efficient, burning much less gasoline for each mile of driving and therefore being a great deal more economical to run. Thus foreign car manufacturers gained a head start over their American counterparts, garnering valuable experience in producing small fuel-efficient vehicles, products that in the 1970s the American consumers began to demand.

The changing pattern of the percentage shares of car sales in the United States by domestic and foreign automakers told a striking story. In 1975 the percentage shares were as follows: the General Motors Corporation, 43.3; the Ford Motor Company, 23.1; the Chrysler Corporation, 11.7; the American Motors Corporation and the rest of the domestic producers, 3.7; and foreign manufacturers, 18.2. But the purchase of foreign makes accounted for an ever-increasing part of the total car sales in the United States. In 1980 the percentage shares were: General Motors, 46.1; Ford, 16.5; Chrysler, 7.4; American Motors and the rest of the domestic producers, 3.5; and foreign manufacturers, 26.5. And of the purchase of imported vehicles in the United States, the Japanese makes constituted approximately 80 percent. In 1980 the domestic automobile industry had its worst sales year since 1961. The number of cars sold by the American producers in 1961 was approximately 5.6 million. In 1979 it was about 8.2 million, but in 1980 it fell to about 6.6 million (a devastating decrease from the 1979 figure). Early in the 1980s American car manufacturers had their own plant lots and the lots of their dealers filled with a huge inventory of vehicles for which there were virtually no prospective buyers. They cut back their operations, closing down plants and laying off tens of thousands of workers. Of the "Big Three"—General Motors, Ford, and Chrysler—the latter two were annually "in the red" hundreds of millions of dollars. As a matter of fact, Chrysler was in such straits that it resorted to asking for federal government guarantees of repayment of loans it was desperately seeking from private banks in order to escape bankruptcy—and the government complied. By the early 1980s the American automobile manufacturers, in response to the public's demand for small fuel-efficient cars, began in earnest to turn them out in large numbers, setting themselves the formidable task of first catching up with and then surpassing the foreign competition in sales of small economically run cars.

THE AIRPLANE. In 1960 the airlines flew, both in and outside the United States, about 58 million passengers a total of about 36 billion miles; in 1970 they flew about 170 million passengers about 132 billion miles; and in 1980 they flew about 297 million passengers about 254 billion miles. Until 1958 the planes used by the American airlines were of the piston-engine and propellor type, but in that year jet-engine aircraft were introduced. Impressively outperforming the "prop" airplanes, jet airplanes soon outnumbered them in the sky. Early in the 1960s the largest "jets" could carry about 150 passengers; in the mid-1970s the largest could hold about 500. By the mid-1970s, as a result of advances in aeronautical engineering, jets sped along at approximately six hundred miles an hour at a height of about 30,000 feet, with their passengers ensconced in comfort, and receiving solicitous treatment from personable flight attendants. Highly sophisticated electronic devices, including radar, made flying vastly safer during conditions of poor visibility or bad weather. In 1981, of the eighty domestic airlines in operation the top half a dozen in terms of revenue were, in order, United Airlines, Eastern Airlines, Delta Air Lines, Pan American World Airways, Trans World Airlines, and American Airlines; but at the same time three of them—United, Eastern, and Pan American—actually suffered a loss in profit.

During the early 1980s the airlines faced a crisis—a severe drop in income, with some airlines even having a few successive annual deficits of tens of millions of dollars. The most important factors leading to the situation were the following: the airlines were compelled to pay soaring amounts for fuel because of the demands of the Organization of Petroleum Exporting Countries; in order to compete, the airlines retained many routes and offered frequent flights so as to provide convenient service and thus attract and hold a clientele, often resorting to the grossly uneconomical practice of dispatching planes with many seats unoccupied; the airlines had to contend with a dwindling demand for their service as prospective passengers, facing both high inflation and unemployment or the threat of it, forsook air travel for vacations, and turned to something more modest.

THE RAILROADS. The level of freight handling by the railroads remained relatively firm and constant from the 1930s on. But this was not the case with passenger travel on the rail systems. In 1940 the nation's airlines annually carried fewer than 5 percent of the number of passengers domestically that the railroads did; in 1960 the railroads carried fewer than 5 percent of the number of passengers domestically that the airlines did! And during the next two decades or so the situation was basically the same.

In 1970 Congress established the National Railway Passenger Corporation, called Amtrak, the unified national railroad system. In order to revitalize and repopularize rail transportation the federal government committed itself to expending large sums of money to help pay for not only the daily running but also improvements in the efficiency and comfort of passenger trains. But with the difficult economic conditions of the early 1980s, the executive branch proposed to reduce federal government subsidies to Amtrak by approximately 35 percent, a decrease that would result in the discontinuance of most passenger travel service outside the relatively heavily used northeastern route from Boston to Washington, D.C. By 1980, just as the competition from overseas jet air travel brought the ship travel business, except for cruises, to almost total extinction, the competition from domestic jet air travel severely weakened the train travel business, a condition that seemed all but irreversible.

Medicine. Significant developments in medicine included the improvements in cancer therapy, the transplanting of vital organs, and the use of new methods in the treatment of heart disease. A grave medical problem of the period was drug abuse.

THE MEDICARE ACT. The Kennedy administration presented to Congress a plan to provide medical care for the aged. Congress twice rejected the proposal. An important factor in the measure's defeat was the antipathy of the American Medical Association, which repeatedly and vigorously characterized the plan as a step toward "socialized medicine." Ultimately, however, in 1965, during the Johnson administration, Congress enacted the plan called Medicare to provide medical care for those sixty-five and over, to be financed from payments under Social Security.

CANCER THERAPY. During the 1970s about 1 million new cases of cancer among the American people were diagnosed annually and about 400,000 died of the disease, which, after heart disease, was the principal cause of death in the nation. At its present incidence, approximately 25 percent of Americans will be stricken with it. In 1940 about 20 percent of those having cancer could be expected to live for five years; in 1980 about 40 percent were expected to do so—and the survival rate was improving rapidly. In 1971 Congress passed the National Cancer Act, which provided extensive funds for research into the causes and treatment of cancer. The gains in a patient's chances of surviving during the 1970s reflected improvements in the use of the traditional methods of treatment—surgery, radiation, and chemotherapy—and in the use of new methods, such as hyperthermia (treatment with heat) and immunotherapy, which is based on the person's natural production of antibodies and includes the employment of a recently developed, exceedingly costly drug named interferon.

ORGAN TRANSPLANTS. An astonishing advance in medicine during the 1960s and 1970s was the transplanting of vital organs from one person to another. The first kidney transplant was performed in

1954 in Boston; within a few years the operation was considered routine, with hundreds and soon thousands being done in the United States annually. In 1963 the first liver transplant was done in Denver, Colorado. In 1967 the South African Dr. Christiaan N. Barnard performed the first successful transplant of a human heart. Over the following decade approximately 350 heart transplants were performed, almost 50 percent of them in the United States.

TREATMENT OF HEART DISEASE. By 1980 the annual number of heart transplants declined because of the shortage of donors and because of the destruction of the transplanted organs by the patients' natural immune defenses, which recognized the organs as foreign and rejected them. The transplant operation was largely superseded by either the performance of coronary bypass surgery (in which the functions of damaged arteries are taken over by sections of the patient's own veins which are grafted onto the heart), with by 1980 about 100,000 such operations being performed annually, or the placing within the body of a pacemaker, with by 1980 about 600,000 people having electronic packages that kept their hearts beating in a steady rhythm.

DRUG ABUSE. One of the most serious medical problems of the 1960s and 1970s was drug abuse, often resulting in the ruining of the users' health. In addition, the unwarranted taking of drugs led to grave social problems, such as that of drug addicts dropping out of ordinary activities or even engaging in criminal acts, including robbing and burglarizing to obtain money for "the habit." By far the most widely used drug was marijuana, with 25 percent of adults trying it at least a few times and 22 percent of youths smoking on a fairly regular basis what was familiarly called "pot" or "grass." Of the hundreds of millions of pills that were "popped" (swallowed), there were two basic categories: the "uppers" (amphetamines), used to stimulate, and the "downers" (barbiturates and tranquilizers), to sedate. The approximately 2 million people who were "on" (using) cocaine, which was usually "snorted" (inhaled in powdered form through the nostrils), had to spend an average of $10,000 a year to assure a steady supply for a "fix" (a dose of a drug). Those addicted to the exceedingly potent drug heroin who "mainlined" (injected it into a vein) numbered in 1980 about 500,000. Undergoing the extreme hallucinatory effects of LSD (the popular designation of lysergic acid diethylamide), many who ingested it did bodily injury to themselves while on a "trip" (a psychedelic drug experience), such as by jumping out of windows under the impression that they were able to fly. And amid the illegal use of drugs was the legal consumption of alcoholic beverages. In 1980 about 11 million adults were alcoholics or frequently drank to excess.

DEVELOPMENT OF HEALTH CONSCIOUSNESS. During the 1970s there was a tremendous increase in the number of Americans who became avidly committed to sustaining good health through a regimen of prudent physical conduct. In order to achieve better health, people altered their life-styles in four basic ways: they stopped over-eating, stopped heavy drinking of alcoholic beverages, stopped smoking, and engaged in regular exercise. From 1970 to 1980 the portion of the population that exercised regularly rose from approximately 26 percent to approximately 47 percent. By 1980 among the most favored forms of exercise were tennis (engaged in by about 18 million people), bicycling (engaged in by about 16 million), and jogging (by about 10 million). Physical-fitness establishments, often called "health spas," sprouted up throughout the nation, with many types of pulley-operated weighted machines to decrease fat and increase muscles. The result of all the health consciousness was that once-paunchy Americans galore could boast that they felt better and were frequently told that they looked better than they had in years.

CULTURE

No better period than that of the 1960s and 1970s can be offered in all American history as an example of one when a close link existed between social change and cultural development. To one degree or another each facet of the advance of art, literature, music, motion pictures, television, and sports strikingly reflected some aspect of the social climate of the period. An influential school of painters seemed to indict a society that had become consumer-oriented and assembly-line-dominated; architects created buildings that were abundantly diverse in conception and execution, a diversity that reflected the increasing differences of life-styles among the nation's various economic, social, and age groups. In a reciprocal manner, one aspect of social change nurtured a segment of literature and that segment of literature fostered that aspect of social change: alienation from long-established principles of social conduct was the guiding force of an important stratum of literature, and that stratum made stronger the alienation of some groups, particularly the young. Newspaper and periodical publishing was a classic example of the fortunes of a business being thoroughly affected by changing economic and social patterns. Primarily because of technological developments of the period, the television industry, with the tremendous advantage of enabling the comfort and convenience of being entertained at home, overtook the motion-picture industry, which was compelled to operate in a much altered way. In the field of music two components enjoyed huge success: one was a very old and once the most exclusive aspect of the performing arts—ballet; the other was a new form appealing to the young in particular—rock 'n' roll. As for sports, no other area of American cultural development manifested such significant gains in status by blacks.

Art. In both major areas of American art important new developments took place during the 1960s and 1970s: in painting a movement emerged that repudiated the nonrepresentational mode of the preceding period and was boldly representational; in sculpture the construction of massive pieces became predominant. In the field of architecture there evolved a tendency toward stylistic diversity.

PAINTING. In the late 1950s there was a growing disdain among some painters for abstract expressionism because of what they considered its overly austere quality and a kind of elitist commitment to that quality by its exponents. The demonstration of this feeling rapidly grew into a full-scale movement called "pop art" ("pop" was short for "popular"). The members of this movement attempted to produce works of art that would be both appealing and understandable to the masses. The new school realistically depicted ordinary objects, particularly consumer-oriented ones, from everyday American life. Its members adopted the style of commercial illustration and the techniques of printing. They appeared to be making a gently humorous indictment of the pervasive influence upon American society of a rampant consumerism fostered by the mass media.

Important in the pop-art movement were Andy Warhol and Roy Lichtenstein. The distinguishing feature of Warhol's work is the presentation of an image repeated to a point approaching mcnotony, a device which was interpreted by art critics as a wry commentary on the bombardment of the senses by standardized assembly-line products. Two of Warhol's most representative works are *100 Cans* (1962), which shows row upon row of soup cans on the shelves of a supermarket, and *Marilyn Six-Pack* (1962), a painting, produced by the silk-screen process, of three rows of two identical portraits of the film star Marilyn Monroe, based upon a single newspaper photograph. Lichtenstein won recognition for his large-scale paintings, sharply defined and faithful in all details, of well-known comic strips, sometimes executed in their regular panel form, boldly mimicking the printing techniques that newspapers used to produce the original strips.

SCULPTURE. The dominant movement in American sculpture was the use of welded metal to create abstract forms. One of the first practitioners of this style was the exceedingly imaginative David Smith. His most famous sculpture is *Hudson River Landscape* (1951), an early work which, through a complex array of twisted steel strands, conveys a sense of a body of water meandering through wilderness. It was not long before members of this school turned frequently to creating massive pieces made of a metal (such as steel or aluminum) or an alloy of metals (such as bronze or brass), many of which were on such an immense scale that they could not fit into a building but had to be placed outdoors in open spaces. Those works needed to be cut out and put together by professional welders and riveters following the design and under the supervision of the sculptors.

During the period of monumentalism in sculpture Louise Nevelson became known for constructing on a smaller scale wall reliefs consisting of ordered arrangements of an accumulation of found wooden or metal objects, used whole or in pieces, each sculpture of which was painted a uniform black, white, or gold.

ARCHITECTURE. The trend in American architecture was an almost total abandonment of the International Style in favor of a diversity of styles—a movement that came to be called Post-Modernism. What virtually every architect forsook was quite discernible—buildings that were glass-and-steel boxes. Their own direction was still unclear. The only rule seemed to be that there should be "no rules." A prominent development was the returning to the old, often with a recommitment to lavish decoration. An outstanding example was a work of Philip Johnson, who had been an apostle of the International Style. He designed the new headquarters of the American Telephone and Telegraph Company (1983) in New York

City in the manner of the Renaissance style. The structure has as its base a traditional arch, above which is a granite tower capped by a huge pediment, scooped out at its apex. The most compelling structure of another leading architect of the period, the brilliantly conservative Chinese-American I. M. (Ieoh Ming) Pei, was the East Building (1978) of the National Gallery of Art in Washington, D.C. Magnificently integrated with its surroundings, this structure consists of two triangular buildings united by a skylight and connected by a plaza to the neoclassical original building.

Literature. The writings of most of the established novelists and poets were very little, if at all, influenced by the period's literary movement called the "beat generation," which did, however, have a significant effect upon society itself. As was the case early in the twentieth century, an important segment of American drama came under the influence of European playwrights, persons this time who forswore the traditional elements of plays. Newspaper and periodical publishing, for a host of economic and social reasons, faced the most difficult set of circumstances with which it had been confronted in this century.

THE NOVEL. Among the best writers of the period were Saul Bellow, John Updike, and Philip Roth. Bellow, in such novels as the highly regarded *Herzog* (1964) and *Mr. Sammler's Planet* (1970), focused on the human being's seemingly futile attempts to discover from within an always apathetic, often hostile society a justification for existence. Updike achieved fame with *Rabbit, Run* (1960). In a brilliantly subdued style this novel portrays a young man who, consumed by a restless longing for the time when he was a high-school basketball star and unable to cope with his situation as an adult member of society, in a simple act of supreme frustration runs away from his wife, child, and job. Roth, with a biting humor, depicted the fixed customs along with the thoughts and feelings of middle-class American Jews. In his best-known novel, *Portnoy's Complaint* (1969), the protagonist experiences agonizing guilt about the effect upon his suffocatingly attentive mother of his many and varied sexual escapades with non-Jewish women.

The writings of the beat-generation movement, which began in the mid-1950s and lasted into the early 1970s, enjoyed a wide popularity and had a notable impact upon a number of groups, especially the hippies. Beat writers consisted of a small group of novelists and poets who in their works renounced the long-held attitudes of conventional American society, especially that which esteemed the acquiring of material wealth. They extolled the deep pleasure to be derived from a variety of experiences, including drug use; many and varied forms of sexual encounters; and the acceptance of an Asian religion, particularly Zen Buddhism, which would lead to a condition of complete bliss, or beatitude (hence the origin of the phrase the "beat generation"). In literary style, they disdained the traditional forms and techniques and employed almost exclusively the patterns of vernacular American speech, including vulgarisms. They also relied heavily on the vocabulary of jazz. Jack Kerouac's *On the Road* (1967) is considered the epitome of the movement's thought and style. The novel portrays the sheer exhilaration of hitchhiking throughout the country, and in the process being exposed to such elements as drugs, unfettered sex, and Zen Buddhism.

POETRY. Widely acknowledged as the most influential American poet of his period, Robert Lowell had a technique that was notably inventive in the choice and setting of words. Lowell's early works were overwhelmingly religious in theme, filled with imagery, and complex in form. In the mid-1950s he started in a new direction, writing simply constructed secular verse that came to be called "confessional poetry." Through it he expresses human apprehensions and perplexities and the therapeutic value of relating them. The great work of this stage of his career is *Life Studies* (1959), a wrenchingly autobiographical collection of poetry and some prose.

The most representative poet of the beat generation was Allen Ginsberg, whose most famous work, *Howl* (1956), is a blistering censure of American social attitudes.

DRAMA. The most significant influence in American drama was theater of the absurd, which was developed largely from the works of the Rumanian-born Frenchman Eugene Ionesco and the Irish-born Frenchman Samuel Beckett. This movement renounced such conventional elements of drama as readily perceivable plot, characters, and dialogue in order to convey a human existence so desperately bewildering that it becomes meaningless, even unreal. Edward Albee was not only the leading American advocate of theater of the absurd but also the most creative of the nation's contemporary playwrights. Crafted in a more conventional form than many of his other works is his best-known play, *Who's Afraid of Virginia Woolf?* (1962). It deals with a middle-aged college professor and his wife (played to harrowing effect in the film version by Richard Burton and Elizabeth Taylor), who during a night of drinking with a younger faculty couple mercilessly torment each other, revealing a marriage permeated with seething malice. Finally, in a supreme effort to put an end to their shared illusions, they "kill off" their imaginary child, signifying that now they have only each other, a relationship—no matter what its nature—they both desperately need.

NEWSPAPERS AND MAGAZINES. Beginning early in the 1960s and continuing beyond the 1970s a number of the nation's metropolitan newspapers were forced, because of revenue losses from a sharp decline in circulation and advertising, either to merge with other papers or to cease publication. The reasons were not difficult to ascertain: the increasing movement of middle-class people out of the cities; strong competition from television news and public-affairs coverage and from suburban newspapers; sharply rising expenses of production; and the costly effects of strikes, mostly for higher wages, particularly by the printers' union. The trend grew with such swiftness that by the mid-1960s only in New York City, Boston, and Washington, D.C., were there still three or more separately operated and competing dailies with large circulations. Among the large-circulation newspapers that closed down were in 1967 the *New York World-Journal-Tribune* (established the previous year by a merger of the *New York Herald Tribune,* the *New York Journal-American,* and the *New York World-Telegram and The Sun*), in 1972 the *Newark Evening News*, in 1978 the *Chicago Daily News*, and in 1982 the *Philadelphia Bulletin.*

In 1980, of the approximately 1750 dailies being published, the top five in order of circulation were the *New York Daily News,* the *Los Angeles Times,* the *New York Times,* the *Chicago Tribune,* and the *Chicago Sun-Times.* Generally regarded as the best major dailies (for comprehensively covering international, national, and local news; presenting a balanced body of opinion by its political columnists; committing itself to investigative reporting; and, withal, being interesting, thought-provoking, and enjoyable to read) were the following: the *New York Times,* with its long-standing reputation for dignity and thoroughness still intact; the *Washington Post,* with its judicious and lucid editorial-page analysis and its incomparably perceptive treatment of political affairs; the *Wall Street Journal,* with its well-presented conservative interpretations of news events and its heavy focus on economic, particularly business, matters; and the *Louisville Courier-Journal,* with its steadfast undertaking of socially conscious investigative journalism still inviolate.

As for periodical publishing, the trend begun in the 1940s and 1950s of producing special-interest magazines continued unabated throughout the 1960s and 1970s. For example, the organization that published the extraordinarily successful weekly *TV Guide* brought forth in 1980 what seemed destined to be a highly popular monthly, *Panorama,* a sleek-looking magazine filled with all sorts of articles to attract video enthusiasts. A rather unusual case of a successfully launched general-interest magazine was the weekly *People,* which was published by the firm founded by Henry R. Luce and his colleagues; appearing in 1974, the new magazine gave accounts, with plenty of photographs, of the comings and goings of celebrities, particularly the young and attractive in the entertainment field. But the most significant aspect of periodical publishing was (due in large part to soaring production costs) the grimly uncertain future of old successful general-interest magazines and the enormous difficulty of establishing new magazines of whatever type. In 1980 alone three of the nation's most distinguished periodicals, on the brink of closing down, were rescued by new owners: the monthly *Harper's,* established in 1850; *The Atlantic Monthly,* founded in 1857; and the weekly *Saturday Review,* launched as *The Saturday Review of Literature* in 1924. Each started out as solely a literary magazine, but later also carried notably perceptive articles on current political and social matters. Each year during the 1970s approximately three hundred new magazines were begun. About 10 percent survived.

Music. The 1960s and 1970s saw what was perhaps the zenith of musical activity in twentieth-century America. Symphony orchestras were ably led and the Metropolitan Opera House, along with opera companies throughout the nation, attracted ever-larger audiences. Ballet enjoyed for the first time a high level of popular esteem. And in the field of popular music, rock 'n' roll quickly captured the loyalty of the young.

ORCHESTRAL COMPOSERS AND CONDUCTORS. The works of the traditionalist Samuel Barber and the experimentalist John Cage represented the best of the opposite ends of the broad spectrum of orchestral musical composition. Barber's music, except for some dissonance and complex rhythmic patterns in his later compositions, was smoothly melodic. A very early piece, *Adagio for Strings* (1936), enjoyed constant and wide appeal over the years. In addition to producing many orchestral works in a wide variety of forms, he composed the music for two operas, *Vanessa* (1958) and *Antony and Cleopatra* (1966), the latter commissioned to inaugurate the new home of the Metropolitan Opera Company in New York City's Lincoln Center for the Performing Arts. Cage was the supreme avant-gardist of the period. He often composed music that was devoid of harmonic and rhythmic patterns and that gave prominence to percussion instruments. He sometimes composed music by "chance"—for example, determining such basic elements as the pitch and duration of notes by drawing a playing card or throwing dice. He even composed music that left to the performers the order of executing sections of a work or the deletion of sections. His most famous piece is an early work, *4'33"* (1952), which requires a pianist to be seated at the keyboard for four minutes and thirty-three seconds without playing any notes while the stillness is interrupted only by haphazard sounds that might occur in the concert hall.

In 1978 the Bombay-born Zubin Mehta became music director of the New York Philharmonic Symphony Orchestra. He brought to the post a pleasingly restrained flamboyance and became well known for his interpretations of the late-nineteenth-century romantic and, to a lesser degree, the early-twentieth-century innovative masters. In 1973 the Boston Symphony Orchestra chose the Japanese Seiji Ozawa as its music director. He was noted for intensely projecting the spirit of each work he conducted. The permanent conductor of the Chicago Symphony Orchestra during the 1970s was the Hungarian-born Georg Solti, a literalist who was particularly respected for his authoritative renditions of the works of Wagner. For fifty years, ending with his death in 1979, Arthur Fiedler conducted the Boston Pops Orchestra (the Boston Symphony minus its principal players). With a showmanlike manner, he brought "serious" music to millions of Americans, presenting programs that were a potpourri of "heavy" classics, "light" classics, and popular tunes mainly from the musical theater.

CONCERT VIRTUOSOS. Three of the most widely admired concert virtuosos were the violinists Isaac Stern and Itzhak Perlman and the pianist Rudolf Serkin. The exuberant Stern gave dazzling performances on what he called his "fiddle." The Israeli-American Perlman (seated while he played because he had been a polio victim) enveloped his listeners with a lush sound, while conveying an irresistible love of producing music. Perhaps no one could equal the extraordinary sensitivity that the Austrian-American Serkin, with his elegant style, brought to the piano.

OPERA. Throughout the nation opera enjoyed a period of tremendous popularity. Attendance at the performances of both the major companies in the large cities and the lesser companies in the small communities broke twentieth-century attendance records. During the summer seasons, formerly devoid of opera, many opera festivals were held. The television networks presented greater and more varied opera fare. Little-known works of the repertory were presented, often to the acclaim of opera fans.

In 1974 the position of one all-powerful general manager of the Metropolitan Opera Company was discontinued in favor of a triumvirate consisting of former lawyer Anthony Bliss as executive director, James Levine as music director and principal conductor, and John Dexter as production director. Six years later Bliss became general manager, with Levine in charge of music and production matters and as the principal conductor. While Levine exhibited a particular insight in interpreting operas in the nineteenth-century Italian repertory, he also commendably performed more recent works. In 1977 there was a live telecast of Puccini's *La Bohème,* the first in what was to become an annual series of live presentations of several operas in their entirety directly from the stage of the Metropolitan.

As had always been the case, the premier opera house attracted virtually all the world's finest singers. Soprano Maria Callas made her debut at the Metropolitan in 1956. Although plagued by some serious vocal limitations, she possessed a magnetic stage presence that captured audiences. Callas is credited with reviving the bel canto ("beautiful song") style, which emphasizes the lyrical quality of singing over the declamatory. This led to the resurrection in opera houses both in the United States and abroad of bel canto works of the nineteenth-century composers Rossini, Donizetti, and Bellini. The two greatest stars of the Metropolitan were the Australian soprano Joan Sutherland and the Italian tenor Luciano Pavarotti. Having a gorgeous sheen to her voice, Sutherland was considered unequaled in the bel canto repertory; she was especially associated with the title role in Donizetti's *Lucia di Lammermoor.* Compared with the tenor Enrico Caruso (the standard against which any subsequent operatic tenor was judged), Pavarotti was considered just as good. The penetrating yet rapturously warm character of his voice and his power to communicate with audiences were unmatched. His singing of Rodolfo in Puccini's *La Bohème* was acknowledged to be unsurpassed. Another much-admired tenor of the Metropolitan was the Spanish-born Placido Domingo, whose voice exhibited both a firm power and a mellow sonority and whose repertory included approximately eighty roles in Italian and French operas, with a concentration on Puccini and Verdi. Two outstanding American singers were the black soprano Leontyne Price, thought to give the period's finest interpretation of the title role in Verdi's *Aida,* and mezzo-soprano Marilyn Horne, who was acclaimed for her renditions of a broad variety of roles in the Italian and French repertory.

Widely acknowledged as the nation's most distinguished operatic company after the Metropolitan was the San Francisco Opera Company, founded in 1923. The company's reputation was regarded as a testament to the tremendous energy and perfectionism of the Austrian-born Kurt Herbert Adler, its general director for twenty-eight years, beginning in 1953. Another leading opera house was the New York City Opera Company, established in 1944. During a twenty-three-year tenure that began in 1957, the Austrian-born director Julius Rudel achieved distinction for being notably progressive in staging little-known operas, particularly in seeing to the presentation of contemporary American works. The star of the house for many years was the ebullient soprano Beverly Sills, a theatrically skillful performer who specialized in the bel canto repertory. Toward the end of her singing career Sills appeared at the Metropolitan. She subsequently succeeded Rudel as director of the New York City Opera Company, in which capacity she immediately proved thoroughly competent in administration and exceedingly effective in public relations.

BALLET. The 1970s were a "golden age" of ballet in the United States. The most rapidly developing performing art in the nation during the period was dance; that is, both ballet and modern dance. In 1970 there were about 425 amateur and professional dance companies in the nation. By 1980 there were about 850 companies; approximately 130 of them were professional, of which about 55 were ballet companies that in addition to giving performances, developed dancers, ballet masters (who train and direct dancers and sometimes do choreography), and choreographers. In 1979 approximately 22 million Americans attended dance performances, compared with about 15 million two years earlier, and only about 1 million three years before that. And New York City became the dance—including ballet—center of the world.

The ascendancy of ballet had not occurred quickly. For the first three decades of the twentieth century there was practically no ballet in the United States, and, as in the preceding century, what little existed was imported from Europe. (The great Russian ballerina Anna Pavlova made many tours of the United States from 1910 to the mid-1920s. The Russian ballet impresario Sergei Diaghilev brought to the United States his world-famed company, the Ballets Russes; the first time was in 1916 when in the troupe was probably the finest male ballet dancer of the twentieth century, the Russian Vaslav Nijinsky.) In 1934 the American Ballet company was founded by Lincoln Kirstein and some associates. In addition to offering programs of high quality, the company made a noteworthy contribution to the development of ballet through the activities of its associated company, the School of American Ballet, the nation's first major organization for the training of ballet dancers. In 1948 the New York City Ballet was established, having been created from the American Ballet company. The New York City Ballet eventually became not only the premier ballet company in the United States but also ranked with the leading companies of the world.

Associated with the American Ballet company and the New York City Ballet was the Russian-born and Russian-trained George Balanchine. A principal dancer and choreographer with Diaghilev's Ballets Russes in the mid-1920s and director of ballet for the Metropolitan Opera House in the mid-1930s, he served as the director and principal choreographer of the American Ballet company from its founding and as the artistic director and principal choreographer of the New York City Ballet from its founding to the present. Balanchine is acknowledged as the undisputed master of American ballet choreography. He created close to a hundred ballets, most with little or no plot and with greatly simplified costuming and staging, focusing on the execution of the dance itself. Along with a few other contemporary choreographers in the United States, he was greatly responsible for transforming the conventional role of the male dancer from being merely supportive of the female dancer to being given the opportunity to exhibit a graceful physical prowess, much of it in solo segments. Two of Balanchine's most popular works were *Entente Cordiale* (1958–1977), a spectacular ballet consisting of three acts, "Stars and Stripes," "Union Jack," and "Tricolore," in celebration of the unique character of each of three nations—the United States, Great Britain, and France—and of their historical interrelationship; and *Jewels* (1967), an abstract ballet comprising three movements, "Emeralds," "Rubies," and "Diamonds," each brilliantly conveying the gem's quality through the manner of the dance and the simple costumes and minimal sets.

One of Balanchine's most gifted colleagues, Jerome Robbins, was the associate artistic director and a choreographer of the New York City Ballet from 1949 to 1963, and has continued to the present to create some ballets for the company and to serve as its ballet master. During the same period he directed or choreographed, or both, a number of popular musicals, including *West Side Story* (1957) and *Fiddler on the Roof* (1964). The first ballet he created was *Fancy Free* (1944), which is about three sailors on leave searching for fun and excitement—and female companionship. A skillful blend of the techniques of classical ballet and popular dance, the work was warmly received by the public.

Among the acclaimed principal dancers with the New York City Ballet were Maria Tallchief, Patricia McBride, Edward Villela, and Peter Martins, all of whom had studied at least for a time with Balanchine. Tallchief, of American Indian background, as prima (head) ballerina during an eighteen-year association with the company ending in the mid-1960s, specialized in the traditional works. The petite yet physically strong McBride, who created major roles in more than thirty ballets, was admired not only for her exquisitely delicate interpretations but also for her skill as a technician. Villela, whose dazzling style was noted for its masculine athleticism, performed in a wide and varied number of roles in both the classical and modern repertory, winning particular acclaim for dancing the title role in the approximately thirty-year-old *The Prodigal Son* (1929), a ballet choreographed by Balanchine. The Dane Martins was coolly elegant as he performed with what was widely acknowledged as the closest to technical perfection a dancer could hope to achieve. In the late 1970s he began to do choreography with much success.

The second leading ballet company in the nation was the American Ballet Theatre, founded in 1939 as the Ballet Theatre. Force-

fully directed for thirty-five years by Lucia Chase and Oliver
Smith, it premiered a number of acclaimed ballets, including Robbins's *Fancy Free,* and advanced the cause of ballet in the United
States through magnificent performances during tours in every
state.

Three of the world's finest dancers, Rudolph Nureyev, Natalia
Makarova, and Mikhail Baryshnikov, all members of the famous
Kirov Ballet of Leningrad, defected (Nureyev early in the 1960s
and the other two in the 1970s) from the Soviet Union while on
tour and settled in the United States to pursue careers outside the
Soviet sphere of influence. They declared that they were motivated
by a desire for artistic freedom, particularly flexibility in assuming
and developing dancing roles. Nureyev is considered the greatest
interpreter of his time of the male classical ballet roles. Displaying
robust yet elegant movements, heightened by an impassioned de-
meanor, he won plaudits from dance critics and fans alike for his
electrifying performances, which encompassed fresh approaches, in
such long-cherished nineteenth-century ballets as *Giselle, The
Sleeping Beauty,* and *Swan Lake.* Makarova, who upon her defec-
tion joined the American Ballet Theatre, was one of the most expressive ballerinas, able to convey to an audience the most intensely
dramatic feeling with a single movement of her incredibly supple
body. The short and somewhat stocky Baryshnikov, who particularly delighted viewers with his remarkably high and protracted bal-
letic leaps, first danced with the American Ballet Theatre and then,
for the opportunity of working with Balanchine, joined the New
York City Ballet. Of the three from the Kirov company, Baryshnikov was the most professionally adventuresome, attempting roles in
the recent repertory of American ballet that were unfamiliar in the
Soviet Union. In 1980 he turned his attention to another aspect of
ballet by accepting the artistic directorship of the American Ballet
Theatre.

During the 1960s and 1970s the choreography of new works of
ballet, as well as that of musical-theater dancing, was very much
influenced by the philosophy and style of modern dance, from
which it received a fresh spirit and texture. It became a common
occurrence for ballet companies, and musical-theater productions
too, to have talented modern-dance performers appear with them
and to have highly regarded modern-dance choreographers create
works for them. By 1980 the once well-entrenched and easily recog-

nizable differences among all three dance forms—ballet, musical theater, and modern—had been blurred.

MUSICAL THEATER. Stephen Sondheim was a composer and lyricist of musicals who during the 1960s and 1970s by himself creatively effected a basic change in the integration of music and lyrics in this field. Of his most original works, the biggest success was *Company* (1970), which starred Elaine Stritch and contains the song "Side by Side by Side." Disregarding the established practice, Sondheim in this musical did not use the talents of singers and dancers, but had his actors do the singing and dancing in order to achieve optimum naturalness. *Company* had no story but was about marriage among the New York City middle class in the 1970s, achieving its intent by presenting a body of interrelated and wittily perceptive vignettes. More conventional than Sondheim's works but nevertheless expertly crafted and clearly showing—even advancing—the Rodgers and Hammerstein legacy of the well-integrated musical were the three top hits of the period: *Hello, Dolly!* (1964), which was adapted from the play *The Matchmaker* by Thornton Wilder, had music and lyrics by Jerry Herman, was choreographed by Gower Champion, starred Carol Channing, and contains the title song "Hello, Dolly!"; *Fiddler on the Roof* (1964), which was based on Yiddish short stories by the Russian-American writer Sholem Aleichem, had music by Jerry Bock and lyrics by Sheldon Harnick, was choreographed by Jerome Robbins, starred Zero Mostel, and contains the songs "If I Were a Rich Man" and "Sunrise, Sunset"; and *A Chorus Line* (1975), which dealt with the varied anguish and triumph experienced by dancers auditioning for the chorus of a musical about to go into production, had music by Marvin Hamlisch and lyrics by Edward Kleban, was choreographed by Michael Bennett, and contains the song "What I Did for Love."

ROCK 'N' ROLL. In the mid-1950s a new type of music appeared that was called "rock 'n' roll." Although a number of musical styles went into the making up of rock 'n' roll, it was primarily a blending of black blues and white country and western. Instrumentally, there was a heavy reliance on the guitar and drums. The music quickly won an intense and sustained allegiance among the nation's youth. The lyrics usually dealt with the concerns of young men and women, such as being subjected to an unsatisfying formal education, living with parents who did not understand their needs, and, particularly, experiencing the agonies of "first love." The exaggerated beat, excessive volume, and energetic body movements of the performers made rock 'n' roll a musical symbol in the early 1960s of the antipathy of youth toward the quiet and orderly aspects of established American society. The top performer was Elvis Presley, who, while playing the guitar to accompany his singing, which was characterized by a howling quality, would rotate his pelvis for emphasis, an action that would send his young fans into raptures. Two of his most popular songs were "Heartbreak Hotel" and "Hound Dog."

In the mid-1960s the nature of rock 'n' roll was altered, and the form became increasingly referred to simply as "rock." The new direction stemmed from the influence of a number of British performing groups, particularly The Beatles and the Rolling Stones. The Beatles were John Lennon, Paul McCartney, George Harrison, and Ringo Starr, the first three playing guitars and the last on the drums. Lennon and McCartney composed the music and wrote the lyrics for most of their songs. Wearing their longish hair in bangs and speaking with pronounced Liverpudlian accents, The Beatles were a smash hit with young audiences whenever they made one of their many visits to the United States. The Rolling Stones, with Mick Jagger as the lead performer, were in their attire and manner blatantly sexual. Under the pervasive influence of British rock groups, there was a deepening commitment to the black blues aspect of rock and a lessening attachment to the white country and western element. The playing (on instruments whose sounds were electronically amplified) and the singing became even louder and the body movements even more frenetic.

Soon after rock 'n' roll had been changed by British performing groups there occurred an equally significant modification of the style through its melding with folk music, resulting in what was called "folk rock." Primarily responsible for and the leading exponent of this new development was Bob Dylan. He was greatly influenced by an earlier generation both of blues singers, such as Huddie ("Leadbelly") Leadbetter and, even more so, of folk singers, particularly Woody Guthrie, who composed the well-known song "This Land Is Your Land" (1956). After composing and singing in the Guthrie style his own songs of social protest, including "Blowin' in the Wind" (1962), Dylan began to absorb the elements of rock, writing and performing new songs with lyrics that angrily expressed the disaffection of the nation's young people. It was not long before most rock groups were giving performances that were to one degree or another drug-oriented: in the kinds of sounds, which conveyed a sense of drug-induced experiences; in the substance of the lyrics; and in the manner of the staging, particularly the lighting. Beginning in the 1970s a number of new performing groups became popular less for the music they played and sang than for their flagrant attire, immoderate physical actions, and extreme stage effects.

Motion Pictures. In order to continue as a viable part of the field of popular entertainment, the motion-picture industry felt compelled to accommodate itself to changing economic and social conditions. It did so. And despite difficult circumstances, great films with great performances were still made.

NEW TRENDS. Three factors in particular were most responsible for significant new trends in filmmaking: the steeply climbing costs of production, particularly during the inflationary economy of the 1970s; the developing public taste for realism over romanticism, with a readier acceptance of, even a desire for, the depiction of violence and explicit sexual activity; and, finally, the constant competition of television. The solution arrived at by the heads of the film industry was to make fewer but better movies. Shooting on location (always done to some extent) became the rule, with directors, performers, and crews hardly ever to be found in Hollywood, but off filming wherever in the United States or abroad the action of the story took place. The reason for this was twofold: to bring forth a more realistic work and to take advantage of lower production costs in part achieved through the use of local extras and some local technicians.

In 1968 the film industry adopted what many considered a flexible and enlightened Motion Picture Code and Rating Program to replace what seemed the rigid and outdated Motion Picture Production Code, which had been in existence for close to forty years. According to the new code, as revised in 1970, a film was issued for public viewing with one of four ratings: G—general audiences; PG—audiences of all ages, but parental guidance suggested; R—restricted audiences, with no one under the age of seventeen admitted without a parent or adult; X—no one under seventeen admitted. As for the relationship between the motion-picture and television industries, by the 1970s the two had come to terms with each other in a resolution satisfactory to both. At first the studios sold to the television networks individual films that had already been shown in movie houses; later they sold in package deals large portions of their entire stock of already screened films. Further, the studios began to make films specifically for television viewing. Ironically, by 1980 Americans were seeing more movies than ever in the past, but they were seeing them at home on television.

DIRECTORS. Beginning early in the 1970s two young directors, Francis Ford Coppola and Peter Bogdanovich, gained prominence for their works and showed promise of even greater achievement from their considerable talent. Each asserted that in order to attain an end product of high quality it was essential that he have undisputed control of all the key factors of the filmmaking process, including, in addition to directing, the writing of the screenplay and the producing of the completed work as both a creative and financial enterprise. Coppola's *The Godfather* (1972) and *The Godfather, Part II* (1974), which were done on a grand scale, soon achieved legendary status in motion-picture history. His *Apocalypse Now* (1979), which dealt with an army officer's assignment to kill an American general who had resorted to independent operations during the Vietnam War, may prove to be the classic war film of its time. Bogdanovich's *The Last Picture Show* (1971) offered a haunting image of a hamlet in Texas during the 1950s as some of its inhabitants affected one another and *Paper Moon* (1973) presented an unforgettable delineation of a slick and wily door-to-door Bible salesman and a nimble-witted little girl who became his associate as they "worked" the Midwest during the 1930s.

STARS. During the 1960s and 1970s film stars were of a different kind from those of the preceding decades. On the whole, they disdained a life of glamour off the screen, preferring to be seen in public engaging in ordinary activities and dressed in casual clothes, often including the symbolic jeans. They thought of themselves as serious practitioners of the fine craft of acting and essayed a wide variety of roles instead of being a "type" that a studio head and his publicity department had created. Such were top stars Paul Newman, Robert Redford, Jane Fonda, and Barbra Streisand. Newman, handsome and muscular, often played a coolly confident loner, with an easy smile and a ready quip, both of which conveyed a measure of defiance. Like Newman, Redford was good-looking and well built and frequently depicted a self-assured individualist, but Redford's characters were more idealistic than Newman's. In keeping with her own well-known social consciousness, Fonda increasingly chose roles that appealed for the eradication of social injustices and of militarism, assignments in which she could demonstrate her considerable acting ability. Streisand, with a face that brought to mind an ancient royal Egyptian, was a spirited actress who was able to deliver a song in a rich soprano that could be caressingly soft or brassily loud.

MUSICALS. In the mid-1950s there began a Hollywood trend of making fewer musicals that were conceived and executed for the screen and turning more to the musical theater for material. By the end of the 1970s almost all the top hit musicals of Broadway had been adapted to the screen. Among them were *Oklahoma!* (1955), with Gordon MacRae; *South Pacific* (1958), with Mitzi Gaynor; *My Fair Lady* (1964), with Rex Harrison and Audrey Hepburn; *The Sound of Music* (1965), with Julie Andrews; *Hello, Dolly!* (1969), with Barbra Streisand; and *Fiddler on the Roof* (1971), with the Israeli Chaim Topol. Many film critics believed that although the motion-picture industry gained a measure of security by screening an already established hit, it lost something in integral spontaneity.

COMEDIES. After about two decades of a relatively small output of comedies, most of them unnoteworthy, the genre burst forth with a new vigor in the 1960s and 1970s. Situations which in the past had been only hinted at were now met head-on; hardly any topic was now considered too delicate for a blatantly comedic treatment. All this was due in large part to the talent of two filmmakers who wrote or co-wrote the screenplays for, directed, and acted in, their productions—Mel Brooks and Woody Allen. *Blazing Saddles* (1974) by Brooks, abounding in ridiculous spoken jokes and sight gags, lampooned the typical western, placing a black sheriff in an all-white community. Allen's finely crafted *Annie Hall* (1977) included scene after scene of cerebral comedy; underscoring them all was the love between a man and a woman (portrayed by Allen and Diane Keaton) that could not overcome their widely divergent backgrounds and personalities.

GANGSTER FILMS. The enthusiasm of the public for gangster films during the 1930s was spent soon after that decade. It was not until the 1960s and 1970s that the enthusiasm was revived by the appearance of three extraordinarily fine productions with new perceptions of the genre, particularly in presenting characters in well-rounded completeness and showing violence realistically. In *Bonnie and Clyde* (1967) Faye Dunaway and Warren Beatty vividly played the leaders of an actual 1930s gang of cold-blooded bank robbers; at the end of the film the two were shot to death, their bullet-ridden and blood-spattered bodies falling, in a memorable use of slow-motion cinematography. Francis Ford Coppola's *The Godfather* (1972) and *The Godfather, Part II* (1974), based on Mario Puzo's best-selling novel and starring Marlon Brando in the first film and Al Pacino in both the first and the second, were impressive treatments of a Mafia family in twentieth-century America.

HORROR FILMS. Creatures of horror in both human and nonhuman form were top box-office draws, giving terror-filled pleasure to movie fans. Director Alfred Hitchcock's *Psycho* (1960), starring Anthony Perkins, was about a psychotic young man who assumed the identity of his mother, whom he had apparently murdered, and in her guise went on to stab to death two strangers. In *Rosemary's Baby* (1968), under the critically acclaimed direction of the Polish-born Roman Polanski, a young married woman was chosen by a coven of witches to be impregnated by the devil and have his child. *The Exorcist* (1973), directed by William Friedkin, dealt with a girl who was possessed by the devil and two priests who ultimately drove out the evil force.

WESTERNS. During the 1960s westerns began to appear that, except for the setting and the background of the characters, were so different from past westerns that the public had some difficulty recognizing them as in the same category. No longer was it a simple matter of "good guys" against "bad guys"; it was a probing of the motives, often complex, of individuals and an examination of the issues pertaining to the period and locale. An excellent example of this development was *The Misfits* (1961), with a screenplay by Arthur Miller, directed by John Huston, and starring Clark Gable, Marilyn Monroe, and Montgomery Clift. It was a study of three cowboys who, in order to earn a living, resorted to capturing wild horses to be killed for pet food and of their female companion who tried to convince them that their action was a desecration both of nature and of their honor. *Butch Cassidy and the Sundance Kid* (1969), starring Paul Newman and Robert Redford, was a breezy account of the unrelenting pursuit by a posse of two appealingly personable outlaws noted for their escapades of derring-do.

WAR FILMS. Whereas the vast majority of war movies during the preceding period treated the motives and actions of the United States and its allies as totally good and those of the enemy as totally bad, and romanticized actual combat, the films of the 1960s and 1970s were more balanced, most of them tending to condemn war itself and to present battle scenes in a gruesomely realistic manner. *Patton* (1970) was about World War II, with George C. Scott memorably playing the role of the tough commander and brilliant tactician Major General George S. Patton, Jr. *M*A*S*H* (1970), under the impressive direction of Robert Altman, probed with devastating wit the devil-may-care attitude and irreverent conduct of the surgeons and staff of an Army field hospital who with capability and concern treat soldiers wounded in the Korean War. *The Deer Hunter* (1979) presented Robert De Niro as the central figure of three young friends whose lives, as well as the lives of those they left behind, were seriously, even destructively, affected by their military experience in the Vietnam War.

SCIENCE-FICTION FILMS. The exploration of space was a natural impetus to the making of a spate of science-fiction movies, and advanced technology enabled special-effects experts to make scenes that were wondrous to behold. The great science-fiction films of the period were striking testimony to the remarkably creative talent of their directors. *2001: A Space Odyssey* (1968), directed by Stanley Kubrick, dealt with travel in space by animate beings and inanimate objects in terms of journeys in the far past and in the near and distant futures. In *Star Wars* (1977), directed by George Lucas, the theme of heroes against villains, the staple of the old adventure films in such settings as ancient Rome, medieval Europe, and nineteenth-century Africa, was transferred to outer space of the future, where humans contended with a variety of strange beings, both friendly and unfriendly, good and evil. In *Close Encounters of the Third Kind* (1977), directed by Steven Spielberg, a spaceship with beings from a distant part of the universe landed on earth, where a select group of humans boarded the craft to join them for a journey into outer space.

Television. Simply put, by the 1960s and 1970s no technological instrument that served social and cultural purposes had a more pervasive influence upon everyday life in America than did television.

WIDE APPEAL. The number of families having television sets increased from about 45.8 million in 1960 to about 76.3 million in

1980. In 1960 approximately 90 percent of America's households contained sets and in 1980 approximately 99 percent did. In 1980 viewing was done on an average of approximately six hours a day.

VARIETY SHOWS. Although variety shows declined in popularity during the 1960s and 1970s, two of the period's most successful programs were of this type. In *The Carol Burnett Show* star Burnett, one of the most appealingly versatile performers ever to appear on television, was well served by a regular cast of solidly dependable comedians. Particularly enjoyed by audiences were the sketches that satirized motion-picture classics and well-known television shows. The extraordinarily creative *Rowan and Martin's Laugh-In,* starring Dan Rowan and Dick Martin and with a regular cast at any one time of about a dozen young and capable comedians, all quite individualistic in style and exceedingly personable, was a notable trend-setter. An immediate hit, the show was a continually fast-moving package of virtually all the devices associated with the field of comedy, including sketches, sight gags, slapstick, insults, and clever quips. The television audience soon came to expect on each installment a host of inventive short routines. After the program had achieved tremendous success, celebrities, many of them quite dignified and not from the field of entertainment, would make brief surprise appearances, usually delivering one of the recurring catch-expressions associated with the show, such as "Sock it to me!"

SITUATION COMEDIES. The long trend in situation comedies was precipitately altered by the appearance in 1971 of one series—*All in the Family.* Unlike its predecessors in the genre, this show did not rely on constrainedly "tame" subject matter but focused openly on controversial topics, such as racial, religious, and ethnic prejudice and sexual conduct—in a sharply humorous manner. The program starred Carroll O'Connor as the supreme bigot and ultraconservative Archie Bunker and Jean Stapleton as his obtuse but lovingly generous wife Edith. The rest of the family was made up of their vivacious daughter and her intellectual and ultraliberal husband, whose views and Polish background made him the frequent object of his father-in-law's jibes. And the television audience soon came to love it all. Consistently popular was *The Mary Tyler Moore Show,* starring Moore as an attractive and sprightly young single woman pursuing a career in the news department of a Minneapolis television station. A major strength of the program was that the indisputably talented star was supported by an ensemble of unusually fine actors; the characters they portrayed included the outwardly cranky but inwardly softhearted chief of the news department; the none-too-bright, egocentric news anchorman; and the leading character's sardonic neighbor-friend who was furiously hunting for a husband.

TALK SHOWS. Retaining its long-standing record as the most-watched offering in this genre was *The Tonight Show.* Johnny Carson, who became the host of the program in 1962, began each installment with a comedy monologue containing teasing comments regarding people and events recently in the news. In conversing with guest celebrities, he was smooth and easygoing, often doing a classic double take (delayed reaction to the meaning of an idea or action). Unlike the hosts of other talk shows, Carson rarely discussed controversial topics, preferring to keep the mood light throughout.

MINI-SERIES DRAMA. During the 1970s there appeared on television a new form of dramatic production, called the "mini-series," which consisted of about half a dozen installments usually telecast on successive evenings over a period of a week or so during prime-time scheduling. In this category was the eight-part *Roots.* Based on a semifictional account by black author Alex Haley of his own "roots," the program traced the writer's ancestry from a West African youth, who was brought as a slave to the American colonies in the late eighteenth century, to that slave's great-grandson, who was a blacksmith during the late nineteenth century. A competent cast of almost forty helped the production strikingly capture the various nuances of a century-long stretch of black-white relations in America. *Roots* was the most-viewed entertainment presentation in the history of the medium, attracting on the average approximately 66 percent of the television audience and being viewed, all or in part, by about 125 million people, with close to 50 percent of the population watching the concluding episode. Two years later *Roots: The Next Generation,* gleaned from the end of Haley's book and then expanded, told the stories of his businessman grandfather and his college-professor father, concluding in the mid-1960s with his own story. The sequel attracted a large audience but nothing comparable to that of the original production. Another eminently successful mini-series was the four-part *Holocaust,* which dealt with the destruction of all but one member of a Berlin Jewish family by the

Nazi regime. The program prompted tens of millions of viewers to engage in moral reflection on the annihilation of approximately 6 million European Jews during the late 1930s and the early 1940s.

BRITISH DRAMA IMPORTS. By 1980 members of more than 45 million households viewed public television with some regularity. The close to three hundred stations in the nationwide noncommercial system earned a reputation for telecasting both American and foreign programs of high quality. They concentrated on dramas; classical music; and documentaries, many of which dealt with art, literature, and music as well as with the natural sciences.

The most successful by far of public television's offerings was an annual series entitled *Masterpiece Theater,* comprising a number of British dramatic productions, which premiered in 1970 and has continued running to the present. Elegantly hosted by the British-born social commentator Alistair Cooke, the series of finely crafted literary fare held the unswerving loyalty of several million fans who found it almost impossible to stir from the television set while an episode was on. Among the most popular works were *I, Claudius,* an adaptation of the Briton Robert Graves's historical novel dealing with Roman political intrigues immediately before and during the reign of the first-century emperor Claudius I; *The Six Wives of Henry VIII,* with each installment devoted to one wife of the English monarch; *Elizabeth R,* treating the life and times of the sixteenth-century queen of England; *The Pallisers,* based on the political novels of the nineteenth-century English author Anthony Trollope; *The Duchess of Duke Street,* patterned after the life of a well-known London cook and hotel proprietor of the early twentieth century; *Upstairs, Downstairs,* a highbrow soap opera about a British household from around 1900 to 1930, focusing on the contrasts and interaction between an upper class family and its servants; *Edward and Mrs. Simpson,* treating the abdication of Edward VIII of Great Britain because of the opposition to his marrying a divorced American woman; and *Danger UXB,* dealing with a World War II British bomb-disposal squad.

NEWS AND PUBLIC AFFAIRS. The most popular program in the field of news and public affairs during the 1970s was *60 Minutes.* For part of the decade it was also one of the ten top-rated television series, a unique distinction for a program in its genre. A single installment of this documentary series almost always covered three news stories, each quite different from the others in content and treatment, resulting in a diversified package that easily appealed to a wide audience. Among the news correspondents narrating the stories were Mike Wallace, Dan Rather, Harry Reasoner, and Morley Safer; the former two could be quite aggressive and were regularly assigned to the more controversial pieces, while the latter two seemed comfortably easygoing and usually handled the lighter segments that were often of a human-interest nature. In households with individuals viewing the nightly news programs on the three major commercial networks (the American Broadcasting Company, the Columbia Broadcasting System, and the National Broadcasting Company), their number went from about 24 million in 1970 to close to 29 million in 1975 to about 34 million in 1980.

In 1979, after more than three decades of sometimes heated discussion by its members of all aspects of the move, the House of Representatives began telecasting its routine proceedings on public television and on a few cable television systems, quickly gaining a rather large audience throughout the nation. Rejecting the commercial television networks' offers of coverage, over which the House would not have had complete authority, the legislative body set up its own equipment for and maintained full control over the telecasting procedure. Although the Senate for many years had permitted the telecasting of its committee hearings, it was still considering, albeit moving closer and closer to, the telecasting of its routine proceedings. The telecasting of proceedings of the United States Supreme Court, which was strongly opposed by a majority of the Court's members, including the chief justice, appeared to be far in the future.

COLOR. It was to be expected, of course, that color television would eventually make its appearance. In 1956 WNBQ-TV (later renamed WMAQ-TV) in Chicago became the first station in the United States to telecast all its local programs in color. By the late 1960s the three major commercial networks were telecasting all their programs in color. In 1965 about 3 million households had color television sets; in 1970, about 24 million households did; in 1980, about 76 million households (virtually all that owned television sets) did. The color television camera contained three tubes (one for each of the three primary colors of light—red, green, and blue), each of which produced a separate electronic impulse, the three of which were then combined as a single signal and transmitted. The color television set had one picture tube containing three electron guns, each of which received one of the three primary colors transmitted and shot a beam of electrons to the screen of the picture tube covered with a myriad of tiny dots of a substance called "phosphur," each dot being hit by and thus giving off one of the three primary colors, with the three colors ultimately blending to result in an image in full color.

CABLE. In the 1950s cable television was introduced on a small scale. By 1960 about 650,000 of the approximately 45.8 million households with television had cable. By 1980 about 15.5 million of the approximately 76.3 million households with television had cable, and only one year later about 19.5 of the approximately 77.8 million households that had television were hooked into one of the approximately 4350 cable television companies in existence.

Initially, cable television was installed in areas where the images on sets hooked up to rooftop antennas to pull television signals from the atmosphere were of poor quality because of the physical remoteness of the regions or because of interference from land formations. The cables brought in (much in the manner of telephone wires relaying calls) sharp images and clear sounds to the sets. With the late 1970s, however, most families subscribing to cable television did so less for the sharper images and more for the greater variety of program offerings (including numerous motion pictures and sports events) than could be obtained on the commercial network and public-television channels. For a monthly charge of about ten dollars a subscriber to cable television, through the use of a small handheld console supplied by the cable company, had access to more than thirty channels drawn from a wide diversity of sources, as opposed to the dozen or so channels available on a set connected to a rooftop antenna. And for additional fees a subscriber could have activated one or more other cable channels that featured a specialized type of program, such as motion-picture classics, recent feature films, nightclub floor shows, and sports events.

VIDEO CASSETTE RECORDERS. One of the most important developments in television during the period was the introduction in 1978 of the video cassette recorder (VCR). Within four years approximately 4 million American homes had the device. With a VCR television viewing was not controlled by telecasting schedules. By setting the timer on the VCR, which was connected to the television set, one could automatically record programs while absent and later view the tapes on the television set; one could record one program while viewing another, thereby "catching" two telecasts during the same or in overlapping time slots; one could build a collection of personally recorded or commercially produced video cassettes of favorite programs, including movies, that could be viewed over and over on the television set.

VIDEO DISC PLAYERS. Introduced in 1979 was the video disc player, another device that made it possible for one to determine exactly what to view on the television set and when to view it. In 1980 about 10,000 video disc players were in use in the United States; by the next year about 70,000 were. The video disc player, which resembled a regular phonograph, was connected to the television set. It played a commercially produced, prerecorded disc, which resembled a regular phonograph platter, holding images and sounds that were cast onto the screen of the television set for viewing. The stock of video discs continually expanded to encompass many offerings within each of a wide variety of categories, including motion pictures, sports events, and at-home instructional courses and demonstrations. The advantage of the video-disc-player system over the video-cassette-recorder system was that it provided both images and sounds of far superior quality; its disadvantage was that it could play only commercially produced discs and could not record programs from the television set as the video-cassette-recorder system could.

Sports. Throughout the 1960s and 1970s professional athletics attracted, in addition to the very many spectators who watched on television screens, huge numbers of spectators in actual attendance. As the 1980s approached, the annual attendance at major-league baseball games was about 40 million and at minor-league games, about 15 million; at college football games it was about 35 million and at professional games, about 15 million; at college basketball games it was about 30 million and at professional games, about 10 million.

Two notable developments occurred in sports. First, after the long-standing policy of refusing to hire blacks was abandoned in the 1940s and 1950s, teams, particularly in football and basketball, were more and more dominated both in numbers and skills by black players. Second, women finally came into their own in professional athletics, especially in tennis.

BASEBALL. Despite the increasingly strong popularity of the other spectator sports, baseball retained its image as a kind of national game of the United States. Among the outstanding pitchers of the 1960s was Sanford ("Sandy") Koufax, who played for the Brooklyn Dodgers and the Los Angeles Dodgers. Throwing a remarkable fastball and a spectacular curve ball, the left-handed Koufax struck out 2396 batters during a relatively short twelve-year career that was terminated by arthritis in his pitching arm. Two of the greatest batters in the history of the sport were Mickey Charles Mantle and Louis Henry ("Hank") Aaron. Mantle, a New York Yankee centerfielder for almost twenty years before retiring in the late 1960s, hit a total of 536 home runs and had a lifetime batting average of .298. Aaron was a superior outfielder, mostly for the Milwaukee Braves and the Atlanta Braves. In 1974 he broke Babe Ruth's almost forty-year-old record of 714 home runs in regular-season major-league play, finishing the season with 733. He completed his career two years later, having set a batting record of hitting a total of 755 home runs in regular-season major-league play. Frank Robinson became the first black manager in major-league baseball when in 1975 he was hired to manage the Cleveland Indians; he had been an outfielder with the Cincinnati Reds and the Baltimore Orioles.

BOXING. If one person were to be chosen as the preeminent athlete of the 1960s and 1970s, it would certainly be the magnetic black boxer Muhammad Ali. (He was originally named Cassius Marcellus Clay, Jr., but adopted a new name after becoming a Black Muslim.) Ali was the first person to win the heavyweight championship three times. He initially took the crown in 1964. Three years later he was stripped of his title and prohibited from fighting by the boxing authorities because of his refusal, based on his religious beliefs, to be inducted into the armed services, but in 1970 he was granted a license to fight again. In 1974 he regained the title, in the spring of 1978 lost it and in the fall of that year regained it, and in 1979 he retired. In 1981, after coming out of retirement and unsuccessfully attempting to win the crown for the fourth time, he retired permanently. Famous for a lightning speed in arms and legs, he was also noted for predicting his victory in an impending bout through the delivery of an inimitably boastful bit of verse.

FOOTBALL. During the 1960s and 1970s professional football captured fans in a manner reminiscent of the sport's popularity in the 1920s. This was due in large part to the achievements of a number of extraordinarily able and charismatic coaches and players. The outstanding coach of the 1960s was Vincent Thomas ("Vince") Lombardi. He was the personification of tough-mindedness: "Winning isn't everything, it's the only thing!" was his announced philosophy. After coaching on the high-school level, for two universities, and one professional team, he served as head coach of the Green Bay Packers from 1958 to 1968 and of the Washington Redskins in 1969, leading the former team to five championships in the National Football League. During his career with the two clubs he compiled a record of 141 wins, 39 losses, and 4 ties. Among the most accomplished players of the period were James Nathaniel ("Jimmy") Brown, John Constantine ("Johnny") Unitas, and Joseph William ("Joe") Namath. Brown, who played for the Cleveland Browns for nine years, was one of the greatest fullbacks in football history. His career scoring record of a total of 126 touchdowns and of gaining a total of 12,312 yards rushing have not yet been surpassed. Unitas, a superb quarterback for the Baltimore Colts, set career records of completing a total of 2830 passes for a total of 40,239 yards gained. Quarterback Namath (dubbed "Broadway Joe" because of his carefree, fun-loving way of life) played masterfully for the New York Jets, setting a record by completing passes for a total of 4007 yards during a single season (1967). Namath's demanding and receiving a quite favorable contract that provided for a high salary precipitated a sharp competition between the National Football League, in existence since 1922, and the American Football League, established in 1960, to sign up outstanding former college players. This prompted the two leagues in 1967 to engage in a joint selection of players and then two years later to merge.

BASKETBALL. During the 1960s and 1970s professional basketball reached the height of its popularity, with teams increasingly being dominated by black players who had earlier enjoyed highly successful college basketball careers. Exerting a profound influence upon professional basketball in the 1960s with his brilliant athletic technique was William Felton ("Bill") Russell, a center for the Boston Celtics from 1956 to 1969. Considered the finest defensive player in basketball history, Russell led his team to eleven championships in the National Basketball Association (NBA). Oscar Robertson (called the "Big O"), as a guard first for the Cincinnati Royals and then the Milwaukee Bucks, scored a career total of 28,620 points and was credited with more than 9000 assists, the latter remaining a career record. Wilton Norman ("Wilt") Chamberlain is regarded as the best offensive player of all time in professional basketball. He was with several teams, including the Philadelphia Warriors and the San Francisco Warriors. The 7-foot, 1-inch Chamberlain set a truly remarkable array of scoring records in the NBA: he scored a career total of 31,419 points; the most points for seven consecutive seasons; the highest per game point average (50.4) for a season; and the most points (100) in one game. About a half-inch taller than Chamberlain was Kareem Abdul-Jabbar. (Originally named Ferdinand Lewis [Lew] Alcindor, he assumed a new name after becoming a Black Muslim.) A center for the Milwaukee Bucks and the Los Angeles Lakers, Abdul-Jabbar exhibited his prowess by consistently being one of the leading scorers every season during the 1970s.

TENNIS. Held in high regard by tennis fans was James Scott ("Jimmy") Connors. In addition to winning other titles before and since, in his banner year of 1974 he took the United States, British, and Australian men's singles championships. In 1979, 1980, and 1981 John McEnroe won the United States men's singles championship, making him the first player since the extraordinary Bill Tilden of the 1920s to capture a national title three consecutive times. The left-hander McEnroe was a brilliant player with a murderously powerful serve, whose displays of hot temper during matches, usually in reaction to umpires' decisions, earned him a reputation as the "bad boy" of tennis.

If there was one sport in which women came into their own, it was professional tennis, with fans following the careers of female players as eagerly as they did those of male players. The two top women stars of the game were Billie Jean King and Christine Marie ("Chris") Evert Lloyd. From 1966 to 1975 the hard-hitting King won the United States women's singles championship four times, the British six times, and the French and Australian once each. She helped to develop interest in women's participation in sports in general and tennis in particular when in a highly publicized match in 1973 she overwhelmingly defeated Robert Larimore ("Bobby") Riggs, a two-time winner of the United States men's singles and a three-time winner of the United States professional championships, who had vociferously maintained that the male athlete was absolutely superior to the female, even one younger than he and in her prime years. A dedicated participant in the women's liberation movement, King strongly espoused equal pay for men and women. The coolly determined Evert Lloyd strikingly made her appearance in the world of tennis in 1971 at the age of sixteen, and over the next decade won the United States women's singles championship six times, the British three times, and the French three times. If the still very young—and exceedingly hard to beat—Evert Lloyd were to continue to perform in the same way for but a few more years and capture but a few more championships, she would wind up her career being the best woman player in the history of the sport.

GOLF. Foremost in professional golf were Arnold Daniel Palmer and Jack William Nicklaus. As a dedicated and skilled athlete, Palmer helped during the early 1960s to revive interest in his sport. Between 1958 and 1964 he won the Master's title four times (thus becoming the first person ever to win it that number of times), the United States Open title once, and the British Open title twice. Nicklaus is perhaps the greatest player in the history of professional golf. After winning the United States Amateur title in 1959 and 1961, he turned professional and went on to win gloriously, between 1962 and 1980, the following titles: the Master's five times (thus becoming the first person ever to win it that many times), the United States Open four times, and the British Open three times.

PRESIDENTS

1. George Washington   1789–1797
2. John Adams   1797–1801
3. Thomas Jefferson   1801–1809
4. James Madison   1809–1817
5. James Monroe   1817–1825
6. John Quincy Adams   1825–1829
7. Andrew Jackson   1829–1837
8. Martin Van Buren   1837–1841
9. William Henry Harrison   1841
10. John Tyler   1841–1845
11. James Knox Polk   1845–1849
12. Zachary Taylor   1849–1850
13. Millard Fillmore   1850–1853
14. Franklin Pierce   1853–1857
15. James Buchanan   1857–1861
16. Abraham Lincoln   1861–1865
17. Andrew Johnson   1865–1869
18. Ulysses S. Grant   1869–1877
19. Rutherford B. Hayes   1877–1881
20. James A. Garfield   1881
21. Chester A. Arthur   1881–1885
22. Grover Cleveland   1885–1889
23. Benjamin Harrison   1889–1893
24. Grover Cleveland   1893–1897
25. William McKinley   1897–1901
26. Theodore Roosevelt   1901–1909
27. William H. Taft   1909–1913
28. Woodrow Wilson   1913–1921
29. Warren G. Harding   1921–1923
30. Calvin Coolidge   1923–1929
31. Herbert C. Hoover   1929–1933
32. Franklin D. Roosevelt   1933–1945
33. Harry S. Truman   1945–1953
34. Dwight D. Eisenhower   1953–1961

35.	John F. Kennedy	1961–1963
36.	Lyndon B. Johnson	1963–1969
37.	Richard M. Nixon	1969–1974
38.	Gerald R. Ford	1974–1977
39.	Jimmy Carter	1977–1981
40.	Ronald Reagan	1981–

SUGGESTED BOOKS FOR FURTHER READING

Acuña, Rodolfo. *Occupied America: A History of Chicanos* (1980).

Allen, Frederick Lewis. *The Big Change: America Transforms Itself, 1900–1950* (1952).

————. *Only Yesterday: An Informal History of the Nineteen-Twenties* (1931).

Banner, Lois S. *Women in Modern America* (1974).

Barnouw, Erik. *Tube of Plenty: The Evolution of American Television* (1975).

Blesh, Rudi. *Shining Trumpets: A History of Jazz* (1975).

Bogan, Louise. *Achievement in American Poetry, 1900–1950* (1951).

Bono, Philip, and Gotland, Kenneth. *Frontiers of Space* (1976).

Burchard, John, and Bush-Brown, Albert. *The Architecture of America: A Social and Cultural History* (1966).

Cochran, Thomas C. *The American Business System: A Historical Perspective, 1900–1955* (1957).

Curti, Merle. *The Growth of American Thought* (1981).

Dinnerstein, Leonard, and Jaher, Frederick Cople, eds. *The Aliens: A History of Ethnic Minorities in America* (1970).

Dolan, Paul J., and Quinn, Edward G., eds. *The Sense of the 70s: A Rhetorical Reader* (1978).

Downer, Alan S. *Fifty Years of American Drama, 1900–1950* (1951).

Durso, Joseph. *The All-American Dollar: The Big Business of Sport* (1971).

Ekirch, Arthur A., Jr. *Ideologies and Utopias: The Impact of the New Deal on American Thought* (1969).

Ewen, David. *Composers for the American Musical Theatre* (1968).

Franklin, John Hope. *From Slavery to Freedom: A History of Negro Americans* (1974).

Freeman, Jo. *The Politics of Women's Liberation* (1975).

Goldman, Eric F. *The Crucial Decade—and After: America, 1945–1960* (1961).

Gottfried, Martin. *Broadway Musicals* (1979).

Handlin, Oscar. *The American People in the Twentieth Century* (1954).

————. *The Uprooted* (1973).

Heald, Morrell. *The Social Responsibilities of Business: Company and Community, 1900–1960* (1970).

Hoffman, Frederick J. *The Modern Novel in America, 1900–1950* (1951).

Hopkins, Jerry. *The Rock Story* (1970).

Hudson, Winthrop S. *Religion in America* (1973).

Hunter, Sam, and Jacobus, John. *American Art of the 20th Century* (1974).

Josephy, Alvin M., Jr. *Red Power: The American Indians' Fight For Freedom* (1971).

KAHN, E. J., JR. *The American People* (1974).

KNIGHT, EDGAR W. *Fifty Years of American Education* (1951).

KOBRE, SIDNEY. *Development of American Journalism* (1969).

KOLODIN, IRVING. *The Story of the Metropolitan Opera, 1883–1966: A Candid History* (1966).

LINGEMAN, RICHARD R. *Don't You Know There's a War On? The American Home Front, 1941–1945* (1970).

MALONE, BILL C. *Country Music U.S.A.: A Fifty-Year History* (1969).

MAY, HENRY F. *The End of American Innocence: A Study of the First Years of Our Own Time, 1912–1917* (1959).

MAYNARD, OLGA. *The American Ballet* (1959).

MICHENER, JAMES A. *Sports in America* (1976).

MUELLER, JOHN H. *The American Symphony Orchestra: A Social History of Musical Taste* (1951).

OLIVER, JOHN W. *History of American Technology* (1956).

O'NEILL, WILLIAM L. *Coming Apart: An Informal History of America in the 1960s* (1971).

PETERSON, THEODORE. *Magazines in the Twentieth Century* (1964).

RAE, JOHN B. *The Road and the Car in American Life* (1971).

RAYBACK, JOSEPH G. *A History of American Labor* (1966).

ROSE, BARBARA. *American Art Since 1900: A Critical History* (1967).

ROSZAK, THEODORE. *The Making of a Counter Culture* (1969).

SAGE, GEORGE H., ed. *Sport and American Society: Selected Readings* (1980).

SCHICKEL, RICHARD. *Movies: The History of an Art and an Institution* (1965).

SCHNEIDER, HERBERT W. *Religion in 20th Century America* (1952).

SHRYOCK, RICHARD H. *The Development of Modern Medicine: An Interpretation of the Social and Scientific Factors Involved.* (1947).

SIEGEL, MARCIA B. *The Shapes of Change: Images of American Dance* (1979).

SILBERMAN, CHARLES E. *Crisis in the Classroom: The Remaking of American Education* (1970).

SITKOFF, HARVARD. *The Struggle for Black Equality, 1954–1980* (1981).

SKLAR, ROBERT. *Movie-Made America: A Cultural History of American Movies* (1975).

SMITH, BRADLEY. *The American Way of Sex* (1978).

STOVER, JOHN F. *American Railroads* (1961).

TAFT, PHILIP. *Organized Labor in American History* (1964).

TAYLOR, JOHN W. R., and MUNSON, KENNETH. *History of Aviation* (1972).

THORP, WILLARD. *American Writing in the Twentieth Century* (1960).

WARNER, SAM BASS, JR. *The Urban Wilderness: A History of the American City* (1972).

WHITE, LLEWELLYN. *American Radio* (1947).

WOOD, ROBERT C., *Suburbia: Its People and Their Politics* (1959).

ZUBIN, JOSEPH, and MONEY, JOHN, eds. *Contemporary Sexual Behavior: Critical Issues in the 1970s* (1973).

INDEX